DEARBORN™

PASSTRAK® SERIES 63

Uniform Securities Agent State Law Exam

License Exam Manual

18th Edition

Dearborn™
Financial Services
A **Kaplan Professional** Company

At press time, this edition of Series 63 contains the most complete and accurate information currently available for the Series 63 license examination. Owing to the nature of securities license examinations, however, information may have been added recently to the actual test that does not appear in this edition.

Published by Dearborn Financial Institute, Inc.

Printed in the United States of America.

03 10 9 8 7 6 5 4 3 2 1

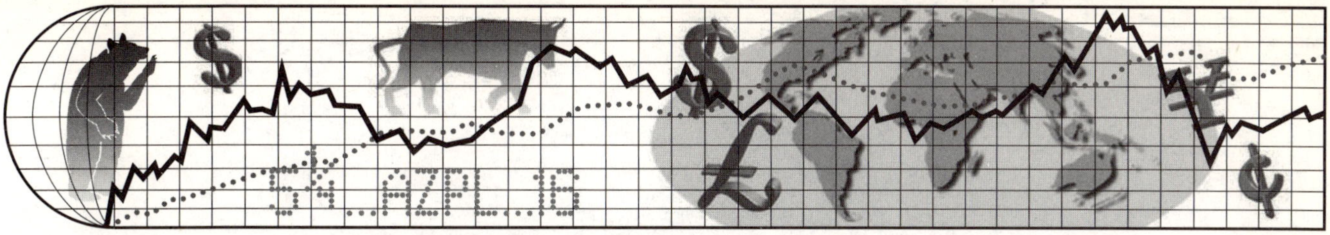

Contents

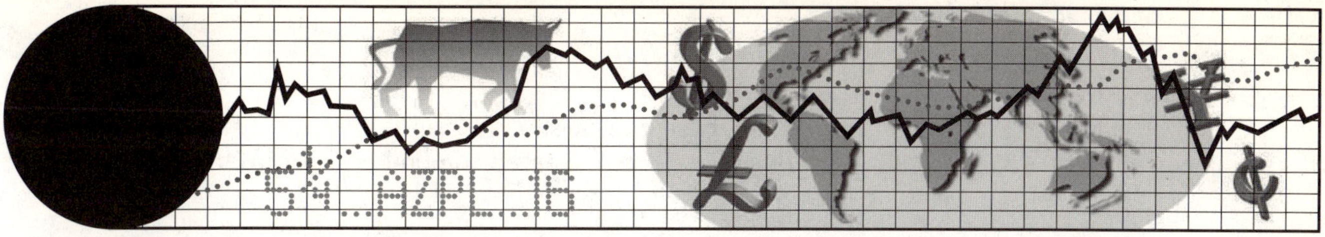

Series 63 Introduction

Thank you for choosing Dearborn's PASSTRAK exam preparation system for your educational needs and welcome to the Series 63 License Exam Manual. This system has been designed with applied adult learning principles to give you the tools you'll need to pass your exam on the first attempt.

Some of these special features include:

- exam-focused questions and content to maximize test preparation;
- an interactive design for the License Exam Manual that integrates content with questions to increase retention; and
- integrated Drill & Practice exam preparation tools to sharpen test-taking skills.

Is there someone I can contact if I have questions as I study?

Dearborn is here to help you with every step of your study process. If you have questions about your study materials, please contact Dearborn's **AnswerPhone** at:

1-800-621-9621 x3598

between 8:00 a.m. and 6:00 p.m. CT, Monday through Friday. AnswerPhone's staff of content experts will answer your questions and clarify the material as needed. If your inquiry is regarding a particular question in the practice exams or in the Drill & Practice, please note the QID number (Question Identifier) as this will allow us to find your question within our testing database.

Test Topic Alert!

Visit our Knowledge Center's Test and Compliance Alerts section at **www.dearborn.com** for industry updates and current exam information.

How is the License Exam Manual organized?

Dearborn's *Series 63 License Exam Manual* consists of Lessons, Lesson Exams, and Practice Final Exams. When an additional point will be valuable to your comprehension, special notes are embedded in the text.

✓ ***For Example:*** These provide situations and numerical instances of the material to illustrate a point for increased comprehension of difficult or technical material.

✓ ***Take Note:*** Tips and examples to amplify important test points.

Test Topic Alert! These highlight content that is likely to appear on the Series 63 exam.

As you read each Lesson, you will also see **Quick Quizzes,** which will help you understand and retain the material covered in that particular section. Quick Quizzes are a brief interactive review of what you just read.

In addition, **Lesson HotSheets** at the end of each lesson summarize the key points in bullet-point format. For your convenience and use as review notes, HotSheets are duplicated at the end of the License Exam Manual on perforated pages.

How is the book organized? The book is made up of Lessons outlined in the same way that the North American Securities Administrators Association (NASAA) has outlined the material for the exam.

- Lesson 1: Administrative Provisions of the Uniform Securities Act (6 questions, or 10%)
- Lesson 2: Securities (15 questions, or 25%)
- Lesson 3: Registration of Persons (18 questions, or 30%)
- Lesson 4: Business Practices (21 questions, or 35%)

A set of Practice Finals complements the Lessons presented in the License Exam Manual. Devote a significant amount of study time to the completion of practice questions and review of rationales.

Preparing for the Exam

How much time should I spend studying? Plan to spend approximately 40 to 60 hours reading the material and working through the questions. Devote a significant amount of your study time to the practice questions and review of rationales. Your actual time, of course, may vary from this figure depending on your reading rate, comprehension, professional background, and study environment.

Spread your study time over the three to four weeks before the date on which you are scheduled to take the Series 63 exam. Select a time and place for studying that will allow you to concentrate your full attention on the material. Be sure to give yourself enough time to learn the material—and then test your retention by taking the Practice Finals.

What is the best way to structure my study time?

The following schedule is suggested to help you obtain maximum retention from your study efforts. Remember, this is intended as a *guideline only*; each individual may require more or less time to complete the steps.

For the License Exam Manual: As you read through each Lesson, pause to complete each Quick Quiz and be sure to complete the Lesson Exam at the end. Review rationales for all questions whether you scored them right or wrong.

✓ ***Take Note:*** Do not be overly concerned with your score on the first attempt at any exam. Instead, take the opportunity to learn from your mistakes.

Repeat the above two steps for each lesson until you have completed all of the Lessons in the workbook (13–20 hours per lesson). Then direct your attention to the corresponding HotSheet to remind yourself of the points that are highlighted for you (7–10 hours). The last step is to complete all of the Practice Finals. Give yourself enough time to take a complete 60-question exam in one sitting (10–20 hours for all exams).

For the CD-ROM: If your study materials include the Series 63 Drill & Practice, this Dearborn CD-ROM includes a large bank of questions that are similar in style and content to those you will encounter on the exam. You can use it to generate exams by specific topic or to create practice finals that are similar in difficulty and topic proportion to the actual Series 63 exam.

On the CD-ROM, create and complete an exam for each topic included under each Lesson heading. For best results, select the maximum number of questions within each topic. Carefully review all rationales. Do an additional exam on any topic on which you score under 60%. After you have completed all lesson exams, create a 60-question exam comprised of all Lesson topics. Repeat this 60-question exam until you score at least 70% (5–10 hours).

Complete at least five of the 60-question Practice Finals. Complete more exams as necessary to achieve a score of at least 80–90%. Create and complete additional topic exams as necessary to correct problem areas (10–20 hours).

Do I need to take all of the exams?

The Practice Finals test the same knowledge you will need to answer the questions on the Series 63 exam. By completing all the exams and checking your answers against the rationale, you should be able to pinpoint areas with which you are still having difficulty. Review questions you miss, paying particular attention to the rationale for those questions.

If a subject still seems troublesome, go back and review the section covering that topic.

The Series 63 Exam

Why do I need to pass the Series 63 exam?

State securities laws require individuals to pass a qualification exam in order to sell securities within their states.

✓ ***Take Note:*** Almost all states require representatives to pass the Series 63 exam (blue-sky test) as a condition of state registration.

What is the Series 63 exam like?

The Series 63 is a 75 minute, 60-question exam administered by the NASD. It is offered as a computer-based test at testing sites around the country. A pencil-and-paper exam is available to candidates who get permission from the NASD to take a written exam. There will be five extra questions (for a total of 65 questions) but these five questions are experimental testing questions that do not count against your score.

Which topics will I see covered on the exam?

The Series 63 exam is divided into four areas. Dearborn's License Exam Manual has four Lessons, outlined the same way the North American Securities Administrators Association (NASAA) has outlined the material for the exam. This course will take you through the following topic areas that the NASAA has outlined as essential to the Series 63 Uniform Securities Agent.

What score must I achieve to pass?

You must answer correctly at least 70% of the questions on the Series 63 exam to pass and become eligible for registration.

How long does the exam take?

You are allowed 75 minutes to finish the exam. If you are taking the computerized version, you will be given additional time before the test—up to half an hour—to take the computer exam tutorial and become familiar with the terminal.

How do I enroll for the exam?

To obtain an admission ticket to the Series 63 exam, your firm must file the proper application form and fees with the NASD. The NASD will then send you a directory of Prometric Centers and an enrollment valid for a stated number of days. To take the exam during this period, you must make an appointment with a Prometric Center as far in advance as possible of the date on which you would like to sit for the test. You can contact Prometric Center at 1-800-578-6273.

What should I take to the exam?

Take one form of personal identification that bears your signature and your photograph as issued by a government agency. You cannot take reference materials or anything else into the testing area. Calculators are available upon request; you cannot use a personal calculator. Scratch paper and pencils will be provided by the testing center, although you will not be permitted to take them with you when you leave.

How is the exam administered?

The Series 63 exam, like many professional licensing examinations, is administered on a nationwide, interactive computer system designed for the administration and delivery of qualifications examinations. Included with your enrollment is a brochure describing how the exam is formatted as well as how to use the computer terminal to answer the questions.

When you have completed the exam, the system scores your answers and displays your grade for the exam on the terminal screen.

How well can I expect to do on the exam?

The examinations administered by the NASD are not easy. You will be required to display considerable understanding and knowledge of the topics presented in this course in order to pass the Series 63 exam and qualify for registration. If you study and complete all of the sections of the course, and consistently score at least 80% on the exams, you should be well prepared to pass the Series 63 exam.

Successful Test-Taking Tips

Passing any NASD Series exam depends not only on how well you learn the subject matter, but also on how well you take tests. You can develop your test-taking skills (and improve your score) by learning a few techniques:

- Read the full question
- Avoid jumping to conclusions—watch for hedge clauses
- Interpret the unfamiliar question
- Look for key words and phrases
- Identify the intent of the question
- Recognize synonymous terms
- Eliminate/short-list Roman numeral choices
- Use a calculator
- Beware of changing answers
- Pace yourself

Each of these pointers is explained below, including examples that show how to use them to improve performance on the NASD exams.

Note: The examples below are not specific to the Series 63 exam.

Read the full question

You can't expect to answer a question correctly if you don't know what it is asking. If you see a question that *seems* familiar and easy, you might anticipate the answer and move on before you finish reading it. This is a serious mistake. Be sure to read the full question before answering—questions are often written to trap people who assume too much. Here is an example of how a quick assumption can produce a wrong answer.

1. What is the term for an underwriting of securities that is priced through a bidding process involving more than one investment banking firm?

    A. Eastern
    B. Western
    C. Negotiated
    D. Competitive

1. **D**. *The answer is D—the question describes a situation in which competitive bidding determines the offering price.*

This is an easy question to answer only for someone who has read the full question, because the point is made in the second half. If you read the question too quickly, you might get to the word "divided" and assume that you are being asked to remember whether a divided underwriting is called an Eastern or Western underwriting.

Avoid jumping to conclusions—watch for hedge clauses

The questions on NASD exams are often embellished with deceptive distractors as choices. To avoid being taken in by seemingly obvious answers, make it a practice to read each question and each answer twice before selecting your choice. Doing so will provide you with a better chance of doing well on the test.

Watch out for hedge clauses embedded in the question. Examples of hedge clauses include the terms *if, not, all, none,* and *except*. In the case of *if* statements, the question can only be answered correctly by taking into account the qualifier. If you ignore the qualifier, you will not answer correctly. Qualifiers are sometimes combined in a question. You will frequently see ***all*** with ***except*** and ***none*** with ***except***. In general, when a question starts with ***all*** or ***none*** and ends with ***except***, you are looking for an answer that is opposite to what the question appears to be asking.

2. All of the following are characteristics of Treasury bills EXCEPT that they

    I. mature in more than one year
    II. are sold at a discount
    III. pay interest semiannually
    IV. are very safe investments

    A. I and II
    B. I and III
    C. II and III
    D. II and IV

2. **B**. *If you neglect to read the "except", you will look for the choices that are characteristics of T-bills. In fact, the question asks which choices are NOT characteristics of T-bills. T-bills mature in one year or less and do not pay periodic interest; therefore, choices (I) and (III) are incorrect.*

Interpret the unfamiliar question

Do not be surprised if some questions on the test seem unfamiliar at first. If you have studied your material, you will have the information to answer all the questions correctly. The challenge may be a matter of understanding what the question is asking. Very often, questions present information indirectly and you have to interpret the meaning of certain elements before you can answer the question. The following two examples concerning bond yields and prices highlight this point:

3. What is the effect of a decline in purchasing power on the current yields of outstanding bonds?

   A. The yields decrease.
   B. The yields increase.
   C. The yields stay the same.
   D. This cannot be determined with the information given.

*3. **B**. This question is asking you to apply knowledge of economics, investment recommendations, and the relationship between bond prices and yields. Consumer purchasing power declines during periods of inflation. Inflation causes interest rates to rise, and this in turn causes prices of outstanding bonds to decrease. When a bond declines in price or sells at a discount, the current yield increases (B).*

This same content could have been tested in a different way, as illustrated by the next example.

4. What is the effect of tight money on bond prices?

   A. Bond prices decrease.
   B. Bond prices increase.
   C. Bond prices stay the same.
   D. This cannot be determined with the information given.

*4. **A**. Tight money is closely related to high interest rates. When money is scarce (tight), interest rates rise. When interest rates rise, prices of outstanding bonds decrease (A).*

At first glance, the two questions appear very different, but in fact they test the same relationship—the relationship between a bond's price and its yield. Be aware that the exam may approach a concept from different angles.

Look for key words and phrases

Look for words that are clues to the situation presented. For example, if you see the word "prospectus" in the question stem, you know the question is about a new issue. Sometimes a question will even supply you with the answer if you can recognize the key words it contains. The following is an example of how a key word can help you answer correctly:

5. Whose Social Security number must appear on an account under the Uniform Gifts to Minors Act?

   A. Minor
   B. Donor
   C. Legal guardian
   D. Parent

5. ***A.*** *Looking at the answers, choice A seems a likely candidate. Under UGMA, the minor is the owner of the securities. As the owner, the minor's Social Security number must be listed on the account. Few questions provide clues as blatant as this one, but many do offer key words that can guide you to selecting the correct answer—if you pay attention.*

Be sure to read all instructional phrases carefully, as illustrated in the next example.

6. Rank the following persons in descending order of their claims against a corporation's assets when the corporation is forced into liquidation.

   I. General creditors
   II. Preferred stockholders
   III. Bondholders
   IV. Common stockholders

   A. I, II, III, IV
   B. I, III, II, IV
   C. III, I, II, IV
   D. III, II, IV, I

6. ***C.*** *The most important aspect of this question is identifying the key word—descending. A descending order ranks a list from highest to lowest—in this question, the highest claim on assets to the lowest claim on assets. (The answer is C: bondholders, general creditors, preferred stockholders, common stockholders.) The question could have asked for the ascending order—lowest to highest. Or it could have asked you to rank the choices from junior claim to senior claim or vice versa.*

Take time to identify the key words to answer this type of question correctly.

Identify the intent of the question

Many questions on NASD exams supply so much information that it is easy to lose track of what is being asked. Learn to separate the "story" from the question. For example:

7. You have decided to buy 100 shares of ABC Mutual Fund, which prices its shares at 5:00 p.m. every business day. You turn in your order at 3:00 p.m.

when the shares are priced at $10 NAV, $10.86 POP. The sales load is 7.9%. What will your 100 shares cost?

A. $1,000
B. $1,079
C. $1,086
D. 100 times the offering price that will be calculated at 5:00 p.m.

*7. **D.** A clue to the answer is presented in the first sentence—the fund price at 5:00 p.m. Orders for mutual funds are executed based on the next price calculated (forward pricing), so the answer to this question is D. You do not need to calculate anything.*

Take the time to identify what the question is asking. Of course, your ability to do so assumes you have studied sufficiently. There is no method for answering questions if you don't know the material.

Recognize synonymous terms

The securities industry has a tendency to abbreviate terms and use acronyms. Terms may be used interchangeably throughout the test, and you should be able to recognize them.

Industry Term	Synonyms or Acronym
effective date	release date
Self Regulatory Organization	SRO
registered representative (RR) account executive (AE)	agent
Fidelity bond	Surety bond
filing	notice filing

Eliminate/short-list Roman numeral choices

Roman numeral questions are common on NASD exams and they require you to distinguish between several likely answers. When you are confronted with Roman numeral choices, try to eliminate one or two of them to help narrow your choices. For example, if you can eliminate choice II in a Roman numeral question, and three of the four answers contain choice II, you have narrowed down your options to the correct answer by process of elimination.

8. An owner of common stock has which of the following rights?

I. Right to determine when dividends will be issued
II. Right to vote at stockholders' meetings or by proxy
III. Right to determine the amount of any dividends issued
IV. Right to buy redeemed shares before they are offered to the public

A. I, III and IV only
B. II only
C. II, III and IV only
D. II and IV only

8. ***B.*** *Stockholders have the right to vote on certain corporate matters and the right to dividends if and when declared. Stockholders do not vote on when a dividend is to be paid, nor on the amount of dividend to be paid. Knowing this, you can eliminate answers A and C.*

Beware of changing answers If you are unsure of an answer, your first hunch is most likely to be correct. **Do not** change answers on the exam without a good reason. In general, change an answer only if you discover that you did not read the question correctly or find new or additional helpful information in another question.

Pace yourself Some people finish the exam early; others use the entire time, and some cannot finish all the questions. Watch the time carefully (time remaining will be displayed on your computer screen) and pace yourself through the exam. Do not dwell on a question if you simply do not know the answer. Make your best guess, mark the question *Record for Review,* and return if time allows.

Dearborn Class Scheduling

Dearborn offers many exam preparation classes throughout the country. For scheduling information, contact

Dearborn Customer Service at 1-800-824-8742

Our efficient and friendly Customer Service team will be happy to help you with your exam preparation scheduling.

And remember to visit **www.dearborn.com** for updated industry information and *free* Test Alerts!

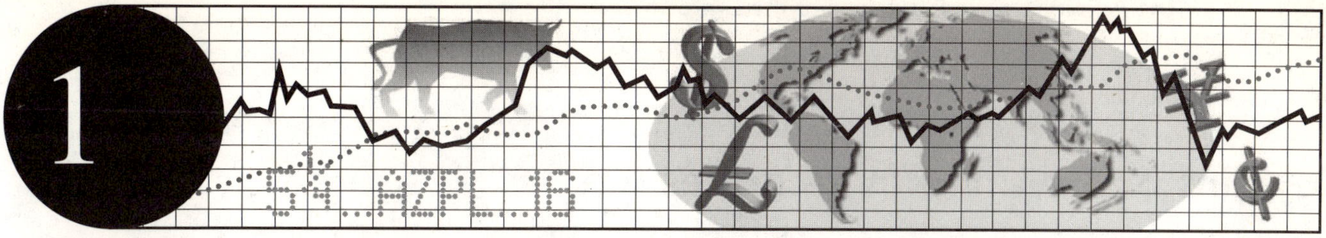

1 The Administrative Provisions of the Uniform Securities Act

INTRODUCTION

This lesson discusses the origins of the **Uniform Securities Act** (**USA**) and addresses the jurisdiction and the powers that the state securities Administrator has to enforce compliance with the legislation.

The USA is model legislation that arose in an effort to unify numerous state securities laws, known as **blue-sky laws**. Under the USA, the state Administrator has jurisdiction over securities transactions that originate in, are directed into, or are accepted in the Administrator's state. For those individuals or transactions that fall within the jurisdiction of the Administrator, the Administrator has power to make rules and orders; conduct investigations and issue subpoenas; issue cease and desist orders; and deny, suspend, or revoke registrations.

The USA provides both civil liabilities and criminal penalties for violating the act. Civil liabilities enable an investor to recover attorneys fees and losses resulting from securities sold in violation of the USA. Criminal penalties in addition to the civil liabilities may be levied against those who engage in fraudulent activities under the act.

The Series 63 exam will include approximately 6 questions on the material presented in this lesson.

LESSON OBJECTIVES

When you have completed this lesson, you should be able to:

- understand the relationship between state and national securities laws;
- recognize the jurisdiction of the state securities Administrator;
- list the powers of the Administrator within its jurisdiction;
- describe the rights of recovery for a security's sale or for investment advice purchased in violation of the USA; and
- contrast civil and criminal penalties for violation of the act.

Origins of the Uniform Securities Act

Financial markets developed along with the industrialization of the United States. As a result of new commercial opportunities, corporations issued securities to the public to fund their growth and development. Each state enacted securities laws to regulate the sale of these securities within their states.

The first state to enact a securities law, known as a **blue-sky law**, was Kansas in 1911. The term *blue-sky* was coined by a Kansas Supreme Court justice who considered some of these newly-issued securities as nothing more than "speculative schemes that have no more basis than so many feet of blue sky." By 1919, more than 30 states had passed blue-sky or securities laws.

National securities markets developed rapidly. Unfortunately, fraudulent sales and issuances of securities arose with equal vigor. In 1933, to protect an unsuspecting public, the United States Congress stepped in by enacting the first national securities law, the **Securities Act of 1933**.

The Securities Act of 1933, known as the **Paper Act**, requires corporations that sell securities in interstate commerce to provide full and fair disclosure to the public and to register their securities with the **Securities and Exchange Commission** (**SEC**). The SEC is the federal agency created under the Securities and Exchange Act of 1934. Corporations register with the SEC by filing a registration statement (hence the term "Paper Act").

✓ ***Take Note:*** The purpose of the Act of 1933 is to prevent fraud by providing investors with accurate information on corporations issuing securities to the public (full and fair disclosure). Full and fair disclosure is the guiding principle behind both national and state securities legislation. Complete and accurate information helps prevent fraud.

USA as Model State Legislation

With the enactment of national securities legislation (e.g., the Securities Act of 1933 and the Securities and Exchange Act of 1934) and numerous states' blue-sky laws, the need for uniformity in securities laws among the states arose. In 1956, the **National Conference of Commissioners on Uniform State Laws** (**NCCUSL**), a national organization of lawyers devoted to unifying state laws, drafted the original Uniform Securities Act.

The **Uniform Securities Act** (**USA**) is model (ideal) legislation, not actual legislation. In other words, the USA is a template or guide that each state uses in drafting its securities legislation. The securities laws of most states follow the USA very closely, and, in many cases, follow it almost exactly.

Test Topic Alert!

The Series 63 exam tests your knowledge of the USA, not the specifics of your state's securities legislation. The USA is periodically updated to adjust to developments in the securities markets. You will be tested on the latest version of the USA used by the **North American Securities Administrators Association (NASAA)**, the advisory body of state securities regulators, in constructing the content of the Series 63 exam.

Test Topic Alert!

The Series 63 is a "law" exam and unlike other securities exams. NASAA requires that you not only know what the law says, but are able to apply the law to concrete examples; general knowledge of the law is not enough. On the test you will be asked to apply the law to situations that you have not seen before.

USA Reflects National Securities Markets Improvement Act of 1996 and Securities Litigation Uniform Standards Act of 1998

While the USA was drafted by the NCCUSL to unify the blue-sky laws among the states, the **National Securities Markets Improvement Act of 1996 (NSMIA)** was enacted by Congress to eliminate conflicts between federal and state laws. In an effort to foster market efficiency, NSMIA charged the SEC with the duty to eliminate overlapping (or dual) state and federal securities regulation. Under NSMIA, securities regulatory responsibilities are divided between federal and state governments. Those securities and transactions regulated by federal law are referred to as **federal covered securities** or **federal covered transactions**.

The Securities Litigation Uniform Standards Act of 1998 (SLUSA) allows federal courts to preempt state courts in class action fraud cases. The Act ensures that state securities class actions will be governed by the uniform standards of federal law.

Federal Covered Securities and Transactions

NSMIA prohibits states from regulating public offerings, proxy solicitations, and the required disclosures of securities that trade on national or regional exchanges. NSMIA also prohibits states from requiring state registration of securities regulated by a national regulatory body such as the SEC. These securities and transactions are **covered (regulated)** by federal laws (e.g., the Securities Act of 1933 and the Investment Company Act of 1940) and cannot be regulated by the state law.

✓ ***For Example:*** A security traded on the New York Stock Exchange (e.g., IBM) is a federal covered security because it trades nationally in interstate commerce; therefore, must register its securities with the SEC. Under NSMIA, a state could not also require IBM to register its securities with the state because its securities are covered by federal legislation (in this case, the Securities Act of 1933).

Examples of federal covered securities are securities:

- issued by an open-end mutual fund, closed-end investment company, unit investment trust, or face amount certificate company that is registered under the Investment Company Act of 1940;
- offered pursuant to the provisions of Rule 506 of Regulation D under the Securities Act of 1933;
- offered by a municipal/governmental issuer, unless the issuer is located in the state in which the securities are being offered; and
- offered by an issuer exclusively to its existing security holders where no commissions or other remuneration is paid directly or indirectly for soliciting the exchange.

The Administrator of the Uniform Securities Act

Administrator The state official charged with enforcement of the USA in the state is called the **Administrator**. The Administrator can be an individual (such as a securities commissioner) or a division within a larger state agency (such as the office of the Secretary of State).

✓ ***Take Note:*** Like most securities legislation, the USA is designed to prevent fraud in the sale of securities to the general public. To guard against fraud, the USA grants the Administrator broad powers over the issuance of securities and registration of individuals who deal in those securities within the Administrator's state.

Quick Quiz 1.1

True or False?

___ 1. The Uniform Securities Act is not the actual law of any state or territory of the United States.

___ 2. The National Securities Markets Improvement Act of 1996 requires states and the national government to have identical registration requirements.

___ 3. The state securities Administrator has responsibility for the enforcement and administration of a state's securities law.

Answers

*1. **T.** The Uniform Securities Act is not the actual law of any state or territory of the United States; it is model legislation that states use as a guide in drafting their own securities law.*

*2. **F.** The National Securities Markets Improvement Act of 1996 does not require the states and national government to have identical registration requirements. The purpose of NSMIA is to eliminate dual regulation and registration.*

3. *T. The state securities Administrator has responsibility for the enforcement and administration of a state's securities law. The SEC is a national regulatory agency, not a state agency.*

Jurisdiction and Powers of the State Administrator

The jurisdiction and powers of the Administrator extend to activities related to the sale of securities.

Terminology

Sale or Sell

The USA defines the term "**sale**" or "**sell**" to include every contract of sale of, contract to sell, and disposition of a security or interest in a security for value.

✓ ***Take Note:*** Any transfer of a security in which money or some other valuable consideration is involved is covered by this definition and subject to the act.

Offer or Offer to Sell

The USA defines the terms "**offer**" or "**offer to sell**" to include every attempt or offer to dispose of, or solicitation of an offer to buy a security or interest in a security for value. These terms include any:

- security given or delivered with, or as a bonus on account of, any purchase of securities or other items constituting part of the purchase;
- gift of assessable stock (assessable stock is stock issued below par for which the issuer has the right to assess shareholders for the balance of unpaid par); or
- warrant or right to purchase or subscribe to another security (an offer of the other security is considered to be included in the warrant or right).

✓ ***For Example:*** If a car dealer, as an essential part of a sale, offers $1,000 in corporate bonds as an incentive, such sale falls under the jurisdiction of the state securities Administrator.

✓ ***Take Note:*** When assessable stock is given as a gift, the Administrator has jurisdiction over the transaction because the issuer can, at some future date, require payment.

These terms do not include any:

- bona fide pledge or loan;
- stock dividend, if nothing of value is given by the stockholders for the dividend;

- class vote by stockholders, pursuant to the certificate of incorporation or the applicable corporation statute, on a merger, consolidation, reclassification of securities, or sale of corporate assets in consideration of the issuance of securities of another corporation; or
- act incident to a judicially-approved reorganization with which a security is issued in exchange for one or more outstanding securities, claims, or property interest, or partly in such exchange and partly for cash.

Jurisdiction of the Administrator

Under law, for any agent of a state (e.g., the Administrator) to have authority over an activity such as a sale or offer of securities, it must have **legal jurisdiction** to act. Jurisdiction under the USA specifically means the **legal authority** to regulate securities activities that take place in the state.

The USA describes those activities considered to have taken place in the state. They are defined as any offer to buy or sell a security, as well as any acceptance of the offer, if the offer:

- **originated in** the Administrator's state;
- is **directed to** the Administrator's state; or
- is **accepted in** the Administrator's state.

✓ ***Take Note:*** Since securities transactions often involve several states, more than one Administrator may have jurisdiction over a security or a transaction.

Case Study: Offer Originated in Administrator's State

Situation: Mr. Thompson (a registered agent in Illinois), on the recommendation of his best client (Mr. Bixby), phones a friend of Mr. Bixby's in Indiana. Mr. Thompson sells a security to Mr. Bixby's friend, Ms. Gordon, who then drives to Mr. Thompson's office in Illinois to meet him and pay for the securities.

***Analysis*:** The Administrators of both Illinois and Indiana have jurisdiction—the Administrator of Indiana has jurisdiction because the offer was *accepted* by Ms. Gordon in Indiana and the Administrator of Illinois also has jurisdiction because the call (offer) originated in Illinois.

Case Study: Offer Directed to Administrator's State

Situation: On the day after he completed his first transaction with Ms. Gordon, Mr. Thompson mails sales offering materials to her home address in Indiana. Ms. Gordon is now not in a position to buy securities, so she discards the material without reading it.

Analysis: By sending sales materials to Ms. Gordon's home address in Indiana, Mr. Thompson directed the offer to Indiana. Even though Ms. Gordon discarded the information, the Administrator in Indiana has jurisdiction because the sales offer was directed to Indiana. The Administrator of Illinois also has jurisdiction because the offer originated in Illinois.

Case Study: Offer Accepted in an Administrator's State

Situation: Mr. Thompson sends additional offers to Ms. Gordon in Indiana who is now on a three-month summer vacation in Florida. Ms. Gordon has her mail forwarded to her in Florida. Upon receiving Mr. Thompson's materials in Florida, she decides to purchase the securities. She pays for the securities by mailing a check to Mr. Thompson drawn on her local bank in Indiana.

Analysis: The offer is accepted by Ms. Gordon while she was in Florida and, therefore, the Administrator of Florida has jurisdiction. Additionally, the Administrator in Illinois has jurisdiction because the offer originated in Illinois and the Administrator in Indiana has jurisdiction because the offer was directed to Indiana. This is a situation where the Administrator's of three different states have jurisdiction.

Publishing and Broadcast Exceptions to Jurisdiction

There are special rules regarding the Administrator's jurisdiction over offers made through a TV or radio broadcast or through a bona fide newspaper.

The USA specifies that an offer would not be made in an Administrator's state and, therefore, the Administrator would not have jurisdiction if it was made under any of the following circumstances.

- Television or radio broadcast that originated outside of the state
- Bona fide newspaper or periodical published outside of the state
- Newspaper or periodical published inside the state but has more than two-thirds (66%) of its circulation outside the state in the last year

✓ ***Take Note:*** A bona fide newspaper is a newspaper of general interest and circulation, such as *The New York Times*. Private investment advisory newsletters, usually distributed by subscription, are not bona fide newspapers and, therefore, do not fall under the publishing exception, nor under the regulatory jurisdiction of the state securities Administrator.

Case Study: Publishing and Broadcast Exemptions

Situation: First Securities & Co., broker-dealers with offices in New York State and Illinois, offers to sell shares in a new retail shoe chain store located in New York. First Securities advertises the offering in the local newspaper, the *New York Gazette*, to residents of New York. First Securities also advertises through the *Gazette's* wholly-owned radio station. The *Gazette* and its radio station are both located in western New York near the Pennsylvania border. About 55% of the *Gazette's* readers and listeners live in Pennsylvania.

Analysis: Although more than half the readers and listeners of the *Gazette* live in Pennsylvania, under the terms of the publishing and broadcasting exemption of the USA, the offer is *not* made in Pennsylvania—the Administrator of New York State has sole jurisdiction over the offering. No dual or multiple jurisdiction applies in this case unless the offer is actually accepted in Pennsylvania. The fact that First Securities is registered in Illinois in addition to

New York is not relevant to this offering because no securities were sold there, nor were any offers or advertising directed to the state.

✓ ***Take Note:*** The term "investment contract" includes interests in a limited partnership, a limited liability company, or a limited liability partnership, or an investment in a viatical settlement or similar agreement.

The United States Supreme Court in the Howey Decision determined that an investment contract constitutes an investment in a common enterprise with the expectation of profits to be derived primarily from the efforts of a person other than the investor.

A "common enterprise" means an enterprise in which the fortunes of the investor are interwoven with those of either the person offering the investment, a third party or other investors. Any instrument that is an investment contract is included in the term security.

Quick Quiz 1.2

True or False?

___ 1. The state's securities Administrator has jurisdiction over a securities offering if it was directed to, originated in, or was accepted in the state.

___ 2. A state Administrator only has jurisdiction over a securities transaction if the the transaction is accepted in the state.

___ 3. An Administrator has jurisdiction over an offer to sell securities if it is made in a newspaper published out of state with 60% of its circulation in the state.

Answers

*1. **T.** The state Administrator has jurisdiction over a security offering if it was directed to, originated in, or was accepted in the state. An offer made by radio broadcast in a state is not under the jurisdiction of the Administrator of the state in which the broadcast was heard unless an offer was accepted by an investor in that state.*

*2. **F.** A state Administrator has jurisdiction over a securities transaction if the transaction is accepted in, originated in, or was directed to the state.*

*3. **F.** A state Administrator has jurisdiction over a securities offering made in a bona fide newspaper published out of state but whose circulation is two-thirds, or 66.6% or more, in the state.*

Powers of the Administrator

The USA not only establishes the jurisdiction of the Administrator but also outlines the **powers** that the Administrator has within that jurisdiction. The USA provides the Administrator with four broad powers with which to enforce and administer the act.

The Administrator has the power or authority to:

- make, amend, or rescind rules and orders;
- conduct investigations and issue subpoenas;
- issue cease and desist orders and seek injunctions; and
- deny, suspend, cancel, or revoke registrations and licenses.

Prohibition Against Personal Profit or Gain

While the Administrator and his employees have powers to enforce the act for the benefit of the public, the Administrator also has the obligation not to misuse the office for personal gain.

✓ ***For Example:*** The Administrator, the officers, and the employees are prohibited from using, for their own benefit, any information derived from their official responsibilities that has not been made public.

Make, Amend, or Rescind Rules and Orders

To enforce the USA, the Administrator has authority to **make**, **amend**, or **rescind rules** necessary to administer the act and the Administrator may also issue interpretive letters. The USA requires that all rules and orders be published. A rule or order of the Administrator has the same authority as a provision of the act itself but these rules and orders are not part of the USA itself. An individual may challenge an order of the Administrator in court within 60 days of order issuance.

While the Administrator has the power to make and amend rules for complying with state blue-sky law, he does not have the power to alter the law itself.

✓ ***Take Note:*** The Administrator has the power to determine the rules for compliance with the law, but does not have the power to make law.

The composition or content of state securities law is the responsibility of the state legislature and not that of administrative agencies. Rules for administration and compliance with the law are the responsibility of the securities Administrator.

Case Study: Rules and Orders of the Administrator

Situation: The Iowa state securities Administrator requires by rule that all companies registering their securities in Iowa must supply financial statements in the specific form and with content prescribed by the Administrator. However, the Administrator does not publish the rule because the rule is too long and complex.

Analysis: The USA allows state Administrators to issue rules and orders in carrying out their regulatory functions and the Iowa Administrator acted quite properly in designing the form and content for financial reports. However, it is required by the USA that Administrators publish all rules and orders. The Administrator, despite the latitude given it in administering the USA, cannot suspend any provision of the USA itself. The Iowa Administrator acted within its authority in designing the forms but acted without authority—that is, he violated the USA—by suspending the requirement that all rules and orders be published.

Conduct Investigations and Issue Subpoenas

The Administrator has broad discretionary authority to **conduct investigations** and **issue subpoenas**. These investigations may be made in public or in private and may occur within or outside of the Administrator's state.

In conducting an investigation, the Administrator has the power to:

- require statements in writing, under oath, as to all matters relating to the issue under investigation;
- publish and make public the facts and circumstances concerning the issue to be investigated;
- subpoena witnesses and compel their attendance and testimony; and
- take evidence and require the production of books, papers, correspondence, and any other documents deemed relevant.

✓ ***Take Note:*** In addition to the power to conduct investigations, the Administrator may enforce subpoenas issued by Administrators in other states on the same basis as if the alleged offense took place in the Administrator's state.

Immunity Under the Fifth Amendment

An individual under investigation by an Administrator may not refuse to testify against himself. In other words, an individual's testimony can be **compelled**. However, the individual cannot be tried or convicted on the basis of the information he was forced to deliver. In effect, the individual is given immunity from prosecution based upon compelled information as guaranteed by the Fifth Amendment's right against self-incrimination.

Case Study: Forced Testimony and the Fifth Amendment

***Situation*:** In the course of an investigation of Mr. Thompson (a registered agent with First Securities Corporation's office in Illinois) the state Administrator required Thompson to testify regarding private memoranda involving securities trades under the Administrator's investigation. Thompson refused. The Administrator then sought (petitioned for) a court order to compel Thompson's testimony and submission of documents. Mr. Thompson's documents and forced testimony were incriminating. The Administrator then issued a cease and desist order to Thompson for violating the USA, but the Administrator was unable to have Thompson prosecuted.

Analysis: In an investigation, an Administrator can compel the testimony of the party under investigation. The reason that Mr. Thompson, who was under investigation, could not subsequently be prosecuted even though he had violated the law was that he had been compelled to testify against himself. Under the Fifth Amendment of the United States Constitution, a person may not be prosecuted if forced to testify against himself. In effect, Mr. Thompson was granted immunity from prosecution on the basis of the incriminating testimony. By granting immunity for the testimony, the safeguards of the Fifth Amendment's right against self-incrimination were preserved.

Cease and Desist Orders

If an Administrator determines that a person is about to engage in an activity that constitutes a violation of the USA, the Administrator may issue a **cease and desist order** without a hearing. The Administrator is granted this power to prevent potential violations before they occur.

Although the Administrator has the power to issue cease and desist orders, it does not have the legal power to compel compliance with the order. To compel compliance in the face of an individual's resistance, the Administrator must apply to a court with jurisdiction for an **injunction**. Only judicial officers can compel compliance by issuing injunctions and imposing penalties for violation of them.

Case Study: Cease and Desist Orders

Situation: Mr.Thompson, properly registered to conduct business in the state of Illinois, makes plans to sell a security within the next few days but the Administrator considers this security ineligible for sale in the state. The Administrator orders Thompson to immediately stop his sales procedures.

Analysis: The Administrator of Illinois issued a cease and desist order to Thompson because there was not sufficient time to conduct a public hearing prior to the sale to determine if the security was eligible for sale in the state.

Contumacy and Contempt

Contumacy is the term used to refer to an individual's refusal to comply with an Administrator's order. **Contempt** is the term used to refer an individual's refusal to comply with a judicial order.

Case Study: Contumacy and Contempt

Situation: Thompson refuses to stop his sales activity because he is convinced that his activities are legal. Upon learning of Thompson's refusal, the Illinois state securities Administrator applies to a court for an order to compel Thompson to stop his sales activity. The Administrator is granted an injunction from the Illinois State Supreme Court which orders Thompson to stop. Thompson continues despite the court order.

Analysis: In refusing to obey the Administrator of Illinois, Thompson has committed contumacy. In refusing to obey the injunction of the Illinois State Supreme Court, he is in contempt of court.

✓ ***Take Note:*** For **contumacy** you get taken to court; for **contempt** you get taken to jail.

Deny, Suspend, Cancel, or Revoke Registrations

The Administrator has the power to deny, suspend, cancel, or revoke the registration of securities professionals.

Securities Professionals

To justify a denial, revocation, or suspension of the license of a **securities professional**, the Administrator must find that the order is in the public interest and also find that the individual:

- has filed an incomplete, false, or misleading registration application;
- willfully violated the Uniform Securities Act;
- has been convicted of a securities-related misdemeanor within the last 10 years;
- has been convicted of a felony within the last 10 years;
- has been enjoined by law from engaging in the securities business;
- is subject to an Administrator's denial, revocation, or suspension;
- is engaged in dishonest or unethical securities practices;
- is insolvent;
- has failed to pay application filing fees; or
- is unqualified on the basis of training, or lack of experience or knowledge.

✓ ***Take Note:*** The public's best interest is not reason enough for the denial, suspension, or revocation of a registration. There must be a further reason, such as described above.

The Administrator must notify the registrant of any reason to postpone, suspend, revoke, or cancel a registration, and, if asked in writing, must provide a hearing within 15 days. The Administrator may not stop a registration on the basis of facts that were known to the Administrator at the time the registration became effective (unless the proceedings are initiated within 30 days).

Securities Issuers

As is the case with a securities professional, a securities Administrator may deny, suspend, cancel, or revoke the registration of a **securities issuer** if the order is in the public's interest and the securities registrant:

- files a misleading or incomplete registration statement;
- has an officer who has been convicted of a securities crime;
- is engaged in an offering that is fraudulent or made on unfair, unjust, or inequitable terms;
- charges offering fees that are excessive or unreasonable;
- is subject to a court injunction; or
- is engaged in a method of business that is illegal.

✓ ***Take Note:*** There are different reasons for stopping the registrations of securities professionals and of issuers. For example, the Administrator can deny a registration if an underwriter charges offering fees that are excessive. No such provision applies to a securities professional registering for a license.

Quick Quiz 1.3

True or False?

___ 1. The Administrator must seek an injunction to issue a cease and desist order.

___ 2. The USA requires an Administrator conduct a full hearing, public or private, prior to issuing a cease and desist order.

___ 3. The USA grants the Administrator the power to issue injunctions to force compliance with the provisions of the USA.

___ 4. In conducting an investigation, an Administrator can compel the testimony of witnesses.

___ 5. Investigations of serious violations must be held in public.

___ 6. An Administrator in Illinois may only enforce subpoenas from South Carolina if the violation originally occurred in Illinois.

Answers

1. ***F.*** *The Administrator need not seek an injunction to issue a cease and desist order. If an individual refuses to comply with a cease and desist order he is expressing contumacy toward the Administrator. The Administrator can then seek an injunction from a court to compel compliance.*

2. ***F.*** *The USA does not require that an Administrator conduct a public or private hearing prior to issuing a cease and desist order. When time does not permit, the Administrator may issue a cease and desist prior to a hearing to prevent a pending violation.*

3. ***F.*** *The USA does not grant the Administrator the power to issue injunctions to force compliance with the act. The act permits the Administrator to issue cease and desist orders and, if they do not work, the Administrator may seek an injunction from a court with jurisdiction. A cease and desist order is an administrative order whereas an injunction is a judicial order.*

4. ***T.*** *An Administrator can compel the testimony of witnesses when conducting an investigation. However, a person compelled to testify cannot be prosecuted on the basis of the compelled testimony.*

5. ***F.*** *Investigation of serious violations need not be held in public.*

6. ***F.*** *An Administrator in Illinois may enforce subpoenas from South Carolina whether the violation occurred in Illinois or not.*

Nonpunitive Terminations of Registration

A registration can be terminated even if there has not been a violation of the Uniform Securities Act. A request for withdrawal, lack of qualification, and cancellation are all reasons for cancellation. Additionally, there is a prohibition against personal profit or gain.

Withdrawal A person, on their own initiative, may request a **withdrawal** of a registration. The withdrawal is effective 30 days after the Administrator receives it, provided no revocation or suspension proceedings are in process against the person making the request.

Lack of Qualification An Administrator may not base a denial of a an individual's registration solely on their **lack of experience**. However, the USA allows the Administrator to restrict an applicant's registration for an investment adviser's license to that of a sales agent or registered representative if that person is not qualified to function as an investment adviser.

Cancellation If an Administrator finds that an applicant or a registrant no longer exists or has ceased to transact business, the Administrator may **cancel** the registration. The Administrator may also cancel a registration if a person is declared mentally incompetent.

✓ ***Take Note:*** Be familiar with the distinctions between cancellation and denial, suspension, or revocation. Cancellation does not result from violations or a failure to follow the provisions of the act. Cancellation occurs as the result of death, dissolution, or mental incompetency.

Quick Quiz 1.4

True or False?

___ 1. A registration may never be withdrawn.

___ 2. An Administrator may deny or revoke a registration of a securities professional solely on the basis of insolvency.

___ 3. An Administrator may revoke the registration of a person who is declared mentally incompetent.

Answers

1. ***F.*** *A person may request a withdrawal of a registration. Withdrawals become effective after 30 days if there are no revocation or denial proceedings in process. An Administrator may not deny a registration solely being on the basis of an individual's lack of experience, but can limit the registrant's activities to brokerage activities if they are not qualified to be an investment adviser.*

2. **F.** *An Administrator may not deny or revoke a registration of a securities professional solely on the basis of insolvency. The denial or revocation must also be in the public's interest.*

3. **F.** *An Administrator does not revoke the registration of a person who is declared mentally incompetent but cancels such registration; this is a nonpunitive administrative action.*

Penalties for Violations of the Uniform Securities Act

The USA provides both **civil liabilities** and **criminal penalties** for persons who violate the USA. In addition, the act provides for recovery by a client of financial loss that results from the fraudulent sale of a security or investment advice.

✓ ***Take Note:*** Fraud is the deliberate or willful concealment, misrepresentation, or omission of material information or the truth in order to deceive or manipulate another person for unlawful or unfair gain.

Civil Liabilities

Securities professionals who sell securities or who offer investment advice in violation of the USA are subject to **civil liabilities** (as well as criminal penalties). Enforcement of civil liabilities under the USA is subject to the Securities Litigation Uniform Standards Act of 1998.

The purchaser of securities sold in violation of the act may sue the seller to recover financial loss.

The purchaser can sue for recovery if the:

- securities were sold in violation of the registration provisions of USA;
- securities professional omits or makes an untrue statement of material fact;
- securities were sold by an agent who should have been but was not registered under the act; or
- securities were sold in violation of a rule or order of the securities Administrator.

Case Study: Fraudulent Sale of Securities

Situation: Mr. Thompson, the registered sales agent, *knowingly* omitted the fact that the shares of a company he sold to his client, Mr. Bixby, were downgraded to speculative grade and that their bonds were placed on a credit watch by one of the major credit rating agencies. A month after the sale, the shares became worthless.

***Analysis*:** Mr. Thompson sold these securities to Mr. Bixby in violation of the Uniform Securities Act because he deliberately or knowingly failed to mention material information, information that was important for Mr. Bixby to know in order for him to make an informed investment decision. Mr. Bixby has the right to recover the financial losses that result from the sale.

✓ ***Take Note:*** Under the USA, the actual seller of the securities or the advice is not the only person liable for the violation of the act. Every person who directly or indirectly controls the person who sold the securities or the advice or is a material aid to the transaction is also liable to the same extent as the person who conducted the transaction.

Statute of Limitations

The time limits, or statute of limitations, for violations of the civil provisions of the Uniform Securities Act is three years from the date of sale (rendering of the investment advice), or two years after discovering the violation, whichever comes first.

Rights of Recovery from Improper Sale of Securities

If the seller of securities discovers that they have made a sale in violation of the USA, the seller may offer to repurchase the securities from the buyer. In this case, the seller is offering the buyer the **right of recission**. To satisfy the buyer's right to recission, the amount paid back to the buyer must include the original purchase price and interest as determined by the Administrator.

By offering to buy back the securities that were sold in violation of the act, the seller can avoid a lawsuit through a **letter of recission**. The buyer has 30 days after receiving the letter of recission to respond. If the buyers does not accept the recission offer within 30 days, the buyer gives up any right to pursue a lawsuit at a later date.

If the buyer accepts the recission offer, he or she may recover:

- the original purchase price of the securities; *plus*
- any interest costs as determined by the Administrator; *plus*
- all reasonable attorney's fees; *minus*
- any income earned during the period that the securities were held.

Rights of Recovery From Improper Investment Advice

A person who buys a security as the result of investment advice received in violation of the USA also has the right of recission. In the case of securities purchased as a result of improper investment advice, the buyer may recover:

- cost of the advice; *plus*
- loss as a result of the advice; *plus*
- all interest costs from date of fee payment as determined by the Administrator; *plus*
- any reasonable attorney's fees.

✓ ***Take Note:*** When securities are sold improperly, the buyer can recover the original purchase price in addition to other losses. When improper investment advice is offered, the purchaser of the advice is entitled to recover the cost of the advice and losses incurred but is not entitled to recover the original purchase price from the adviser.

Criminal Penalties

Persons found guilty of a fraudulent securities transaction are subject to **criminal penalties** (as well as civil liabilities). Upon conviction, a person may be fined, or imprisoned, or both. To be convicted of fraud, the violation must be willful and the registrant must know that the activity is fraudulent.

Statute of Limitations

The statute of limitations for criminal offenses under the USA is five years from the date of the offense.

✓ ***Take Note:*** Remember the sequence of 5-5-3 for the application of *criminal* penalties; five-year statute of limitations, $5,000 maximum fine, and imprisonment of no more than three years. Under the *civil* provisions, the statute of limitations runs for two years from the discovery of the offense or to three years after the act occurred, whichever occurs first.

Judicial Review of Orders

Any person affected by an order of the Administrator may obtain a review of the order in an appropriate court by filing a written petition within 60 days. A copy of the petition must also be served upon the Administrator who then must supply the court with evidence supporting the order. The court may order additional evidence and the Administrator may modify the findings on the basis of this evidence. The court has exclusive jurisdiction to affirm, modify, enforce, or set aside the order in whole or in part. The judgment of the court is final.

Quick Quiz 1.5

True or False?

___ 1. A sales agent who unknowingly commits a violation of the Uniform Securities Act is liable under the act's criminal liability provisions to time in prison.

___ 2. A client who purchased a security in violation of the Uniform Securities Act may recover the original purchase price plus costs involved in filing a lawsuit.

___ 3. The right of recission must be accepted within two years of receipt of the letter of recission.

___ 4. Any person aggrieved by an order of the Administrator may request an appeal of the order within 60 days which, in effect, functions as a stay order during the period.

Answers

1. ***F.*** *In order to be subject to time in prison, a sales agent must knowingly have violated the USA.*

2. ***T.*** *A client who purchased a security in violation of the USA may recover the original purchase price plus costs involved in filing a lawsuit.*

3. ***F.*** *The right of recission must be accepted within 30 days of receipt of the letter of recission, not two years.*

4. ***F.*** *Although any person aggrieved by an order of the Administrator may request an appeal of the order within 60 days, such appeal does not function as a stay order during the appeal process. The person who is subject of the order must comply with the order during the period.*

The Administrative Provisions of the USA HotSheet

USA as Model Legislation:	• USA is not *actual* but *model* legislation for each states' own legislation
NSMIA of 1996:	• Eliminates state and federal registration duplication
Securities Litigation Uniform Standards Act (1998)	• Class actions governed by federal standards
Federal Covered Securities:	• Covered by national, not state, regulation • Includes securities listed on U.S. exchanges, issued by investment companies, or sold to qualified purchasers
Administrator:	• State official responsible for the implementation of the USA
Powers of the Administrator:	• Make rules and orders • Conduct investigations and issue subpoenas • Issue cease and desist orders and seek injunctions • Deny, suspend, cancel, or revoke registrations
Fifth Amendment Protection:	• Forced testimony given immunity under the Fifth Amendment
Fraud:	• Willful misrepresentation for unlawful gain
Civil Liabilities:	• Attorney's costs *plus* losses on investment *plus* interest *minus* any income earned
Recission	• Right to rescind a fraudulent trade
Criminal Penalties:	• Fines or imprisonment, or both
Statute of Limitations:	• Time limits for bringing suit in a case • **Civil**—three years from date of sale or of rendering of advice or two years after discovering violation, whichever occurs first • **Criminal**—five years after date of the transaction

Lesson Exam 1

1. To protect the public, the Administrator may

   I. deny a registration if the registrant does not have sufficient experience to function as a registered representative
   II. limit a registrant's functions to that of a broker if, in the initial application for registration as an investment adviser, the registrant is not qualified to act as an adviser
   III. take into consideration that the registrant will work under the supervision of a registered investment adviser or broker-dealer in approving a registration
   IV. deny a registration, although denial is not in the public's interest if it is prudent in view of a change in the state's political composition

   A. I and II
   B. I, II and III
   C. III and IV
   D. I, II, III and IV

2. Which of the following accurately describes a cease and desist order as authorized by the USA?

   A. An order issued by a federal agency to a brokerage firm to stop an advertising campaign
   B. An order by any administrative agency to refrain from a practice of business found by that agency to be unfair
   C. An order issued by a court requiring a business to stop an unfair practice
   D. An order from one brokerage firm to another brokerage firm to refrain from unfair business practices

3. An Administrator can deny an investment adviser's registration for all of the following reasons EXCEPT

   A. lack of experience
   B. failure to post a surety bond
   C. failure to pass a written exam
   D. not meeting minimum financial standards

4. A person who sells securities in violation of state securities laws is civilly liable for

   I. principal
   II. interest
   III. court costs
   IV. attorney's fees

   A. I, II and IV
   B. I and III
   C. II, III and IV
   D. I, II, III and IV

5. Under the Uniform Securities Act, which of the following persons is responsible for proving that a securities issue is exempt from registration?

   A. Underwriter
   B. Issuer
   C. State Administrator
   D. There is no need to prove eligibility for an exemption.

6. The Administrator may, by rule,

   A. forbid an adviser from taking custody of client funds
   B. allow an agent to waive provisions of the USA
   C. suspend federal law if the Administrator believes it to be in the public interest
   D. suspend the registration of a federal covered adviser because the contract did not meet the requirements for a state sanctioned investment advisory contract

7. If a sales rep (agent) chooses to appeal an Administrator's order, the rep must file for review of the order with the appropriate court
   A. immediately
   B. within 30 days after the entry of the order
   C. within 180 days after the entry of the order
   D. within 60 days after the entry of the order

8. If it is in the public interest to do so, the Uniform Securities Act provides that the state Administrator may deny the registration of a person for all of the following reasons EXCEPT that
   A. the applicant is not qualified owing to lack of experience
   B. a willful violation of the Uniform Securities Act has taken place
   C. the applicant is financially insolvent
   D. the applicant is enjoined temporarily from engaging in the securities business

9. A customer living in one state receives a phone call from an agent in another state. A transaction between the two occurs in a third state. According to the Uniform Securities Act, the transaction falls under the jurisdiction of the Administrator of
   A. the state in which the customer lives
   B. the state in which the agent is registered
   C. the state in which the transaction took place
   D. all three states involved

10. An Administrator in conducting investigations may do all of the following EXCEPT
   A. make public or private investigations both inside or outside the state to determine if a registrant has violated the USA
   B. require or permit any person to file a statement in writing under oath or otherwise whether or not professionally related to the party under investigation
   C. publish information concerning any violation of the USA or of any rule whether or not the party investigated objects
   D. revoke immunity from prosecution from a party who is compelled to testify over Fifth Amendment objections

11. Under the USA, if a sales rep is ordered to appear before the Administrator to answer a complaint and the sales rep refuses to appear, which of the following is TRUE?
   A. The Administrator may cancel the registered representative's license within 10 days.
   B. The rep may plead protection under the Fifth Amendment of the U.S. Constitution and refuse to answer questions.
   C. The rep has demonstrated contumacy toward the Administrator.
   D. The Administrator may issue an injunction.

12. An Administrator may summarily suspend a registration pending final determination of proceedings under the USA. However, the Administrator may not enter an order without

I. appropriate prior notice to the applicant as well as the employer or prospective employer of the applicant
II. opportunity for a hearing
III. findings of fact and conclusions of law
IV. prior written acknowledgment of the applicant

A. I only
B. I and II
C. I, II, and III
D. I, II, III and IV

13. The Administrator has authority to

I. issue a cease and desist order without a hearing
II. issue a cease and desist order only after a hearing
III. convict violators of the 1933 Securities Act in criminal prosecutions
IV. sentence violators of the USA to three years in prison

A. I and III
B. I and IV
C. II and III
D. II and IV

Lesson Exam 1 Answers & Rationale

1. B. The Administrator can deny, suspend, or revoke a registration for many reasons, but it must be in the interest of the public. The Administrator may not deny the registration simply because it is prudent. The Administrator may determine that an applicant, in his initial application for registration for an investment adviser, is not qualified to act as an adviser and thus limit the registration to that of a broker-dealer and the Administrator can also take into consideration whether the registrant will work under the supervision of a registered investment adviser or broker-dealer when approving an application. QID: 38329

2. B. A cease and desist order is a directive from an administrative agency to immediately stop a particular action. The order can come from a federal, state, or judicial body; it is not exclusive to any one. Administrators may issue cease and desist orders with or without a hearing. Brokerage houses cannot issue cease and desist orders to each other. QID: 28940

3. A. Lack of experience, by itself, is not cause for registration denial. QID: 39207

4. D. A person who sells securities illegally is liable for the purchase price of the securities plus interest from the date of purchase, costs and reasonable attorney's fees. QID: 31195

5. B. The burden of proof for claiming eligibility for an exemption falls to the person claiming the exemption. QID: 28884

6. A. The Administrator has considerable discretion to make rules or issue orders. Specifically, the USA allows the Administrator to prohibit custody by rule. However, the USA does not allow the Administrator to waive provisions of the USA, nor can the Administrator suspend federal law. QID: 36703

7. D. Under the USA, a registered person has up to 60 days to appeal any disciplinary finding by the state Administrator. QID: 31090

8. A. Registration may be revoked if the applicant willfully violates the Uniform Securities Act, is financially insolvent, or has been enjoined from engaging in the securities business. If the person qualifies by virtue of training or knowledge, registration cannot be denied for lack of experience only. QID: 28953

9. D. Under the scope of the Uniform Securities Act, if any part of a transaction occurs in a state, the transaction falls under the jurisdiction of the state Administrator. The transaction is under the control of the Administrator of the state in which the customer lives and the Administrator of the state in which the transaction took place. QID: 28932

10. D. The Administrator may not revoke immunity from prosecution if a party is required to testify against his will. Any person compelled to testify over objecting on Fifth Amendment grounds cannot be prosecuted on the basis of the information provided. However, the person compelled is not exempt from prosecution for perjury or contempt committed in the course of his testimony. The Fifth Amendment guarantees the right against self-incrimination. The Administrator can make investigations in public or private both inside or outside the state to determine if a registrant has violated the USA. The Administrator may require or permit any person to file a statement in writing under oath or otherwise, whether or not professionally related to the party under investigation and may publish information concerning any violation of the USA. QID: 36385

11. C. The representative has demonstrated contumacy. Note that the Administrator cannot issue injunctions; only a court with jurisdiction can issue an injunction. QID: 31076

12. C. With the exception of those proceedings awaiting final determination, the Administrator must provide an appropriate prior notice to the applicant as well as the employer or prospective

employer of the applicant and provide the opportunity for a hearing. In addition, the Administrator may only issue a stop order after findings of fact and conclusions of law. An applicant is not required to provide written acknowledgement before an order is issued. QID: 38330

13. B. The Administrator may issue a cease and desist order without a hearing, but does not have the authority to convict violators of the 1933 Securities Act in criminal prosecutions nor sentence violators of the USA. QID: 39209

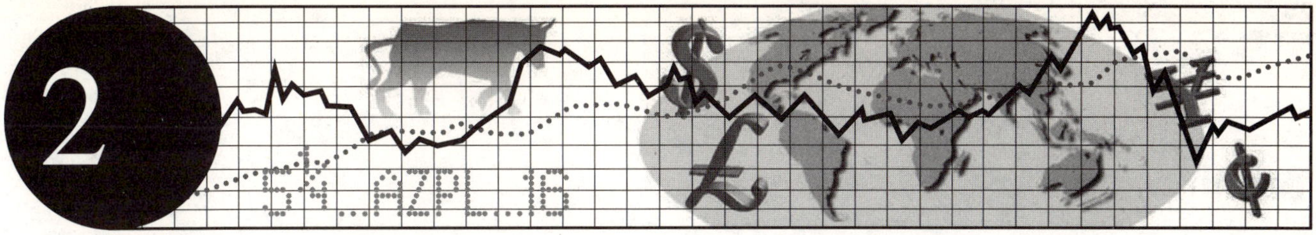

Securities

INTRODUCTION

The Administrator's jurisdiction and powers extend over securities transactions as well as persons engaged in securities transactions. This lesson discusses the procedures for the registration of securities and their exemptions from registration. For a securities transaction to be lawful under the USA, the security itself must be registered unless it is exempt from the act's registration requirements.

The Series 63 exam will include approximately 15 questions on the material presented in this lesson.

LESSON OBJECTIVES

When you have completed this lesson, you should be able to:

- determine who is and is not a security issuer;
- compare and contrast the different methods of securities registration;
- identify instruments that are securities;
- list the categories of exempt securities;
- define an exempt transaction and provide examples; and
- describe the requirements for exemption from registration for private placements.

Terminology

Recognizing and comprehending terms as they are used in the USA is crucial to understanding the scope and meaning of the act.

Security

Perhaps, the most important term in the USA is the term **security**. The provisions of the USA apply to *only* those financial instruments that are included in the term security. Any instrument that is *excluded* from the term security is not covered by the act.

While the USA does not explicitly define a security, it provides a comprehensive list of those financial instruments that are included in the term security and therefore covered by the provisions of the act. Under the USA, **security** includes:

- note;
- stock;
- treasury stock;
- security future;
- bond;
- debenture;
- evidence of indebtedness;
- certificate of interest or participation in a profit-sharing agreement;
- collateral trust certificate;
- preorganization certificate or subscription;
- transferable share;
- investment contract;
- voting rust certificate;
- certificate of deposit for a security;
- fractional undivided interest in oil, gas, or other mineral rights;
- put, call, straddle, option or privilege on a security;
- certificate of deposit, or group or index of securities;
- put, call, straddle, option or privilege entered into on a national securities exchange relating to foreign currency;
- any interest or instrument commonly known as a security; or
- a certificate of interest or participation in, receipt of, guarantee of, or warrant or right to subscribe to or purchase, any of the above.

The term **security** includes both a certificated and an uncertificated security, and those securities that are held in electronic bookkeeping or other nonwritten form.

Not included in the term security are:

- An insurance or endowment policy or annuity contract under which an insurance company promises to pay a fixed sum of money either in a lump sum or periodically
- Interest in a contributory or noncontributory pension or welfare plan subject to the Employee Retirement Income Security Act of 1974

✓ ***Take Note:*** An automobile is not included in the list of terms included in the definition of a security. If a registered agent commits fraud in the sale of his car, he has not committed a violation of the USA. He has violated the antifraud provisions of another act prohibiting fraudulent commercial transactions.

Note also that commodities futures contracts, precious metals, antiques, collectibles, and real estate are not listed above. Under the Uniform Securities Act, they are not securities and therefore not subject to the act's provisions.

✓ ***For Example:*** Interests in farm animals represent an investment of money in a common effort of others, (a breeder or trainer) to realize a profit from the sale of the animals. An individual farmer's direct ownership of a cow is not a security—it is just a cow. However, a farmer's investment of money in a tradable interest in a heard of cattle on which he expects to earn a profit solely as the result of the breeders' efforts is a security because it is an investment contract.

✓ ***Take Note:*** Commodity futures are not securities, but options on commodities are. Annuities with fixed payouts are not securities, but variable annuities are because they are dependent upon the investment performance of securities within the annuity.

✓ ***Take Note:*** The act specifically notes that the term "investment contract" includes interests in a limited partnership, a limited liability company, or a limited liability partnership, or an investment in a viatical settlement or similar agreement. The United States Supreme Court in the **Howey Decision** determined that an investment contract constitutes an investment in a common enterprise with the expectation of profits to be derived primarily from the efforts of a person other than the investor. A **common enterprise** means an enterprise in which the fortunes of the investor are interwoven with those of either the person offering the investment, a third party or other investors. Any instrument that is an investment contract is included in the term security.

Nonexempt Security

If a security is not exempt from registration requirements, it is called a **nonexempt security**. When you see the term **nonexempt**, it means *subject to registration*. When you see the term **exempt**, it means *not subject to registration*.

✓ ***Take Note:*** The methods of registration discussed in this lesson refer to nonexempt securities because if a security is not exempt from registration, it must be registered.

Issuer

An **issuer** is any person who issues (distributes) or proposes to issue a security. The most common issuers of securities are companies or governments (federal, state, and municipal governments and their agencies and their subdivisions).

✓ ***For Example:*** Simus Shoe Co., (a retail chain store) issues shares to the public. Mr. Bixby (a wealthy investor) buys the shares through his broker, Mr. Thompson, at First Securities Corp. Simus Shoe is the issuer, Mr. Bixby is the investor, and First Securities Corp. is the broker-dealer.

Nonissuer Transaction

A **nonissuer transaction** is not directly, or indirectly, for the benefit of the issuer. A nonissuer transaction occurs when the proceeds from the sale of securities go to the seller of the securities who is not the issuer of those shares.

✓ ***Take Note:*** If Mr. Bixby sells 100 shares of stock he owns in Simus Shoe Co. on the New York Stock Exchange (NYSE), Mr. Bixby receives the proceeds from the sale, not Simus Shoes. This is a nonissuer transaction.

Nonissuer transactions are also referred to as **secondary transactions** or transactions between investors.

✓ ***For Example:*** When Mr. Bixby sold his 100 shares of Simus Shoe on the NYSE, he sold those shares to another investor who purchased them from him on the floor of the NYSE. This is a secondary transaction.

Initial or Primary Offering

The first time an issuer distributes securities to the public, it is called a **primary** or **initial public offering (IPO)**. Initial or primary offerings are issuer transactions because the issuer (the company) receives the proceeds.

✓ ***For Example:*** The first time that Simus Shoe Co. issued shares to the public, Simus Shoe engaged in an IPO or a primary offering because it received the proceeds from distributing its shares to the public. After Simus Shoe went public, transactions between investors executed on exchanges through brokerage agents were secondary transactions in nonissuer securities.

Quick Quiz 2.1

1. Which list of instruments below are not securities?

   A. Stock, treasury stock, rights, warrants, transferable shares
   B. Voting trust certificates, interests in oil and gas drilling programs
   C. Commodity futures contracts, fixed payment life insurance contracts
   D. Commodity options contracts, interests in multilevel distributorship arrangements

2. Which of the following is not part of the four-part test for a security?

   A. An investment of money
   B. An expectation of profit
   C. Management activity by owner
   D. Solely from the efforts of others

3. Nonexempt securities

   A. need not be registered in the state in which they are sold
   B. must be registered in the state in which they are sold
   C. need not be registered if sold in an exempt transaction
   D. need not be registered if sold in a nonexempt transaction

4. A nonissuer transaction is a transaction

   A. between two corporations
   B. in which the issuing corporation will not receive the proceeds from the transaction
   C. between a corporation and an issuer
   D. in which the security must be registered

Answers

1. **C.** *Commodity futures contracts and fixed payment life insurance contracts are not securities. Commodity option contracts are securities.*

2. **C.** *Management activity on the part of the owner is not part of the Howey, or four-part, test for an instrument to be a security. The four parts are: (1) an investment of money in (2) a common enterprise with (3) an expectation of profit (4) solely from the effort of others.*

3. **B.** *Nonexempt securities must be registered in the state in which they are sold. Exempt securities need not be registered because they are exempt from registration.*

4. **B.** *A nonissuer transaction is one where the company that issues the shares does not receive the proceeds from the transaction. A nonissuer transaction is a transaction between two investors.*

General Procedures for the Registration of Securities

Under the Uniform Securities Act, it is unlawful for any person to offer or sell a security in a state unless the security, transaction, or offer is exempt from the USA's registration requirements. If the security is not exempt or is a federal covered security, it must be registered in the state or it cannot be lawfully sold in the state.

Registration Procedures

The first step in the registration procedure is for the issuer or its representative to pick up a registration statement or application from the state securities Administrator.

Filing the Registration Statement

State Administrators require every issuer to supply the following information on their applications:

- amount of securities to be issued in the state;
- states in which the security is to be offered; and
- any adverse order or judgement concerning the offering by regulatory authorities, court, or the SEC.

When filing the registration statement with the Administrator, an applicant may include documents that have been filed with the Administrator within the last five years, provided the information is current and accurate. The Administrator may, by rule or order, permit the omission of any information it considers unnecessary.

Filing Fee

The issuer (or any other person on whose behalf the offering is to be made) must pay a filing fee as determined by the Administrator when filing the registration. The filing fees are often based upon a percentage of the total offering price.

✓ ***Take Note:*** If the registration is withdrawn or if the Administrator issues a stop order before the registration is effective, the Administrator may retain a portion of the fee and refund the remainder to the applicant.

Ongoing Reports

The Administrator may require the person who filed the registration statement to file reports to keep the information contained in the registration statement current and to inform the Administrator of the progress of the offering.

✓ ***Take Note:*** These reports cannot be required more than quarterly.

Escrow

As a condition of registration, the Administrator may require that a security be placed in **escrow** if the security is issued:

- within the past three years;
- at a price substantially different than the offering price; or
- to any person for a consideration other than cash.

Special Subscription Form

The Administrator may also require, as a condition of registration, that the issue be sold only on a form specified by the Administrator and that a copy of the form or subscription contract be filed with the Administrator or preserved for up to three years.

Effective Registration Period

A registration is effective for one year after its **effective date** (the date that the Administrator authorizes the issuer to sell the shares). However, there is an exception to this rule—the one-year period may be extended if the issuer or broker-dealer offering the securities has an unsold allotment of shares.

✓ ***Take Note:*** Unlike securities registered under federal law, securities registered under the USA must be reregistered every year.

Withdrawal of Registration Statement

A registration statement may not be withdrawn until one year after its effective date if any securities of the same class are outstanding and may only be withdrawn with the approval of the Administrator.

The Administrator's Powers

The Administrator has the power under the USA to deny, suspend, or revoke the registration of a security; however, the Administrator can only invoke these powers if it is in the public's interest *and* the applicant:

- files a false or incomplete statement;
- is in violation of the USA;
- is engaged in a method of business that is illegal;
- has an officer who has been convicted of a securities-related crime;
- has prepared a fraudulent registration; or
- charges unreasonable fees.

In addition, the Administrator may deny a registration if the applicant fails to pay the filing fee. When the fee is paid, the denial order will be removed provided the applicant is in compliance with all registration procedures.

Quick Quiz 2.2

True or False?

___ 1. Only the issuer of securities itself can file a registration statement with the Administrator.

___ 2. Every applicant for registration of securities in a state must include any adverse order or judgement concerning the offering by any court, other regulatory agency, or the SEC

___ 3. The Administrator may require registrants to file quarterly reports.

Answers

*1. **F.** A registration statement may be filed by the issuer or the issuer's representative (such as a broker-dealer).*

*2. **T.** The applicant must indicate the amount of securities to be registered in the Administrator's state and any adverse order or judgement concerning the offering by any court, other regulatory agency, or the SEC.*

*3. **T.** The Administrator may require registrants to file quarterly reports but may not require reports to be filed more frequently than quarterly.*

Securities Registration and Notice Filings

The USA provides issuers with two methods of registration: coordination and qualification. In addition, the Act allows issuers of federal covered securities to file their federally filed document with the state Administrator. This procedure is called "notice filing."

The National Securities Markets Improvement Act of 1996 preempted state registration of securities issued by investment companies under the Investment Company Act of 1940. Notwithstanding the preemptive provisions of NSMIA, state securities Administrators may require the issuers of federal covered securities to file those documents filed with the SEC to be filed for "notice" purposes and require such issuers to pay filing fees and provide a consent to service of process to the state.

Registration by Coordination

A security may be **registered by coordination** if a registration statement has been filed under the Securities Act of 1933 in connection with the same offering.

In coordinating a federal registration with state registration, issuers must supply the following records in addition to the consent of service of process.

- Copy of the latest form of prospectus filed under the Securities Act of 1933 if the Administrator requires
- Copy of articles of incorporation and bylaws, a copy of the underwriting agreement, or a specimen copy of the security
- If the Administration requests, copies of any other information filed by the issuer under the Securities Act of 1933
- Each amendment to the federal prospectus promptly after it is filed with the Securities and Exchange Commission

Effective Date Registration by coordination becomes effective at the same time the federal registration becomes effective, provided the following conditions are met.

- No stop orders have been issued and no proceedings are pending against the issuer
- Registration has been on file for at least 20 days or a shorter period as the Administrator may specify
- Statement of the maximum and minimum offering prices and underwriting discounts must be on file for two business days

Registration by Qualification

Any security can be **registered by qualification**. Registration by qualification requires a registrant to supply any information that the state securities Administrator requires. Securities not eligible for registration by another method must be registered by qualification. In addition, securities that will be sold only in one state (intrastate) will be registered by qualification.

To register by qualification, an issuer must supply a consent to service of process and the following information.

- Name, address, form of organization, description of property, and nature of business
- Information on directors and officers and every owner of 10% or more of the issuers securities, and the remuneration paid to owners in the last 12 months
- Description of issuers capitalization and long-term debt
- Estimated proceeds and the use to which the proceeds will be put
- Type and amount of securities offered, offering price, and selling and underwriting costs
- Stock options to be created in connection with the offering
- Copy of any prospectus, pamphlet, circular, or sales literature to be used in the offering
- Specimen copy of the security along with opinion of counsel as to the legality of the security being offered

- Audited balance sheet current within four months of the offering with an income statement for three years prior to date of the balance sheet

✓ ***Take Note:*** Additional information may be required by the Administrator by rule or order. The Administrator may require that a prospectus be sent to purchasers prior to the sale and newly-established companies registering their securities for the first time in a state register by qualification.

Effective Date A registration by qualification becomes effective whenever the state Administrator so orders.

Notice Filings For Federal Covered Securities

With respect to an investment company that is a federal covered security, the Administrator may require the issuer to file the following documents as a condition for sale of their securities in the state.

- Documents of a federal registration statement filed with the SEC
- Documents filed as amendments to the initial federal registration statement
- A report as to the value of such federal covered securities offered in the state
- Schedule D and a consent to service of process for those securities covered under the Securities Act of 1933, no later than 15 days after the first sales of the security in the state
- Consent to service of process

✓ ***Take Note:*** The Administrator may waive any or all of the provisions of these rules.Under the USA, the Administrator may require notice filling fees to the extent necessary to compute fees. An Administrator may require issuers to file a report of the value of the securities sold or offered to persons in the state.

Quick Quiz 2.3

True or False?

___ 1. If Simus Shoe Company, a new retail shore store chain, has applied for the registration of its securities with the SEC as required by the Securities Act of 1933 and it also wants to register its securities in the state of Illinois, Simus would most register by coordination.

___ 2. Any company may register by qualification whether or not it files a statement with the SEC.

Answers

*1. **T.** Registration by coordination involves coordinating a state registration with that of a federal registration.*

2. *T. Any company may register by qualification. Companies that are not established or that intend to offer their securities in one state register by qualification.*

Exemptions from Registration

In certain situations, the USA exempts securities and transactions from registration and filing requirements of sales literature and registration. A security, a transaction, or both, can be exempt.

Exempt Securities and Exempt Transactions

An **exempt security** retains its exemption when initially issued and in subsequent trading. However, an **exempt transaction** must be established before each transaction. The two are not mutually exclusive.

✓ ***For Example:*** A transaction can be exempt, but the security involved in that transaction may have to be registered.

The Uniform Securities Act provides for 10 categories of exempt securities and 18 categories of exempt transactions. Those securities that are nonexempt must register under one of three methods—filing (notification), coordination, or qualification. An exempt security retains its exemption upon its initial issue as well as in subsequent trading.

An exemption for a transaction, on the other hand, must be established with each transaction. Provided it is in the public interest, the state Administrator can deny, suspend, or revoke the registration of a security if the issuer files a false or incomplete statement, has been convicted of a securities related crime, is in an illegal business, has filed a fraudulent application, or charges unreasonable fees. Registrants must pay filing fees to the state in which they register.

An **exempt security** is exempt from state registration. Securities are exempt because they are regulated by the federal government or a regulatory agency. The purpose of the USA is to protect the public from fraudulent securities activities. NSMIA eliminated the dual registration of securities; if a security is regulated by the federal government or regulatory agency, states may not regulate these also, hence the securities are exempt from state regulation under the USA.

An **exempt transaction** is exempt from the regulatory control of the state Administrator because of the manner in which a sale is made or because of the person to the sale is made. The USA prohibits the sale of securities in the state unless they are registered in the state, exempt from registration in the state, or subject to an exempt transaction.

✓ ***For Example:*** A registered representative can sell a security that is not exempt in the state if the representative the security is a bank. Because such sale is an exempt transaction, the sale can be made without registration. This means that the securities sold in exempt transactions do not have to be registered in the state. If such securities were not sold in exempt transactions, they would have to be registered in the state.

Exempt Securities

Currently, there are 10 categories of securities exempt from registration and filing of sales literature requirements of the Uniform Securities Act:

1) United States Government and Municipal Securities. These include securities issued, insured, or guaranteed by the United States, by a state, or by their political subdivisions. Certificates of deposits for any these are included in the exemption.

2) Foreign Government Securities. These include securities issued, insured, or guaranteed a foreign government (or any of their political subdivisions) with which the United States maintains diplomatic relations.

3) Depository Institutions and International Banks. These include securities that are issued, guaranteed by, or are a direct obligation of a depository institution or international bank (depository institution means bank, savings institution, or trust organized under the laws of the state).

4) Insurance Company Securities. These include securities issued, insured, or guaranteed by an insurance company authorized to do business in the state.

5) Public Utility Securities. These include any security issued or guaranteed by a railroad, other common carriers, public utility, or public utility holding company registered under the Public Holding Company Act of 1935; regulated as to rates by federal or state authority; subject to the jurisdiction of the Interstate Commerce Commission; or regulated in respect to issuance or guarantee of the security by a governmental authority of the United States, any state, Canada, or any Canadian province.

6) Certain Options and Rights. These include put or call option contracts, warrants, or subscription rights on a federal covered security. Also exempt under this category are options on a security, an index of securities, or foreign currency option issued by a clearing agency registered under the Securities Exchange Act of 1934.

7) Securities Issued by Nonprofit Organizations. These include securities issued by religious, educational, fraternal, charitable, social, athletic, reformatory, or trade associations.

8) Securities Issued by Cooperatives. These include securities issued by a nonprofit membership cooperative to members of that cooperative.

9) Securities of Employee Benefit Plans. This includes any investment contract issued by an employee stock purchase, saving, pension, or profit-sharing plan.

10) Equipment Trust Certificates. Equipment trust certificates issued on leased property by exempt or federal covered issuers. Exemptions from registration extend to **federal covered securities** or those securities listed on the New York Stock Exchange, the American Exchange, the Nasdaq National Market (NNM), and other regional stock exchanges.

✓ ***Take Note:*** These exemptions are known as **blue-chip exemptions**.

✓ ***For Example:*** Shares of investment companies registered under the Investment Company Act of 1940 are exempt as federal covered securities.

Under NSMIA there cannot be dual coverage. However, federal covered securities can be required to pay filing fees with the states in which they are sold.

✓ ***Take Note:*** A promissory note, draft, bill of exchange, or banker's acceptance that matures within nine months, is issued in denominations of at least $50,000, and receives one of the three highest ratings by a nationally recognized rating agency is a federal covered security and also exempt from registration requirements.

Quick Quiz 2.4

1. Which of the following securities are exempt from registration and filing requirements under the USA?

   I. Shares of investment companies registered under the Investment Company Act of 1940
   II. Shares sold on the Nasdaq National Market System
   III. AAA rated promissory notes of $100,000 that mature in 30 days
   IV. Shares sold on the New York Stock Exchange

   A. I only
   B. II and IV
   C. II, III, and IV
   D. I, II, III and IV

2. Which of the following securities is not exempt from the registration and advertising requirements of the USA?

   A. Shares of Commonwealth Edison, a public utility holding company
   B. Securities issued by the Carnegie Endowment for Peace
   C. Securities issued by the National Bank of Canada
   D. Variable annuity contract issued by Prudential Insurance Co.

3. Under the Uniform Securities Act,

   A. an exempt security must be sold in an exempt transaction
   B. if a security is sold in an exempt transaction, the security is automatically exempt
   C. if a security is exempt, the transaction is not automatically exempt
   D. exempt transactions always involve issuers

Answers

1. **D.** *All of the securities are federal covered securities and therefore not subject to the registration requirements of the USA.*

2. **D.** *Variable annuities (whose performance depends upon the securities in a segregated fund) are nonexempt, which means they are covered by the act and have to register. Shares in public utilities, charitable foundations, and foreign banking institutions as listed in choices A, B, and C are federal covered securities and therefore exempt from registration.*

3. **C.** *Under the USA, if a security is exempt, it does not automatically mean that the transaction is exempt.*

Exempt Transactions

The Uniform Securities Act allows exemptions for 18 types of **exempt transactions**. Securities sold in exempt transactions are not subject to the filing or registration and advertising requirements of the act because of the manner in which they are sold.

1) Isolated Nonissuer Transactions. These include secondary (nonissuer) transactions, whether effected through a broker or not, that occur infrequently (which is very few transactions per broker per year; the exact number varies by state).

2) Specified Nonissuer Transactions. These include nonissuer transactions by a registered agent provided that the security has been outstanding in the public's hands for at least 90 days, provided that the issuer has:

- a class of securities registered under the Securities Exchange Act of 1934;

- a class of securities registered under the Investment Company Act of 1940; or
- filed and maintained information comparable to that required under the Securities Exchange Act of 1934 with the Administrator for 180 days.

3) Foreign Nonissuer Transactions. These include nonissuer transactions in securities subject to the Securities Exchange Act of 1934 reporting requirements.

4) Nonissuer Transactions in Securities Subject to Securities Exchange Act Reporting. A nonissuer transaction in an outstanding security if the issuer files reports with the SEC.

5) Nonissuer Transactions in Specified Fixed-Income Securities. Issuer must not be in default nor in the organization stage.

6) Unsolicited Brokerage Transactions. These include transactions initiated by the client, not the agent.

7) Pledges. A nonissuer transaction executed by a bona fide pledgee.

8) Underwriter Transactions. These include transactions between issuer and underwriter as well as those between underwriters themselves.

9) Unit Secured Transactions. These include transactions in a bond backed by a real mortgage or deed of trust provided that the entire mortgage or deed of trust is sold as a unit.

10) Bankruptcy, Guardian, or Conservator Transactions. Transaction by an executor, administrator, sheriff, or trustee in bankruptcy.

11) Institutional Investor Transactions. These are primarily financial institutions and high net worth investors.

✓ ***Take Note:*** Remember the distinction between an **accredited investor** and **institutional investor**.

An **accredited investor** is an investor who meets the accredited investor standards of Regulation D. Reg D standards require that an individual have a net worth greater than $1,000,000 or $200,000 in income for the last two years and the current year, invests for his own account, and has requisite knowledge to evaluate investments.

An **institutional investor** is an investor that manages large amounts of money for other people, such as a mutual fund, an insurance company, or a pension fund.

12) Limited Offering Transactions. These include any offering, called a **private placement**, directed at not more than 10 persons other than institutional investors during the previous 12 consecutive months, provided that:

- the seller believes that all of the noninstitutional buyers are purchasing for investment purposes only;
- no commissions or other remuneration is paid for soliciting noninstitutional investors; and
- no general solicitation or advertising is used.

13) Transactions with Existing Security Holders. No commissions may be paid.

14) Offering when Registered under the USA and the Securities Act of 1933. This includes an offer (but not a sale) of a security for which a registration statement has been filed if no stop order is in effect. In other words, an offer, but not the sale, of a security may take place prior to the effective date of the registration; the actual sale must take place after the registration is effective.

15) Offerings when Registered Under the USA and Exempt from the 1933 Securities Act. These include offerings, but not sales, of a security exempt from registration under the Securities Act of 1933. Offers, but not sales, can be made prior to the effective date of the registration.

16) Control Transactions. This includes mergers, consolidations, or reorganization transactions to which the issuer and the other person or its parent or subsidiary are parties.

17) Recission Offers. These include offers made to rescind an improper transaction.

18) Out-of-State Offers or Sales. This includes an offer or sale of a security to a person who is not a resident of the state and is not present in the state.

The Administrator's Powers

The USA grants the Administrator the authority, by rule or order, to exempt a security, transaction, or offer from the USA's registration and filing requirements. In addition, the Administrator may waive a requirement for an exemption of a transaction or security.

✓ ***For Example:*** Securities and transactions that are exempt from the filing and advertising provisions of the Uniform Securities Act are not exempt from the antifraud provisions of state securities law.

The Administrator may, by rule or order, deny or revoke any exemption with respect to a security or transaction upon prior notice to the interested parties. The Administrator must also provide an opportunity for a hearing. The

Administrator also has the power to summarily deny or revoke exemptions pending final determination of any proceedings.

Under the Uniform Securities Act, the burden of providing an exemption or an exception from a definition falls upon the person claiming it.

Quick Quiz 2.5

Indicate an exempt transaction with **Y** and a non-exempt transaction with **N**.

___ 1. A transaction in a foreign issue is an exempt transaction.

___ 2. Mr. Thompson, an agent with First Securities Inc. (a broker-dealer) receives an unsolicited request to purchase a security for Mary Gordon, a high net worth individual.

___ 3. The sale of an unregistered security in a private, non-publicly advertised transaction to 10 or fewer investors over the last 12 months.

___ 4. The sale of unclaimed securities by the Administrator of securities for the state of New Mexico.

___ 5. Sale of stock of a privately-owned company to the public in an initial public offering.

Answers

1. ***Y.*** *A transaction in a foreign issue is an exempt transaction.*

2. ***Y.*** *Mr. Thompson's receipt of an unsolicited order from Ms. Gordon is a transaction that does not have to be registered.*

3. ***Y.*** *The sale of an unregistered security in a private, non-publicly advertised transaction to 10 or fewer investors over the last 12 months is an exempt transaction (a private placement).*

4. ***Y.*** *The sale of unclaimed securities by the Administrator of securities for the state of New Mexico is an exempt transaction.*

5. ***N.*** *The sale of stock of a privately-owned company to the public in an initial public offering is not an exempt transaction.*

Securities HotSheet

Investment Contract (Howey Decision):	• Investment of money • Common enterprise • Expectation of profits • Solely from efforts of others
Nonexempt Security:	• Must register
Issuer:	• Company, government, or government subdivision that offers or proposes to offer securities
Nonissuer:	• Secondary market transaction • Proceeds do not go to issuer
Primary Offering:	• Initial public offering
Methods of Registration:	• Coordination, Qualification
Notice Filing:	• Federal covered investment company securities – sole documents with states
Exempt Security:	• No registration under USA required • Still subject to antifraud provisions
Exempt Transaction:	• Transaction need not be registered under USA

Lesson Exam 2

1. Under the Uniform Securities Act, which of the following persons is responsible for proving that a securities issue is exempt from registration?

   A. Underwriter
   B. Issuer
   C. State Administrator
   D. There is no need to prove eligibility for an exemption.

2. Under the Uniform Securities Act, an issuer is any person who issues, or proposes to issue, a security. Which of the following is not an issuer according to the USA?

   I. The city of Chicago, which is involved in a distribution of tax-exempt highway improvement bonds
   II. AAA Partnership issues certificates of interest or participation in its oil, gas, and mining titles
   III. The AAA Manufacturing Company, which proposes to offer shares to the public but has not completed the offering
   IV. The United States government, which proposes to offer Treasury bonds

   A. I only
   B. II only
   C. I, II and III
   D. I, II and IV

3. All of the following describe exempt transactions EXCEPT

   A. ABC, a broker-dealer, purchases securities from XYZ corporation
   B. First National Bank sells its entire publicly-traded bond portfolio to Amalgamated National Bank
   C. Amalgamated Nation Bank sells its publicly-traded bond portfolio to ABC Insurance Company
   D. Joe Smith, an employee of Amalgamated Bank, buys securities from ABC Brokerage Corporation

4. Which of the following are exempt securities?

   I. U.S. government securities
   II. unsolicited transactions
   III. transactions between issuers and underwriters
   IV. securities of credit unions

   A. I, II and IV
   B. I and IV
   C. II and III
   D. IV only

5. Which of the following securities is(are) exempt from the registration provisions of the USA?

   I. Issue of a savings and loan association
   II. General obligation municipal bond
   III. Bond issued by a company that has common stock listed on the American Stock Exchange

   A. I only
   B. II only
   C. II and III
   D. I, II and III

6. Which of the following is(are) primary transactions?

I. John inherited securities of the XYZ Corporation from his father who, as a founder to the company, received the shares directly from the company as a result of stock options.
II. John sold the securities he had inherited from his father to his neighbor, Peter, at the market price without charging a commission.
III. John's father, a founder of XYZ corporation, purchased shares of XYZ directly from the corporation subsequent to its founding without paying a commission.
IV. John purchased shares in XYZ Corporation in a Third-Market transaction.

A. I only
B. I and II
C. III only
D. I, II, III and IV

7. Stock of which of the following qualifies for the blue-chip exemption provided by the USA?

A. A corporation with $10 million in net worth
B. A corporation that is listed on the NYSE
C. A bank holding company
D. A municipal issuer

8. Registration statements for securities under the Uniform Securities Act are effective for

A. a period of time determined by the Administrator for each issue
B. one year from the effective date
C. one year from the date of issue
D. one year from the previous January 1st

9. Which of the following is defined as a security under the Uniform Securities Act?

A. A guaranteed, lump-sum payment to a beneficiary
B. Fixed, guaranteed payments made for life or for a specified period
C. Commodity futures contracts
D. Investment contract

10. Which of the following transactions is not exempt?

I. A sale of nonexempt securities by a trustee in bankruptcy which involves numerous commissions
II. A New York Stock Exchange manufacturing company sells its securities to 12 of its employees in a state without charging commissions
III. A manufacturer listed on the New York Stock Exchange offers its securities only to its employees in a state through an agent who charges commissions
IV. A bank headquartered in New York State sells securities of the bank to its employees only through an agent who charges commissions

A. I only
B. II and III
C. II and IV
D. IV only

11. Which of the following transactions are exempt from registration under the USA?

I. A trustee of a corporation in bankruptcy liquidates securities to satisfy debt holders
II. An offer of a securities investment is directed to 10 persons in the state during a 12-month consecutive period
III. An agent frequently engages in nonissuer transactions in unregistered securities on an unsolicited basis
IV. Agents for an entrepreneur offers pre-organization certificates to less then 10 investors in the state for a modest commission

A. I and II
B. I and IV
C. II and IV
D. I, III, and IV

12. The United States Supreme Court in the Howey decision ruled that an instrument that represents the investment of money in a common enterprise with an expectation of profit solely through the managerial efforts of others is a security. In following the Howey decision, the USA would consider which of the following a security?

A. Purchase of a house in a desirable real estate market with the expectation that the house will be resold at a profit within a few years
B. Purchase of jewelry for speculative purposes as opposed to personal use
C. Investment in options to acquire a security
D. Investment in commodities futures

13. A primary issue is

A. the first transaction between two parties in the over-the-counter market
B. a sale between investors of securities traded on the New York Stock Exchange
C. a new offering of an issuer purchased by an investor
D. a secondary market transaction in a security recently offered to the public

Lesson Exam 2 Answers & Rationale

1. B. The burden of proof for claiming eligibility for an exemption falls to the person claiming the exemption. QID: 28884

2. B. Under the Uniform Securities Act, an issuer is any person who issues, or proposes to issue, a security. Examples of issuers are a municipality such as the city of Chicago, which issues tax-exempt highway improvement bonds; the AAA Manufacturing Company, which proposes to offer shares to the public even though it has not completed the offering; and the United States government, when it proposes to offer Treasury bonds. Oil, gas, and mining partnerships are not issuers under the terms of the Uniform Securities Act; however, certificates of interest in them are securities. QID: 38343

3. D. The purchase of securities from a broker-dealer by an employee of a bank is a nonexempt transaction—it is a sale of a security by a broker-dealer to a member of the public and is, therefore, not exempt. Transactions between brokers and issuers, transactions between banks, and transactions between banks and insurance companies are exempt because they are transactions between financial institutions. In most cases, exempt transactions are those that do not affect the public. QID: 37170

4. B. Both unsolicited transactions and transactions between issuers and underwriters are exempt transactions, not exempt securities. U.S. government securities and securities of credit unions are exempt securities, not exempt transactions. QID: 31175

5. D. All the securities listed are exempt. QID: 28837

6. C. A primary transaction is one where the issuer of the securities receives the proceeds of the sale. John's father, although a founder of the company, purchased shares directly from the company. This transaction is a primary transaction because the firm received the funds from the sale of the shares. In all the other instances, the firm, the original issuer of the securities, did not receive the proceeds of the transaction. These transactions are called nonissuer transactions. QID: 38314

7. B. Companies whose securities are listed on a national exchange, such as the NYSE or AMEX, qualify for the blue-chip exemption. Companies that are listed must provide periodic reports concerning their firms and the reports must be available to prospective investors. A company with $10 million in net worth is not of itself evidence that the company has a blue-chip exemption. Municipal issuers are not given a blue-chip exemptions because they are exempt securities to begin with. QID: 28913

8. B. Securities registration statements are effective for one year from the effective date. QID: 28872

9. D. Investment contracts are listed as a security under the Uniform Securities Act; the term is often used as a synonym for a security. A guaranteed, lump-sum payment to a beneficiary is an endowment policy which is excluded from the definition of a security. Fixed, guaranteed payments made for life or for a specified period are fixed annuity contracts which are not defined as securities. Commodity futures contracts are not securities; however, puts and calls on the commodity itself are options which, under the act, are considered securities. QID: 37182

10. B. A New York Stock Exchange manufacturing company that sells its securities to more than 10 persons (whether or not they are employees) is not an exempt transaction, whether commissions are charged or not. In addition, a manufacturer listed on the New York Stock Exchange who offers its securities only to its employees in a state through an agent who

charges commissions is not an exempt transaction. A sale of nonexempt securities by a trustee in bankruptcy which involves numerous commissions is an exempt transaction. A bank headquartered in New York State that sells securities to its employees through an agent who charges commissions is engaging in an exempt transaction; bank securities are exempt whether or not a commission is charged. QID: 36373

11. A. Transactions by fiduciaries, such as a trustee in a bankruptcy reorganization, are exempt from registration. An offer of a securities investment to 10 or fewer persons (called a private placement) is also exempt from registration. Engaging in nonissuer transactions on a regular basis is not exempt from registration, whether or not the trades are unsolicited. Offers of pre-organization certificates are not exempt when commissions are charged. QID: 37153

12. C. The investment in options is the only choice above that meets the definition of a security. It is an investment in a common enterprise with the expectation that the owner will profit as a result of the managerial efforts of others. The purchase of a house or jewelry is a purchase of a real asset or product that may result in a profit for the owner but not as a result of the managerial efforts of a third party. Commodities futures contracts are specifically excluded from the definition of a security. Note that options on futures, however, are securities under the USA. QID: 38315

13. C. A primary transaction is a new offering of an issuer purchased by an investor. The first transaction between two investors in the over-the-counter market refers to a secondary transaction (the market between investors). A sale between investors of securities traded on the New York Stock Exchange is another example of a secondary transaction. QID: 38617

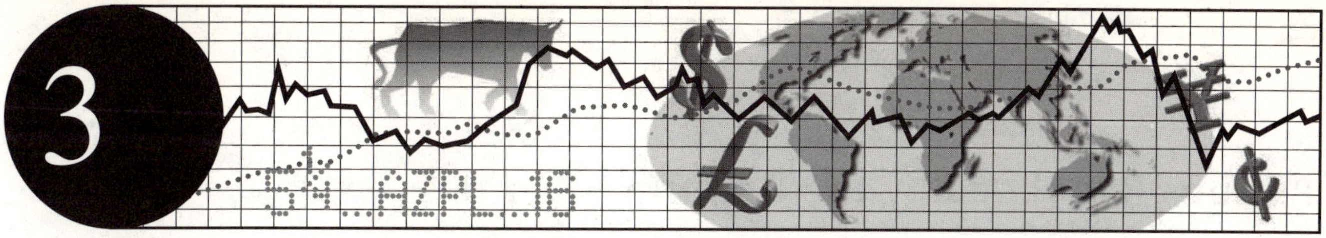

Registration of Persons

INTRODUCTION

The USA defines the jurisdiction and powers of the Administrator over securities, as well as those persons over which the Administrator can apply those powers. For a person to be covered (regulated) by the USA, it must be defined as a **person** for the law (the Administrator) to have jurisdiction. This lesson defines those persons covered by the USA who are subject to the Administrator's jurisdiction and registration requirements.

The USA regulates four classes of persons: broker-dealers, agents, investment advisers, and investment adviser representatives. Persons under the USA can be **persons** (such as agents and investment adviser representatives) or **legal entities** (such as broker-dealers and investment advisory firms). All persons who fall under the definition of agent or broker dealer must register with the Administrator.

The Series 63 exam will include approximately 18 questions on the material presented in this lesson.

LESSON OBJECTIVES

When you have completed this lesson, you should be able to:

- recognize the distinctions between a natural person and a legal person;
- define broker-dealer, agent, investment adviser, and investment adviser representative;
- identify procedures and requirements for registration in a state; and
- describe the differences between exclusions from definitions and exemptions from registration.

Persons Regulated by the Uniform Securities Act

The Uniform Securities Act regulates four classes of **persons**, each of which has a specific meaning within the language of the act. The four classes of persons are: **broker-dealers**, **agents**, **investment advisers**, and **investment adviser representatives**.

Person

The concept of **person** in law can have one of the two following meanings:

- a **natural person** (an individual; human being); or
- a **legal person** (entity) such as a corporation or partnership.

A **natural person** means any individual or person (human being) as the term is used in common, non-legal conversation.

A **legal person** or **legal entity** (such as a corporation) is what is called a legal fiction—it exists as a creature of law. For a legal entity (such as a corporation) to be sued in court, it must have a **legal existence** or **identity**. In addition to corporations, entities such as partnerships and governments are given legal identity as persons under the USA. They can conduct business, commit criminal acts, bear civil liabilities, and be sued in a court of law.

✓ ***Take Note:*** If an individual or organization does not fall within a definition as the term is used in the act, then the individual (human being) or organization (legal person) is not subject to the registration requirements of the USA. If an individual or business organization falls within a definition, it is subject to the regulations of the act. Under the USA, definitions are critical.

"Person" includes any entity such as:

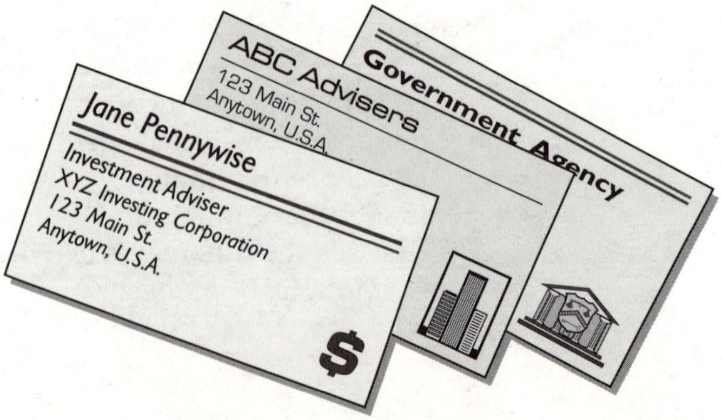

Individual or Business or Government

Quick Quiz 3.1

True or False?

___ 1. A corporation is not a person and therefore the state Administrator does not have jurisdiction over its securities activities.

___ 2. An individual is a natural person and not a legal person subject to the jurisdiction of the Uniform Securities Act.

Answers

1. ***F.*** *A corporation is a person under the law and subject to the jurisdiction of the state Administrator with respect to securities transactions.*

2. ***F.*** *An individual is a natural person and, just like a legal person (e.g., a corporation), may be subject to the Uniform Securities Act.*

The Four Classes of Persons

The four classes of persons that fall within the regulatory authority of the Uniform Securities Act are.

- broker-dealers (legal persons, companies)
- agents (natural persons, individuals)
- investment advisers (legal persons, companies)
- investment adviser representative (natural persons, individuals)

Broker-Dealer

A **broker-dealer** is defined as any person (legal entity) engaged in the business of effecting transactions in securities for the account of others or for its own account. Any legal person (e.g., a securities firm) with an established place of business (an office) in the state that is in the business of buying and selling securities for the accounts of others (customers) and/or for its own proprietary account is a broker-dealer.

✓ ***Take Note:*** When a broker-dealer effects trades for the accounts of others, it is acting in an agency capacity—that is, as a broker. When the broker-dealer engages in trades for its own account, it is acting in a principal capacity—that is, as a dealer. These two capacities explain the hyphenation of the term *broker-dealer*.

Exclusions from the Definition of Broker-Dealer

In the Uniform Securities Act, the term **broker-dealer** does not include **agents** (because they represent the broker-dealer and therefore are *not* the broker-dealer) and **issuers of securities**.

Financial institutions are also excluded from the definition because they are covered (regulated) by federal or other legislation. Financial institutions include banks, savings and loan institutions, trust companies, insurance companies (as defined by the Investment Company Act of 1940), pension and profit-sharing trusts, and other institutional buyers.

Additionally, a person who has no place of business in the state is not a broker-dealer if that person:

- effects transactions in the state exclusively with or through:
  - –issuers;
  - –other broker-dealers;
  - –financial institutions (as described above); or
- is licensed in the state in which he maintains a place of business and effects securities transactions solely with existing customers who are not residents of the state in which the transaction takes place.

✓ ***Take Note:*** The term **exclusion** means not included in or covered by a definition.

Broker-Dealers Excluded From the Term "Broker-Dealer"

Broker-dealers with no place of business in the state who conduct business exclusively with other broker-dealers or other covered institutions such as banks, savings institutions, and investment companies are excluded from the definition. The act also excludes those broker-dealers with no office in the state who solely conduct business with existing customers who are temporarily in the state, such as those people on vacation or remaining in the state for 30 days or less.

✓ ***Take Note:*** A person can effect securities transactions for compensation in a state but not be required to register as a broker-dealer under the state's securities laws.

Case Study: Exclusion from the Definition of Broker-Dealer

Situation: First Securities Corporation is a registered broker-dealer with offices in Illinois. Mr. Thompson, a registered representative in First Securities' Illinois office, recommends the purchase of Simus Shoes stock to his customer, Mr. Bixby, who is temporarily on vacation in Hawaii. Mr. Bixby agree to the purchase of Simus Shoes as well as other securities while in Hawaii.

The Hawaiian state securities Administrator does not issue a cease and desist order against First Securities for unlawfully selling securities as an unregistered broker-dealer in Hawaii.

Analysis: The Hawaiian securities Administrator acted correctly by not issuing a cease and desist order against First Securities. Under the USA, First Securities is not required to register as a broker-dealer in Hawaii because it limits its business to an existing customer, Mr. Bixby, who is temporarily in the state. Since First Securities is properly registered in Illinois, it need not register in Hawaii providing, of course, Mr. Bixby does not take up permanent residence there.

Broker-Dealer Registration Requirements

The USA is very clear regarding the registration requirements of broker-dealers. It states: *"It is unlawful for any person to transact business in this state as a broker-dealer...unless he is registered under this act."*

If a person falls within the definition of a broker-dealer, that person must register. If a person is excluded, they do not have to register.

Financial Requirements

The Administrator may establish **minimum capital requirements** for broker-dealers. These requirements may not exceed those provided for under the Securities Exchange Act of 1934. No minimum financial requirements for agents or investment adviser representatives exist, however, the Administrator may require those broker-dealers who have custody of or discretionary authority over clients funds or securities to post **surety bonds**. The amount of surety bonds, sometimes called **fidelity bonds**, is limited to the amount set by the Securities Exchange Act of 1934.

✓ ***Take Note:*** The Administrator may require that registrants meet certain financial standards. In general, all securities professionals who register in a state must submit an application with the required information, provide a consent to service of process, and pay filing fees to the state.

Case Study: Who is a Broker-Dealer?

Situation: First Securities Corporation of Illinois sells municipal bonds and equity securities to both the general public and to other securities firms. First Securities sells many of its municipal bonds to its biggest customer, Transitions Broker-Dealers, Inc., located in Indiana. Transition Brokers is a wholesale broker-dealer with no offices in Illinois that trades exclusively with other broker-dealers.

First Securities discovers that Transition Brokers-Dealers is not registered in Illinois but does business with other broker-dealers in Illinois. The president of First Securities asks the president of Transition Brokers why his firm is not registered in Illinois and the president of Transition answers that it is because they are not broker-dealers in Illinois. The president of First Securities is baffled—it appears to him that Transition is indeed a broker-dealer.

Analysis**:** First Securities sells both exempt securities (municipal bonds) and nonexempt securities (equities) to the general public and to other broker-dealers. First Securities is a broker-dealer because it is a legal entity with a place of business in the state that effects securities transactions for itself and for the accounts of others and so must register in Illinois.

Like First Securities, Transition Broker-Dealers conducts broker-dealer activities. However, in Illinois confines the business to transactions between itself and other broker-dealers, such as First Securities. The USA specifically excludes from the definition of broker-dealer out-of-state broker-dealers who deal exclusively with other broker-dealers and have no place of business in the state.

While Transition Brokers is in **fact** conducting operations of a broker-dealer in Illinois, it is not under the **law** a broker-dealer subject to the registration with the Illinois securities Administrator. If Transition Brokers were located or had an office in Illinois, it would be a broker-dealer by definition and have to register as such in Illinois.

Quick Quiz 3.2

True or False?

___ 1. In general, a person who effects transactions in securities for itself or for the account of others in the course of business must register in the state as a broker-dealer.

___ 2. Under the Uniform Securities Act, an out-of-state firm that transacts business with an established customer who is on vacation is not considered a broker in the state in which the customer.

___ 3. A person not defined as a broker-dealer in the state under the USA need not register as such.

Answers

1. T. A person who effects transactions in securities for itself or for the account of others must register in the state as a broker-dealer unless specifically excluded from the definition.

2. T. A firm with an out-of-state registration is not considered a broker-dealer in that state if transacting business with a customer who is passing through the state on vacation.

3. T. If a person is excluded from the definition, that person need not register as a broker-dealer; however, if they are not excluded, they must register.

Agent

The Uniform Securities Act defines an **agent** as any individual (human being) who represents a broker-dealer (legal entity) or an issuer (legal entity) in effecting (or attempting to effect) transactions in securities.

Agents are individuals in a sales capacity who represent broker-dealers or issuers of securities. As agents, they act on behalf of others who are known as **principals**. Agents are often referred to as **sales representatives** or **registered representatives** whether selling registered or exempt securities.

✓ ***Take Note:*** The use of the term **individual** here is important. Only an individual, or a natural person, can be an agent. A corporation, such as a brokerage firm, is not a natural person—it is a legal entity. The brokerage firm is the legal person (legal entity) that the agent (natural person) represents in securities transactions.

Nonregistered Employees of Broker-Dealers

Nonregistered employees of a broker-dealer (such as clerical personnel) are generally not agents.

✓ ***For Example:*** Secretaries and sales assistants (known as ministerial personnel) are not agents if their activities are confined to administrative activities. However, if secretaries or sales assistants accept customer transactions or take orders over the phone, they are engaging in securities transactions and are subject to registration as agents.

Employees of Securities Issuers

Unlike the situation with broker-dealers, employees of an issuer may represent their employer in effecting securities transactions without falling within the definition of an agent.

Exclusions From the Definition of "Agent"

The USA excludes from the definition of agent those individuals who represent issuers when effecting transactions in the following three situations:

- securities exempt from registration,
- transactions exempt from registration, and
- with existing employees, partners, or directors of an issuer if no commissions or remuneration is given for soliciting in the state.

Effecting Transactions in Exempt Securities

Securities exempt from registration are called **exempt securities**. An employee of an issuer is not an agent when representing an issuer in the following exempt securities:

- U.S. government and municipal securities;
- Canadian and other specified securities;
- securities of U.S. banks and savings institutions or trust companies;
- commercial paper with in denominations of $50,000 or more with maturities of nine months or less; and
- investment contracts issued in connection with employee's stock purchase, savings, pensions, or profit-sharing plans.

Effecting Exempt Transactions

Transactions exempt from registration are called **exempt transactions**. They are:

- isolated non-issuer transactions;
- transactions between issuer and underwriters; or
- transactions between savings institutions or trust companies.

Effecting Transactions with Existing Employees, Partners, or Directors of an Issuer

An employee of an issuer is not an agent when selling his employer's securities to existing employees, partners, or directors if no commissions are charged. If commissions are charged, the employee would be an agent and have to register as such under the act.

An employee of an issuer is not an agent when representing an issuer if the issue is exempt from registration (e.g., banks, financial institutions, and governments). Additionally, the employee is not an agent when representing an issuer in exempt transactions (transactions between an underwriter and issuer).

The USA exempts these individuals and transactions from registration because these issuer related activities are covered (regulated) by national securities law.

Agent Registration Requirements

The registration requirements for an agent are the same as those for a broker-dealer. The USA states: *It is unlawful for any person to transact business in this state as...an agent unless he is registered under this act.*

Financial Requirements

In general there are no financial requirements, or **net worth requirements**, to register as an agent. However, the Administrator may require an agent who has custody of or discretion over clients' funds or securities to post **surety bonds** up to the amount set by the Securities Exchange Act of 1934. At the discretion of the Administrator, the employing broker may also be required to post surety bonds as well as maintaining net capital requirements.

Case Study: Agent as defined by the USA

Situation: The City of Chicago issues bonds for the maintenance of local recreational facilities. Purchasers have two choices: they can purchase the bonds directly from the city through Charles Stith (an employee of the city responsible for selling the bonds) or they can purchases them from Mr. Thompson (an employee of First Securities Corporation of Chicago). Neither Mr. Stith nor Mr. Thompson charge a commission, although First Securities Corp. is remunerated with an underwriting fee.

Analysis: The City of Chicago is an issuer of exempt securities (municipal bonds). Charles Stith, as an employee of the issuer (City of Chicago), is not an agent as defined in the USA because he is representing the issuer in an exempt security. Therefore, Stith does not need to register with the Administrator of Illinois provided he receives no compensation. However, Thompson, as a representative of First Securities, must register with the Administrator because he represents a broker-dealer in effecting securities transactions in the state. Representatives (agents of broker-dealers) must register in the states in which they sell securities.

✓ ***Take Note:*** Exemptions from registration generally apply to representatives of issuers, rather than to representatives of broker-dealers.

Fee and Commission Sharing Registered agents of broker-dealers may share fees or split commissions with others provided they are registered as agents for the same broker-dealer or for a broker-dealer under common ownership or control.

Quick Quiz 3.3

Write **A** if the person is an agent and **B** if not.

___ 1. Person who effects transactions in municipal securities on behalf of a broker-dealer.

___ 2. A registered representative's salaried secretary who take orders.

___ 3. An employee of a bank that is issuing shares who receives a commission for selling the bank's securities.

___ 4. Individual who represents her nonexempt employer in the sale of its securities to existing employees for a commission.

___ 5. Person who represents an issuer in effecting transactions with underwriters.

Answers

1. ***A****. Persons must be registered as agents when they effect transactions on behalf of broker-dealers whether the securities are exempt or not.*

2. ***A****. A secretary effecting transactions on behalf of a broker-dealer must be registered whether or not they receive a commission.*

3. ***B****. An employee who represents an exempt issuer (a bank) in selling its securities need not register as an agent, even if they receive commissions.*

4. ***A****. A person who represents his employer in selling securities to employees must register as an agent if the person receives a commission. If no commission is paid, registration is not necessary.*

5. ***B****. Persons who represent issuers in securities transactions with underwriters need not register as agents.*

Investment Adviser

Under the USA, an **investment adviser** is defined as any person (legal entity) who, for compensation and as part of a regular business, engages in the business of advising others as to the value of securities or as to the advisability of investing in or selling them. The advice can be delivered in person, through publications or writings, or through research reports concerning securities.

To be an investment adviser, a person must meet the following three requirements. They must:

- provide advice about securities;
- provide that advice as part of an ongoing business; and
- receive compensation for the investment advisory services.

In most cases, investment advisers are legal persons—that is, partnerships or corporations that provide investment advice or portfolio management services on an ongoing basis.

✓ ***Take Note:*** An individual can be an investment adviser if he operates as a **sole proprietorship**.

Exclusions From Definition of Investment Adviser

There are many exclusions from the term **investment adviser**. Excluded are:

- investment adviser representatives (the firm is the investment adviser);
- banks, savings institutions, and trust companies;
- Lawyers, Accountants, Teachers, and Engineers (*LATE*) whose investment advisory services are solely incidental to their professional practices;
- broker-dealers whose investment advisory services are incidental to their brokerage business and who receive no special or separate compensation for offering advice;
- publishers of bona fide newspapers or magazines of general and paid circulation;
- federal covered investment advisers (advisers with more than $30 million under management);
- persons who are excepted from the definition of investment adviser under the Investment Advisers Act of 1940; and
- any other person the Administrator specifies.

Registration Requirements for an Investment Adviser

The registration requirements for an investment adviser are much like those of a broker-dealer. The USA states: *It is unlawful for any person to transact business in this state as an investment adviser...unless he is so registered under this act or is exempt from registration requirements.*

Exemption from Registration for Investment Advisers

The USA specifically exempts from registration certain persons who, although they fall within the definition of an investment adviser, do not have to register as such in the state.

The advisers exempt from registration with the state Administrator are those who have no place of business in the state but are registered in another state, provided their only clients in the state are:

- federal covered advisers;
- institutional investors;
- existing clients who are not residents but are temporarily (up to 30 days) in the state;
- limited to five or fewer clients resident in the state during the preceding 12 months (called the ***di minimus*** exemption); or
- investment advisers the Administrator exempts by rule or order.

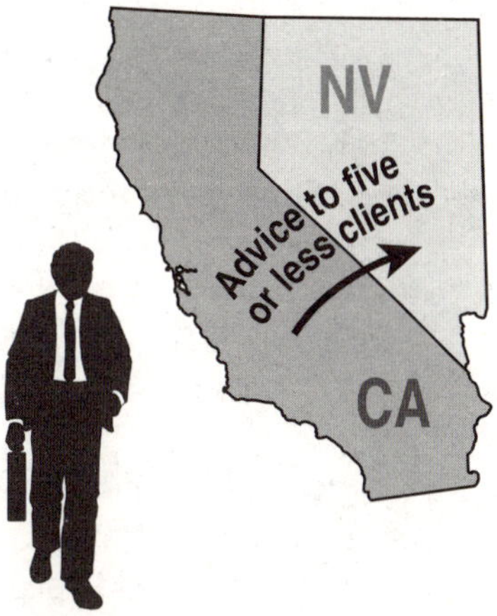

Case Study: Out-of-State Advice

Situation: A California-registered investment adviser has directed investment advice on five separate occasions over the past year to persons in the state of Nevada. Is the investment adviser required to register in the state of Nevada?

Analysis: The answer is no. Registration is not required because the investment adviser does not have an office in Nevada and directs business to five or fewer clients during the year. If the firm had an office in Nevada, registration would be required in that state. Also, even if the firm had no office in Nevada, registration would be required if business had been transacted with six or more clients in the year.

✓ ***Take Note:*** NSMIA eliminated state registration requirement for advisers with $30 million or more in assets under management.Those advisers with between $25 to $30 million have the option to register with either the state or the SEC. Advisers with less than $25 million must register with the state.

✓ ***Take Note:*** Investment advisers exempt from state registration are *not* exempt from paying state filing fees and giving notice to the Administrator.

Case Study: Exclusion from Definition and Exemptions from Registration

Situation: Charles & Goode, a partnership located in Illinois, has been in the business of selling investment advice in the form of research reports and managing securities portfolios for the past 20 years. The partnership has earned a good reputation among investors and has managed less than $25 million until this year. This year they have gained several new clients and now have $50 million in assets under management.

Most of Charles & Goode's clients are wealthy individuals and residents of Illinois, but they have three clients who are residents of Wisconsin and 30 clients who live in Indiana. The principals of Charles & Goode have also formed a separate partnership called the C&G Mutual Fund Advisers, Inc., which manages a small investment company with assets of $15 million. The partners in Charles & Goode are confused as to what they must do to be in compliance with the Uniform Securities Act.

Analysis: As a partnership in the business of managing money for individual clients, Charles & Goode falls within the definition of an investment adviser and must so register with the Illinois securities Administrator until it manages $25 million or more in assets. However, with the addition of new clients as of the current year, Charles & Goode will be exempt from registration with Illinois, although it still falls within the definition of an investment adviser. Charles & Goode is now a federal covered adviser that must register with the SEC because it has more than $30 million in assets.

Prior to becoming a federal covered adviser, Charles & Goode need not register in Wisconsin because they have fewer than five clients in the state; however, they would have to register in Indiana because they have more than five clients there. After becoming federal covered advisers, Charles & Goode does not have to register in Indiana, Wisconsin, or Illinois—after it manages more the $30 million it only has to register with the SEC, not the state Administrator. An adviser with assets between $25 and $30 million may register with either the state or the SEC. Advisers with $30 million or more in assets must register with the SEC only.

The separate partnership, C&G Mutual Fund Advisers Inc., which manages only $15 million, is exempt from registration in Illinois (or any other state) because investment companies are federal covered advisers under the Investment Company Act of 1940 subject to registration with the SEC.

✓ ***Take Note:*** As a general rule, the SEC or federal rules involve bigger numbers than the state rules—large investment advisers must register with the SEC; small investment advisers must register with the state.

Financial Requirements

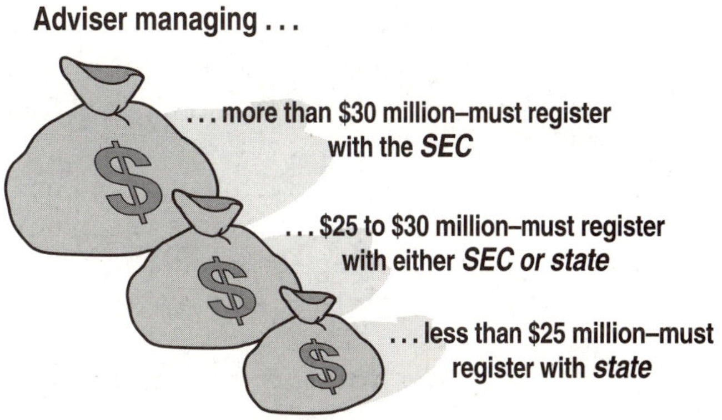

Financial Requirements

The Administrator may, by rule or order, establish minimal financial requirements for an investment adviser registered in the state. The Administrator may require an adviser who has custody of or discretionary authority over client funds or securities to post bonds or another form of security. The financial requirements that the Administrator sets cannot exceed those required by the Investment Advisers Act of 1940.

Like all other persons required to register, an investment adviser must pay a filing fee as determined by the Administrator.

Quick Quiz 3.4

Choose **A** if the phrase describes an investment adviser that must register under the USA and **B** if it does not.

___ 1. Publisher of a newspaper that renders general financial advice.

___ 2. Broker-dealer that charges a fee for providing investment advice over and above commissions from securities transactions.

___ 3. An investment adviser that manages $10 million in assets.

Answers

1. **B.** *Publishers of newspapers and magazines of general circulation that offer general financial advice need not register.*

2. **A.** *Broker-dealers must register as investment advisers if they receive special or separate compensation for giving investment advice.*

3. **A.** *An investment adviser that manages less than $25 million in assets must register as an investment adviser under the USA.*

Investment Adviser Representative

An **investment adviser representative** means any individual (other than an investment adviser or federal covered investment adviser) who represents an investment adviser or federal covered investment adviser when:

- making investment recommendations;
- managing accounts or client portfolios;
- soliciting investment advisory services; or
- supervising employees who perform any of these duties.

✓ ***Take Note:*** Partners, officers, directors, or other employees controlled by an investment adviser who provide the above services also serve in the capacity of investment adviser representatives.

Investment Advisers and Investment Adviser Representatives

Investment Adviser: Business or Individual

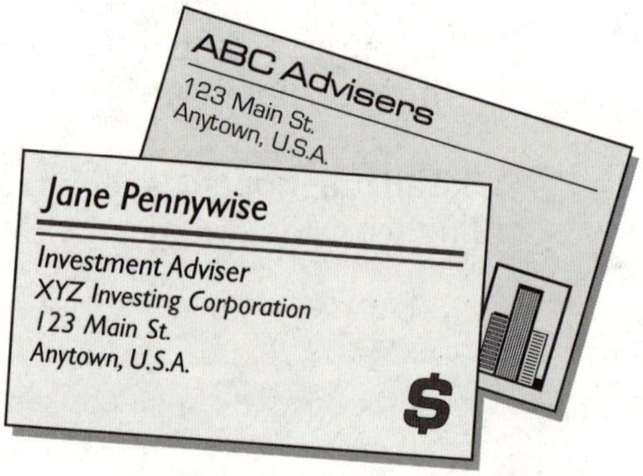

Investment Adviser Representative: Individual Only

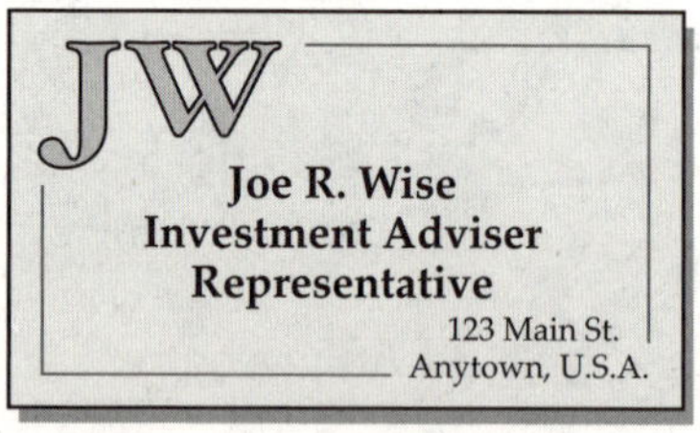

Exclusions From the Definition of "Investment Adviser Representative"

Employees of investment advisory firms are excluded from the term **investment adviser representative,** provided their activities are confined to clerical duties or those activities which are solely incidental to the investment advisory services offered. Should the investment advisory employee receive specific compensation for offering these services, the employee would then have to register as an investment adviser representative.

Quick Quiz 3.5

True or False?

___ 1. An investment adviser representative must register with the SEC if she has clients with assets of $30 million or more under management.

___ 2. A partner in a registered investment management firm is, by definition, an investment adviser and, therefore, cannot be an investment adviser representative.

___ 3. An employee of an investment advisory firm is an investment adviser representative if his duties are confined to clerical activities.

___ 4. A ministerial employee who receives specific compensation for offering investment advisory services is not an investment adviser representative.

___ 5. An employee of an investment advisory firm is an investment adviser representative if his duties involve making investment recommendations.

Answers

1. ***F.*** *An investment adviser (not the investment representative) must register with the SEC if the firm manages assets of $30 million or more. The rep would have to be registered as an investment adviser representative in the state in which his office is located.*

2. ***F.*** *A partner in a registered investment management firm is, by definition, an investment adviser. However, the partner may also be an investment adviser representative if the partner provides the services of an investment adviser representative.*

3. ***F.*** *An employee of an investment advisory firm is not an investment adviser representative if his duties are confined to clerical activities.*

4. ***F.*** *A ministerial employee who receives specific compensation for offering investment advisory services is an investment adviser representative.*

5. ***T.*** *An employee of an investment advisory firm is an investment adviser representative if his duties involve making investment recommendations.*

General Registration Procedures for Securities Professionals

Any person who meets the definition of broker-dealer, agent, investment adviser, or investment adviser representative must register with the state. To register with the state securities Administrator, a person must:

- submit an application;
- provide a consent to service of process;

- pay filing fees;
- post a bond (if required by the Administrator); and
- take an examination (if required by the Administrator).

Submit Application

All persons must complete and submit an **initial application** (as well as renewals) to the state securities Administrator. The application must contain whatever information the Administrator may require by rule, such as:

- form and place of business (broker-dealers and investment advisers);
- proposed method of doing business;
- qualifications and business history (broker-dealers and investment advisers must include the qualifications and history of partners, officers, directors, and other persons with controlling influence over the organization);
- injunctions and administrative orders;
- convictions of misdemeanors involving a security or any aspect of the securities business;
- felony convictions, whether securities related or not;
- financial condition and history; and
- advertising and promotional material, if applicant is an investment adviser.

In the case of an investment adviser, the Administrator also may require that an applicant publish an announcement of the registration in one or more newspapers in the state.

✓ ***Take Note:*** If an agent terminates employment with a broker-dealer, both parties must promptly notify the Administrator. If an agent terminates employment with Broker-Dealer I to join Broker-Dealer II, all three parties must notify the Administrator.

Provide Consent to Service of Process

New applicants for registration must provide the Administrator with a **consent to service of process**. The consent to service of process appoints the Administrator as the applicant's attorney to receive and process noncriminal securities-related complaints against the applicant. Under the consent to service of process, all complaints received by the Administrator have the same legal effect as if they had been served personally on the applicant.

✓ ***Take Note:*** The consent to service of process is submitted with the initial application and remains in force permanently. It does not need to be supplied with each renewal of a registration.

Pay Filing Fees

States require **filing fees** for initial applications as well as for renewal applications. If an application is withdrawn or denied, the Administrator is entitled to retain a portion of the fee. Filing fees for broker-dealers, investment advisers, and their representatives need not be identical. Broker-dealers and investment advisers may file, without a fee, for a successor firm to complete the unexpired portion of the year.

Financial Reports and Recordkeeping Requirements

The USA requires registered broker-dealers and investment advisers to keep such accounts, correspondence, memoranda, papers, books, and other records as the Administrator requires. These records must be preserved for three years by broker-dealers and five years by advisers unless the Administrator prescribes otherwise.

The Administrator may also require registered broker-dealers and investment advisers to file financial reports. The recordkeeping and financial reports required by the state Administrator may *not* exceed those required by the Securities Exchange Act of 1934 or the Investment Advisers Act of 1940.

If any material information in these documents becomes inaccurate or incomplete, the registrant must promptly file a corrected copy with the Administrator. All required documents are subject to reasonable periodic, special, or other examination as the Administrator deems appropriate, in the public interest, or for the protection of the investor.

Post Bonds

The Administrator may, by rule, require **minimum net capital** for broker-dealers. Broker-dealers in compliance with the SEC net capital requirement are exempt from the USA's minimum capital requirements. Agents of broker-dealers do not have net worth requirements; however, the Administrator may require an agent to post a surety bond if the agent has custody of or discretion over client funds or securities.

Quick Quiz 3.6

True or False?

___ 1. A consent to service of process must be submitted with each renewal application.

___ 2. An Administrator may establish net capital requirements for investment adviser representatives.

___ 3. When a securities professional registers in a state, he must provide the state Administrator with a list of all states he intends to register in.

Answers

1. **F.** *A consent to service of process is filed with the initial application and permanently remains on file with the Administrator.*

2. **F.** *The term* net capital requirement *refers to the financial requirements of a broker-dealer, not an investment adviser representative. Investment adviser representatives may be required to post a bond if they maintain discretion or custody of client funds and/or securities.*

3. **F.** *A list of other states in which a securities professional intends to register is not required on a state application for registration.*

Registration of Persons HotSheet

Person:
- Individual, company, or government

Broker-Dealer Registration:
- Must register in state where business is done unless exempt
- Effective after Administrator notification; expires December 31st

Exempt from State Registration as a Broker-Dealer:
- Banks, savings institutions, other financial institutions, agents, issuers
- BDs with no office in state only doing business with institutions
- BDs registered in another state transacting business with a current client passing through a different state

Exemptions from Agent Registration:
- Represents issuer in exempt transaction
- Represents issuer in bankers' acceptances, and commercial paper (270 days or less)
- Represents issuer in sale of employee benefits plans

Agent Registration:
- Broker-dealers can only employ registered agents
- Agents must be registered in state of residence, where securities are offered, and where securities are sold
- Agents who represent broker-dealers must be registered if they sell exempt or nonexempt securities
- Agents who represent issuers must be registered if they sell nonexempt securities
- Effective after Administrator notification; expires December 31
- Notification by agent & old & new employer for employment change
- Automatic registration of partners, officers, and directors when new broker-dealer registers

Investment Adviser Registration:
- Federally registered if adviser manages more than $30 million
- State registered if adviser manages less than $25 million
- Choice between federal and state if adviser manages between $25 and $30 million
- Investment company advisers are always federally registered
- File form ADV and appropriate fees
- Audited balance sheet if custody; unaudited balance sheet if not
- Effective after Administrator notification; expires December 31

Investment Adviser Exemptions:
- No office in state and communications directed to 5 or fewer clients in 12 months
- No office in state and clients are institutions, broker-dealers, or investment advisers only

Investment Adviser Recordkeeping:
- All specific customer and investment adviser records kept for 5 years; must be kept in investment adviser's office for the first 2 years

Lesson Exam 3

1. Under the Uniform Securities Act, any partner, officer, or director is an investment adviser representative if they

   I. offer advice concerning securities
   II. manage client accounts or portfolios
   III. determine securities recommendations for representatives to disseminate
   IV. supervise personnel engaged in the above activities but does not sell these services to the public

   A. I only
   B. I and II
   C. I, II and III
   D. I, II, III and IV

2. Which of the following would be an agent under the terms of the USA?

   I. A sales representative of a licensed broker-dealer who sells secondary securities to the general public
   II. An assistant to the president of a broker-dealer who, for administrative purposes, accepts orders on behalf of the senior partners
   III. A subsidiary of a major commercial bank registered as a broker-dealer that sells securities to the public
   IV. An issuer of nonexempt securities registered in the state and sold to the general public.

   A. I and II
   B. III and IV
   C. I, II and III
   D. I, II, III and IV

3. Under the USA, which of the following is(are) considered a broker-dealer?

   I. Agent
   II. Issuer
   III. Corporation selling interests in an oil and gas limited partnership
   IV. Credit union selling its own stock

   A. I only
   B. I and III
   C. II and IV
   D. III only

4. Which of the following persons is an agent under the Uniform Securities Act?

   A. Silent partner of a broker-dealer
   B. Secretary of a branch office sales manager
   C. Clerk at a broker-dealer who is authorized to take orders
   D. Broker-dealer executive who does not solicit or transact business

5. Under the Uniform Securities Act, which of the following qualifies as an investment adviser representative?

   A. An employee who is highly skilled in evaluating securities and performs administrative or clerical functions for an investment adviser
   B. An individual who renders fee-based advice on precious metals
   C. A solicitor for an advisory firm who is paid a fee for his services
   D. A stockbroker who offers incidental advice on securities as part of his sales commissions

6. Under the USA, which of the following is considered a broker-dealer in a state?

   A. First Federal Company Trust
   B. XYZ broker-dealers with an office in the state where only clients are with insurance companies
   C. An agent effecting transactions for a broker-dealer
   D. A broker-dealer with no place of business in the state who only does business with other broker-dealers

7. An employee of a large, publicly-held company effects transactions with existing employees for the purchase of the company's debentures. Under the USA, the employee

   A. must register as an agent of the issuer
   B. need not register as an agent of the issuer
   C. may receive commissions without registration
   D. must register as an agent if he will receive commissions or remuneration, either directly or indirectly

8. An investment adviser is all of the following EXCEPT a

   I. broker who charges for investment advice
   II. publisher of a financial newspaper
   III. person who sells security analysis
   IV. CPA who, as an incidental part of his practice, charges a fee for constructing a portfolio of tax-sheltered investments

   A. I and II
   B. II and III
   C. II and IV
   D. III and IV

9. Who of the following must register as an agent?

   A. An individual representing a broker-dealer who sells commercial paper
   B. An individual who sells commercial paper for ABC National Bank
   C. A government employee who sells Treasury bonds to the public
   D. An individual who is paid a commission to sell certificates of deposit for ABC National Bank

10. Under the Uniform Securities Act, all of the following persons may provide investment advice incidental to their normal business without requiring registration as an investment adviser EXCEPT a(n)

    A. teacher
    B. economist
    C. lawyer
    D. engineer

11. Under the Uniform Securities Act, an agent is a(n)

    A. broker-dealer who sells registered securities to the general public
    B. individual who represents an issuer in a transaction exempt from the act
    C. individual representing a broker-dealer who sells federal covered securities exempt from registration under the act
    D. individual who represents an issuer in an exempt transaction in which no commissions are paid

12. Which of the following is not a person as defined by the Uniform Securities Act?

    A. XYZ Dry Cleaners, Inc. whose shareholders all work on the premises and who also offers financial advice to those customers who request it
    B. A child prodigy gifted in math, in the custody of his parents, whose parents opened an account at a major securities firm
    C. A small unincorporated investment club
    D. A small city outside of Toronto, Canada that does not maintain investment accounts at a brokerage houses

13. An Administrator can deny an investment adviser's registration for all of the following reasons EXCEPT

    A. lack of experience
    B. failure to post a surety bond
    C. failure to pass a written exam
    D. not meeting minimum financial standards

Lesson Exam 3 Answers & Rationale

1. D. The Uniform Securities Act defines persons associated with an investment adviser as investment adviser representatives, including any partner, officer, or director who offers advice concerning securities. Persons who manage client accounts or portfolios, determine securities recommendations, and supervise personnel engaged in the above activities are investment adviser representatives. QID: 38342

2. A. Under the USA only individuals can be agents. A person who sells securities for a broker-dealer is an agent. An administrative person, such as the assistant to the president of a broker-dealer, is considered an agent if he takes securities orders from the public. Corporate entities are excluded from the definition of an agent. QID: 37144

3. D. A broker-dealer is defined as any person that invests for others or for his own account. A broker-dealer is not an issuer or an agent. QID: 28943

4. C. Anyone who solicits or receives an order while representing a broker-dealer is an agent. Silent partners, secretaries of branch managers, and executives of broker-dealers are not agents under the terms of the USA because they do not solicit or receive orders. Remember, broker-dealers are not agents; agents represent broker-dealers. QID: 28821

5. C. A solicitor is considered an investment adviser representative under the Uniform Securities Act. An employee who performs clerical or administrative functions only is not an investment adviser representative. Precious metals are not securities and, therefore, a person advising on them is not considered an investment representative. A stockbroker is a representative of a broker-dealer. QID: 37163

6. B. A broker-dealer with an office in a state must be registered with the state Administrator even if it only does business with other broker-dealers or institutions. QID: 31208

7. D. Under the USA, an individual is an agent when effecting transactions with an issuer's existing employees if commissions are paid. QID: 28829

8. C. A publisher of a financial newspaper and a CPA who, as an incidental part of his practice, constructs portfolios of tax-sheltered investments are not investment advisers. QID: 28823

9. A. An individual who represents a broker-dealer who sells commercial paper must register under the USA. The securities (commercial paper) are exempt; nevertheless the representative must be registered as an agent of the broker-dealer. An individual who sells commercial paper for ABC National Bank would not have to register because both the transaction and security are exempt from state registration requirements. An employee of the federal government need not register with the state because he represents an exempt issuer and is selling exempt securities. An individual who is paid a commission to sell certificates of deposit for a commercial bank does not have to register as an agent. QID: 37162

10. B. The Uniform Securities Act does not grant an economist exemption from registration. The USA does offer an exemption to a teachers, lawyers, and engineers if the investment advice is incidental to their business. QID: 31206

11. C. An individual employed by a broker-dealer who sells securities to the public is an agent under the Uniform Securities Act. The USA defines an agent as ". . .any individual other than a broker-dealer who represents a broker-dealer or issuer in effecting or attempting to effect purchases or sales of securities." The law excludes from the definition of *agent* those individuals who represent an issuer in exempt transactions, exempt securities, and transactions with issuers' employees when no commission is paid. QID: 37143

12. B. Under the Uniform Securities Act, the term *person* has a specific meaning. Person refers to an individual, corporation, association, joint-stock company, trust, unincorporated organization, government, or a political subdivision of a government. A minor child, no matter how precocious, is not a person legally capable of entering into contracts. Adults must open custodial accounts on behalf of minor children. QID: 37173

13. A. Lack of experience, by itself, is not cause for registration denial QID: 39207

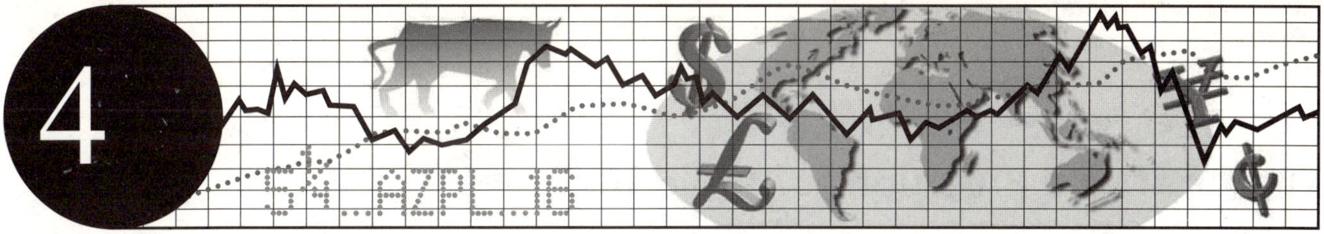

Unethical Business Practices

INTRODUCTION

The Uniform Securities Act was drafted to eliminate conflicts in various state securities legislation and to protect the public from fraudulent securities practices. Courts and self-regulatory agencies have determined those activities that are fraudulent. The securities industry has developed standards of ethics and fair practice that all securities professionals must follow to avoid fraud and to conduct business in an ethical manner.

This lesson discusses practices which are fraudulent under the USA as well as those that, while they do not constitute fraud, are prohibited by law or by the rules of the Administrator or **self-regulatory organizations (SROs)** within the securities industry.

Fraudulent and prohibited practices are the most heavily tested topics. You must know what these practices are and be able to apply the principles that guide ethical behavior to specific situations.

Fraudulent and prohibited practices make up 35% of the exam. The Series 63 exam will include approximately 21 questions on the material presented in this lesson.

LESSON OBJECTIVES

When you have completed this lesson, you should be able to:

- describe the antifraud provisions of the USA;
- recognize specific fraudulent and prohibited practices;
- make distinctions between prohibitions that pertain to sales of securities and those that pertain to the sale of investment advice;
- list the required provisions for investment advisory contracts; and
- identify various types of market manipulation.

The Antifraud Provisions of the USA

The Uniform Securities Act addresses the problem of fraud in two categories. The first category refers to the fraudulent activities when conducting sales or purchases of a securities; the second category refers to responsibilities when providing investment advice.

Fraudulent & Prohibited Practices in the Sale of Securities

Under the USA, it is unlawful for any person, when engaged in the offer, sale, or purchase of any security, directly or indirectly, to:

- employ any device, scheme, or artifice to defraud;
- make any untrue statement of a material fact or omit to state a material fact necessary to make a statement not misleading; or
- engage in any act, practice, or course of business that operates as a fraud or deceit upon a person.

✓ ***Take Note:*** There are no exceptions to the anti-fraud provisions of the Act. They apply to *any* person and any securities transaction whether registered, exempt, or federal covered.

While the USA does not list the prohibited practices, the following have been held by courts, regulatory agencies, and state Administrators to be fraudulent, dishonest, or unethical practices and therefore prohibited.

✓ ***Take Note:*** All such practices are prohibited, whether they are fraudulent or not.

Misleading or Untrue Statements

The USA prohibits any person from making any **misleading** or **untrue statements of material fact** in connection with the purchase or sale of a security.

The following are examples of untrue statements of material fact that constitute fraud if made knowingly and willfully.

- Inaccurate market quotations
- Misstatements of an issuer's earnings or projected earnings or dividends
- Inaccurate statements as to the amount of commissions, markup, or markdown
- Telling a customer that a security will be listed on an exchange without concrete information concerning its listing status
- Informing a client that the registration of a security with the SEC or with the state securities Administrator means that the security has been "approved" by these regulators

- Misrepresenting the status of customer accounts
- Promising a customer services without any intent to perform them or without being properly qualified to perform them
- Representing to customers that the Administrator approves of the broker-dealer or agent's abilities

Case Study: Making Leading or Untrue Statements

***Situation**:* Mr. Thompson, a registered securities agent in Illinois, informs a long-standing client, Ms.Gordon, that her largest equity holding, First Tech Internet Services, Inc., will be listed on the New York Stock Exchange upon completion of its registration. In addition, he exaggerates the earnings by $1.00 per share to make her more comfortable and encourage her to buy more shares. Thompson is convinced the earnings will rise to that amount and does not want Ms. Gordon to sell because he believes the stock will appreciate in price once listed on the exchange.

***Analysis**:* Mr. Thompson violated the USA by deliberately misrepresenting the earnings of First Tech Internet Services. Although Mr. Thompson's motives may have been good, he must be truthful in his effort to encourage clients to purchase more stock—his conviction that stock would rise upon its listing on the NYSE is not sufficient. No violation of the act occurred with respect to First Tech's exchange listing because Mr. Thompson knew that the stock was in registration to be listed on the NYSE.

Failure to State Material Facts

The USA does not require an agent to provide all information about an investment, only that information that is **material** to making an informed investment decision. However, the agent must not fail to mention material information that could have an impact of the price of the security.

In addition, the agent may not state facts that of themselves are not untrue but, as a result of deliberately omitting others, renders the recommendation misleading under the circumstances.

Case Study: Failure to State Material Facts

Situation: Upon acceptance of its registration by the SEC, First Tech Internet Services will publish its financial statements in a newspaper ad. Mr. Thompson deliberately failed to mention this advertisement to Ms. Gordon.

After its listing on the New York Stock Exchange, the research department in Mr. Thompson's firm prepares a very negative report on First Tech. The research department discovered a change in accounting practices that will have a detrimental affect on subsequent earnings reported by First Tech. Mr. Thompson continues to recommend the stock to Ms. Gordon because he believes the increased exposure gained by the exchange listing will outweigh the future decline in earnings. As a result, Thompson neglects to inform Ms. Gordon of the change prior to her purchase of additional shares.

***Analysis**:* Mr. Thompson violated the USA even though he made no misleading statements to Ms. Gordon with respect to First Tech. Mr. Thompson did not have to mention the ad in the paper because it is not material, yet he violated the act when he failed to mention the accounting change that would result in significantly lower earnings. Although an accounting change is not ordinarily a material fact, in this case it was because it would have a detrimental impact on the company's earnings and its market price.

Using Inside Information

Making recommendations based on **material inside information** about an issuer or its securities is prohibited. Should an agent come into possession of inside information, the agent must report the possession of the information to a supervisor or compliance officer.

✓ ***Take Note:*** Material inside information under securities law is any information about a company that has not been communicated to the general marketplace and that would likely have an impact on the value of a security.

Case Study: Using Inside Information

Situation: Mr. Thompson is a friend and neighbor of Mr. Cage, president and owner of more than half of First Tech's securities. Mr. Cage discloses to Mr. Thompson that the company has just discovered a new technology that will double First Tech's earnings within the next year. No one outside of the company, except for Mr. Thompson, knows of this discovery. On this basis, Mr. Thompson buys additional shares of First Tech for Ms. Gordon.

Analysis: The information on First Tech's new technology is material inside information that has not been made public. It is material information that only Mr. Thompson and company officials know. Mr. Thompson violated the USA in acting upon this information. Mr. Thompson should have communicated the possession of the information to his compliance officer and refrained from making recommendations on the basis of this information.

Making Unsuitable Investment Recommendations

Agents must always have reasonable grounds for making recommendations to clients. Prior to making recommendations, the agent must inquire into the client's financial status, investment objectives, and ability to assume financial risk.

The following practices violate the suitability requirements under the USA as well as the rules of fair practice that regulatory agencies have developed. A securities professional may not:

- recommend securities transactions without regard to customer financial situation, needs, or investment objectives;
- induce transactions solely to generate commission (**churning**);
- recommend a security without reasonable grounds;
- make transactions in customer accounts that are excessive in size and frequency in view of the client's financial resources; or
- fail to sufficiently describe the important facts and risks concerning a transaction or security.

Case Study: Making Unsuitable Investment Recommendations

Situation: Mr. Thompson has a wide variety of clients: high net worth individuals, trusts, retirees with limited incomes and resources, and college students. Mr. Thompson has strong beliefs about First Tech, a growth stock that pays no dividends. He forcefully recommends the stock to all his clients without informing them of the volatility of First Tech and the pending downgrade in earnings. He also informs his clients of the new technology breakthrough that Mr. Cage, the president of First Tech, had told him in confidence.

Analysis: Mr. Thompson has violated the USA on several counts. First, he made a recommendation without regard to the separate financial conditions, needs, and objectives of his diverse client base. The recommendation is unsuitable for the investment objectives of his retired clients with fixed incomes and limited financial resources. Additionally, he made the recommendation in an unsuitable manner by failing to reveal the earnings volatility or risk and the downgrade in earnings and he revealed inside information to clients while making recommendations based on that information.

Exercising Discretion Without Prior Written Authority

Securities professionals may not exercise discretion in an account without **prior written authority (power of attorney)** from the client. Prior written authority is also known as **trading authorization.**

Case Study: Discretionary Trading Authorization

Situation: Mr. Thompson's client, Mr. Bixby, has indicated over the phone that he authorizes Mr. Thompson to make trades for him. Mr. Bixby's family lawyer, Mr. Derval, has specific power of attorney over some of Mr. Bixby's businesses. Mr. Bixby promised Mr. Thompson that he would send in the trading authorization within the next day or two to give Thompson discretion over the account. However, Mr. Thompson immediately executes trades in First Tech for Mr. Bixby to take advantage of its impending NYSE listing.

The following week, Mr. Thompson receives Mr. Bixby's written trading authorization. On the day after the authorization arrived Mr. Bixby's attorney, Mr. Derval, indicates that Mr. Bixby would like to buy shares in General Electric. Because Mr. Derval has power of attorney for Mr. Bixby, Mr. Thompson bought the shares.

Analysis: Mr. Thompson violated the USA by trading in Mr. Bixby's account prior to receipt of the written trading authorization. Having authorization in the mail" is not sufficient. Mr. Thompson also violated the USA by accepting the order from Mr. Derval because although he is Bixby's attorney, he was not specifically authorized to trade in Mr. Bixby's securities account. Had Mr. Derval provided Thompson with specific written third-party trading authorization from Mr. Bixby, Mr. Thompson then could have accepted the order for General Electric without a violation of the act.

Borrowing Money or Securities from Clients

Securities professionals may not borrow money or client securities for their personal use unless that person is a bank or securities firm in the business of lending money and/or securities.

Case Study: Borrowing Money or Securities from Clients

Situation: On occasion, Mr. Thompson borrows cash from his discretionary client, Mr. Bixby, when Mr. Bixby's account is not fully invested. Mr. Bixby has given Mr. Thompson much latitude because Mr. Thompson has done well in managing the account and Mr. Thompson always repays the money in time to reinvest Mr. Bixby's funds in new securities purchases. Thompson justifies these borrowings as within the discretionary power Mr. Bixby had granted him. The First National Bank is also a client of Mr. Thompson, but he does not borrow from the bank because it charges unusually high interest rates.

Analysis: Mr. Thompson has engaged in a prohibited practice because securities professionals may not borrow from customers who are not banks. Furthermore, Mr. Thompson violated the USA in exceeding the specific discretionary authority that Mr. Bixby had authorized. Mr. Bixby had authorized Mr. Thompson to trade in securities—not to take his money for personal use.

Commingling Customer Funds and Securities

Securities that are held in customer name must not be **commingled** (mixed) with those of the firm.

✓ ***For Example:*** If a firm has 100,000 shares of General Electric stock in its own proprietary account and its clients separately own an additional 100,000 shares, the firm may not place customer shares in the firm's proprietary account.

To mix shares together would give undue leverage or borrowing power to a firm and could jeopardize the security of clients' securities in the event of default.

Guaranteeing Clients Profits

Securities professionals may not **guarantee** a certain performance, nor may they guarantee against a loss by providing funds to the account.

✓ ***Take Note:*** The term *guaranteed* under the USA means "guaranteed as to payment of principal, interest, or dividends." The regulatory agencies of the securities industry prohibit securities professionals from guaranteeing the performance returns of an investment or portfolio.

Sharing in Client Accounts

Securities professionals cannot share in the profits or losses of client accounts unless the client and the broker-dealer supply prior written approval. Furthermore, the gains and losses must be in proportion to the funds invested. In such a situation, it would be permissible to commingle the agent's and the customer's funds.

✓ ***Take Note:*** An agent and a customer can have a joint account in which they share profits and losses in proportion to the amount invested. However, clients and a broker-dealer cannot have joint accounts.

Market Manipulation

Securities legislation is designed to uphold the integrity of markets and transactions in securities. However, market integrity is violated when transactions misrepresent actual securities prices or market activity. The most common forms of market manipulation are **front running** and **matching purchases**.

Front running is the practice of entering an order for the benefit of a firm or a securities professional before entering those of customers'.

✓ ***For Example:*** If a securities professional receives an order from an institutional client to purchase a large number of shares, the securities representative or firm cannot enter a personal order prior to completing the customer's purchase in an effort to benefit from a likely price rise.

Matched purchases occur when market participants agree to buy and sell securities among themselves to create the appearance of activity or trading in a security. Increased volume in a security can induce unsuspecting investors to purchase the security, thereby bidding up the price. As the price rises, those who initiated the matched purchases sell their securities at a profit.

✓ ***Take Note:*** **Arbitrage** is not a form of market manipulation; it is the simultaneous buying and selling of the same security in different markets to take advantage of different prices. Simultaneously buying a security in one market and selling it in another forces prices to converge and, therefore, provides uniform prices for the general public.

Other Prohibited Practices in the Sale of Securities

Security industry regulatory agencies prohibited a number of practices that violate industry standards of fair practice. Some of prohibited practices are:

- deliberately failing to follow a customer's order;
- effecting transactions with customers not recorded on the books of the employing broker-dealer without express prior written consent;
- failing to bring written customer complaints to the attention of the employing broker-dealer;
- failing to inform customers that certain transactions involve larger than ordinary commissions, taxes, or transaction costs;
- misrepresenting the status of customer accounts;
- promising to perform services for a customer without any intent to perform them or without being properly qualified to perform them;
- soliciting orders for unregistered, nonexempt securities;
- spreading rumors; and
- recommending transactions based on rumors.

Case Study: Prohibited Practices—Trades not on the Books

Situation: Mr. Thompson, a registered agent for First Securities, Inc. of Illinois, is also a part owner of Computer Resources Inc., a privately-traded company in the state. Mr. Thompson is also friends with Mr. Byers, the chairman of Aircraft Parts Inc., a large manufacturing company traded on the New York

Stock Exchange. Mr. Byers has an account with Mr. Thompson at First Securities.

Mr. Thompson decides to sell his shares in Computer Resources to one of his clients. Since the shares are not publicly traded, Mr. Thompson completes the trades without informing First Securities or recording the transaction on their books. Mr. Thompson believes there is no need to inform his employer because the shares are privately traded. On the following day, Mr. Byers calls Mr. Thompson and indicates that he would like to sell his shares in Aircraft Parts. Mr. Thompson, who now has plenty of liquid assets from the sale of his shares in Computer Resources, decides to buy the shares directly from Mr. Byers. Mr. Thompson does not record the trade on the records of First Securities because he considers it a private transaction between himself and Mr. Byers.

Analysis: In both cases Mr. Thompson has engaged in a prohibited practice. A registered agent may not conduct transactions with customers of his employing broker-dealer that are not recorded on the books without prior written consent. It makes no difference whether the shares Mr. Thompson sold were privately traded—when an agent effects trades with clients of the firm, they must be recorded on the books of the firm unless prior written authorization is obtained.

Case Study: Prohibited Practices—Customer Complaints and Front Running

Situation: Upon completion of the sale of his shares in Aircraft Parts, Inc., Mr. Byers has considerable funds to invest. Mr. Thompson then recommends to Byers that he purchase Simus Shoes, a thinly-traded chain store that First Securities analysts have highly recommended subsequent to its initial public offering. Mr. Byers agrees. Just prior to entering Mr. Byers orders, Mr. Thompson purchases several hundred shares for himself. Mr. Byers learned of Mr. Thompson's purchase and wrote him a stinging letter of complaint about it. Since Mr. Thompson considered the transaction a private matter, he did not think it necessary to bring the letter to the attention of First Securities. A few days later, Mr. Thompson personally apologized to Mr. Byers and took him out for a drink.

Analysis: Mr. Thompson has engaged in two practices here that violate industry practice. First, while the recommendation of Simus Shoes was perfectly appropriate, it was not appropriate for Mr. Thompson to enter his personal order for the same shares prior to completing Mr. Byers' purchase. This is known as front running, a prohibited practice. Additionally, Mr. Thompson (as a registered agent) must bring all written complaints to the attention of his employer. Had Mr. Byers simply lodged a verbal complaint, Mr. Thompson would not have been under an obligation to bring it to the attention of the manager of his office. Taking Mr. Byers out for a drink did not violate industry standards.

Quick Quiz 4.1

Write **U** for unlawful or prohibited activities and **L** for lawful activities.

___ 1. An agent guarantees a client that funds invested in mutual funds made up of government securities cannot lose principal.

___ 2. A customer calls his agent and places a buy order for 1,000 shares of any hot internet company. Later in the day, the representative enters an order for 1,000 shares of Global Internet Services.

___ 3. An agent receives a call from his client's spouse advising him to sell her husband's securities. Her husband is out of the country and requested that his wife call the agent. The agent refuses because the wife does not have trading authorization and she complains vigorously to his manager.

___ 4. A client writes a letter of complaint to his agent regarding securities that the agent had recommended. The agent calls the client to apologize and then disposes of the letter because the client seemed satisfied.

___ 5. A registered agent borrows $10,000 from a credit union that is one of her best customers.

___ 6. An agent is convinced that Internet Resources will rise significantly over the next three months. She offers to buy the stock back from her customers at 10% higher than its current price at any time during the next three months.

___ 7. An agent receives an order for the purchase of an obscure foreign security. The agent informs the client that the commissions and charges on this purchase will be much higher than those of domestic securities.

___ 8. A registered rep who works for a small broker that employs no securities analysts assures her clients that she can analyze any publicly-traded security better than any analyst and that she will do it personally for each security purchased by a client regardless of the industry.

___ 9. A securities sales agent recommends that her client buy 1,000 shares of Internet Consultants, Inc., an unregistered nonexempt security with a bright future.

Answers

1. ***U.*** *It is unlawful to guarantee the performance of any security. Government securities, although default-free, have interest rate risk or market price risk that an agent may not guarantee.*

2. ***U.*** *It is unlawful to exercise discretion without prior written authorization. Since the client was a nondiscretionary client, the agent could not, on his own initiative, select which internet company to invest in.*

3. **L.** *An agent must refuse orders from anyone other than the customer unless that person has prior written trading authority.*

4. **U.** *All written customer complaints must be forwarded to a principal of the agent's employing broker-dealer.*

5. **L.** *Agents may borrow from banks or financial institutions that are in the business of lending money to public customers. Agents may not borrow money from their customers who are not in the business of lending money.*

6. **U.** *An agent may not guarantee the performance of a security.*

7. **L.** *It is lawful to charge extra transaction fees when justified as long as the customer is informed prior to the transaction.*

8. **U.** *It is unlawful to promise services that an agent cannot reasonably expect to perform or that the agent is not qualified to perform.*

9. **U.** *It is unlawful to solicit unregistered nonexempt securities except in a private placement.*

Fraudulent & Prohibited Practices When Providing Investment Advice

The fraudulent and prohibited practices described so far have related to the sale of securities. The Uniform Securities Act also prohibits fraudulent activities when providing investment advice.

The USA makes it unlawful for any person who receives compensation (directly or indirectly) for advising another person (whether through analyses or reports) as to the value of securities, to employ any device, scheme, or artifice to defraud the other person. Additionally, they may not engage in any act, practice, or course of business which operates or would operate as a fraud or deceit upon the other person or engage in dishonest or unethical practices as the Administrator may define by rule.

✓ ***Take Note:*** Prohibitions are determined by the nature of the activity, not the registration status of the person engaged in the activity.

✓ ***For Example:*** An agent providing investment advice and an investment adviser engaged in selling are equally subject to the prohibitions against fraud.

Fiduciary Responsibility

When securities professionals act in an investment advisory capacity, they are called **fiduciaries** and are held to higher ethical standards than when they are engaged in the sales of securities.

Fiduciary responsibility exceeds that which is normally required of ordinary business relationships because the fiduciary is in a position of trust. The fiduciary must act for the benefit of the client and place the interests of their clients above their own.

✓ ***Take Note:*** Investment advisers and their representatives are bound by the same restrictions as broker-dealers and their agents. In addition, investment advisers, as fiduciaries, must place the interest of their clients above those of their own and advisers must have written investment advisory contracts with their clients (unless exempted by the Administrator). Those contracts must inform clients of fees and how they are computed and contain a prohibition against assignment (transfer) of the account without the client permission.

Disclosure of Capacity

As a result of the fiduciary relationship that exists between an investment adviser and the client, the Uniform Securities Act places greater disclosure burdens on investment advisers. Prior to the completion of a transaction, an adviser must disclose to clients whether the firm is acting as a principal or broker in the transaction.

Agency Cross Transaction. An **agency cross transaction** is a transaction in which an adviser acts as an investment adviser as well as a broker-dealer for the other side. The adviser must disclose this capacity to clients and receive consent in writing prior to conducting the trade.

✓ ***Take Note:*** In an agency cross transaction, the adviser may not recommend the transaction to both parties of the trade.

An exception to the prior written consent requirement is made when an investment adviser only provides what is called **impersonal investment advice.** Then, an adviser may act as principal without prior written consent from each client, if the adviser discloses that he may be acting as principal.

✓ ***Take Note:*** Impersonal investment advice is advice publicly distributed to 35 or more persons that does not purport to meet the objectives of specific individuals.

Investment Advisory Contracts

The primary relationship between a client and an investment adviser is determined by an **investment advisory contract**. The USA makes it unlawful for an investment adviser to enter into, extend, or renew any investment advisory contract unless in writing or the Administrator, by rule or order, provides otherwise.

All investment advisory contracts must state, in writing, that:

- the investment adviser shall not be compensated on the basis of a share in (percentage of) the capital appreciation of the client's funds;
- no investment advisory contract may be assigned to another adviser without the consent of the client; and
- if a partnership, the client shall be notified of any change in membership of the partnership within a reasonable time after the change.

Case Study: Assignment and Notification of Change in Membership

***Situation**:* Mr. Bixby withdrew $10 million from his account at the end of the year, leaving less than $1 million under management with Market Tech Advisers, Inc., an advisory company incorporated in Illinois. During the course of the year, three officers left the firm. As a matter of corporate policy, Market Tech did not advise Mr. Bixby of these changes.

The following year, Market Tech (without notifying Mr. Bixby) assigned his account to Associated Investment Partners, a small partnership located in California and Mr. Bixby was happy with the new partnership. Shortly after the assignment, Mr. Bixby learned of the death of one of the major partners through an article in the newspaper. He retained his account at Associated even though he had not been informed by them of the partner's death.

***Analysis**:* Market Tech Advisers, Inc. was under no obligation to inform Mr. Bixby of the change in officers because it is a corporation and not a partnership. However they did violate the USA by assigning Mr. Bixby's account to Associated Partners without his consent. Additionally, the USA requires partnerships to inform clients of any change in partner membership within a reasonable amount of time after the change which means that Associated Partners violated the USA by not informing Mr. Bixby of the partner's death.

Investment Advisory Fees

The USA does not allow an investment adviser to share in a client's capital gains. The adviser is allowed to charge the client a fee based upon the total value of a fund averaged over a definite period (e.g., quarterly or annually).

Case Study: Investment Advisory Fees

***Situation**:* Market Tech Advisers, a registered investment advisory company, charges clients a fee of 1% of their assets managed by the firm based upon the average amount of funds in the account each quarter. Last quarter, Market Tech performance was extremely good and, as a result, the fees of one of its largest clients, Mr. Bixby, more than doubled. Next quarter the value of the account dropped by 25% and so did the fee. Mr. Bixby complained that Market Tech was sharing in his capital appreciation in violation of the written advisory contract.

***Analysis**:* Market Tech is in compliance with the USA. Market Tech charged Mr. Bixby a 1% fee based upon the total assets in the account over a designated period. Since the assets more than doubled in the first quarter, so did the fee. Market Tech based its fees on the average value of funds under management, not on a percentage of Mr. Bixby's capital gains—a practice in compliance with the USA. In the subsequent quarter, Market Tech's fee declined by 25% as a result market deterioration. Had Market Tech taken a 5% share in the capital appreciation of Mr. Bixby's funds rather than charging a 1% quarterly fee based upon the total value, Market Tech would then have been in violation of the USA.

Custody of Client Funds and Securities

Under the USA, it is unlawful for an adviser to have custody of client funds and securities if:

- the Administrator in the state prohibits, by rule, advisers from having custody; and
- in absence of a rule, an adviser fails to notify the Administrator that he has custody.

Custody is the physical possession or control of funds and securities. Many advisers do not have custody because their client funds and securities are maintained at a bank or brokerage house. The adviser makes investment decisions under an advisory contract with the client's funds and securities placed in a custodial account at a commercial bank.

Quick Quiz 4.2

1. An investment advisory contract need not include

   A. the fees and their method of their computation
   B. a statement prohibiting assignment of client accounts without client consent
   C. the states in which the adviser is licensed to conduct business
   D. notification requirement upon change in membership if an investment partnership

True or False?

___ 2. An Administrator may not prevent custody of securities or funds if an adviser notifies the Administrator prior to taking custody.

___ 3. An adviser may not sell securities to its customers from its own proprietary account.

___ 4. Under USA antifraud provisions, an investment adviser is bound by the restrictions that apply to sales practices when engaged in sales activities.

Answers

1. C. The USA does not require investment advisers to include in their contracts a list of those states in which they are licensed to do business. The USA does require advisers to include their method of computing fees, a statement prohibiting assignment without client consent, and notification of change in membership of the investment partnership.

2. **F.** *An Administrator may, by rule or order, prevent an adviser from taking custody. If an Administrator prevents custody, an adviser cannot overrule the Administrator by notifying the Administrator first.*

3. **F.** *An adviser may sell securities to clients from its own account provided disclosure is made upon receipt of written consent from the client prior to executing the trade.*

4. **T.** *Investment advisers are bound by the regulations that apply to sales activities as well as those that apply to advisory activities. The reverse is also true. When a sales agent engages in investment advisory activities, the agent is bound by the rules that apply to providing investment advice to others as well as those that apply to sales practices.*

Business Practices HotSheet

Practices Prohibited of All Securities Professionals:

- Misleading or untrue statements
- Failure to state material facts
- Use of insider information
- Unsuitable transactions
- Market manipulation (pegging, front running, wash sales, matched purchases)

Other Prohibited Sales Practices:

- Unauthorized third-party trading
- Borrowing money from customers who are not banks or lending institutions
- Commingling client funds
- Failing to follow client instructions
- Exercising discretion without authority
- Effecting transactions not on the books
- Failing to report written complaints
- Guaranteeing against loss
- Failing to inform clients of higher than normal charges
- Misrepresenting customer account status
- Creating misleading trading activity
- Promising undeliverable services
- Unauthorized sharing in customer accounts
- Solicitation of unregistered, nonexempt securities
- Misrepresenting Administrator approval

Unlawful or Unethical Investment Advisory Practices:

- Unsuitable investments
- Unauthorized discretion
- Unauthorized third-party transactions
- Excessive trading
- Commingling funds
- Misrepresentation of material facts
- Nondisclosure of information sources
- Excessive fees
- Conflicts of interest
- Unauthorized custody of customer funds
- Operating without advisory contracts
- Performance-based compensation, except under unique circumstances
- Failing to disclose material legal action in past 10 years at least 48 hours before contracting with client
- Failing to disclose principal or agent capacity

Series 63 Lesson Exam 4

1. Under the USA, the Administrator may deny or revoke a registration if an agent

   I. borrows money from his wealthy clients' accounts
   II. solicits orders for nonexempt unregistered securities.
   III. buys and sells securities in accounts in order to generate a high level of commissions
   IV. alters market quotations in order to induce a client to invest in an attractive growth stock

   A. I and III
   B. I and IV
   C. I, II and III
   D. I, II, III and IV

2. Which of the following transactions are exempt from the filing and antifraud provisions of the USA?

   A. Transactions in unregistered exempt securities
   B. Nonissuer transactions in securities subject to Section 12 of the Securities Exchange Act of 1934 that have met all required reporting requirements for a one-year period
   C. Transactions between issuers and underwriters
   D. None of the above.

3. A customer is upset with her agent for not servicing her account properly and sends him a complaint letter about his actions. Under the USA, the agent should

   A. call the customer, apologize, and attempt to correct the problem
   B. tell the customer he is willing to make recission
   C. do nothing
   D. bring the customer complaint to the employer immediately

4. Which of the following practices is prohibited under the USA?

   A. Participating in active trading of a security in which an unusually high trading volume has occurred
   B. Offering services that a rep cannot realistically perform because of his broker-dealer's limitations
   C. Altering the customer's order at the request of a customer which subsequently results in a substantial loss
   D. Failing to inform the firm's principal of frequent verbal customer complaints

5. It is legal under the USA for a registered investment adviser to tell a client that

   A. a registered security may lawfully be sold in that state
   B. an exempt security is not required to be registered because it is generally regarded as being safer than a nonexempt security
   C. her qualifications have been found satisfactory by the Administrator
   D. a registered security has been approved for sale in the state by the Administrator

6. According to the USA, which of the following is an example of market manipulation?

   A. Creating the illusion of active trading
   B. Omitting material facts in a presentation
   C. Guaranteeing performance of a security
   D. Transactions in excess of a customer's financial capability

7. Which of the following transactions are prohibited?

   I. Borrowing money or securities from a high net-worth customer
   II. Selling speculative or "hot" issues to a retired couple of modest means on a fixed income
   III. Failing to follow a customer's orders so as to prevent investment in a security not adequately covered by well-known securities analysts
   IV. Backdating confirmations for the benefit of the client's tax reporting

   A. I and II
   B. II and III
   C. I, II and III
   D. I, II, III and IV

8. Under the Uniform Securities Act, an investment adviser may legally have custody of money or securities belonging to a client if the

   I. adviser is registered under the 1940 Act
   II. Administrator has not prohibited custodial arrangements
   III. adviser does not also have discretionary authority over the account
   IV. adviser has notified the Administrator that he has custody

   A. I and III
   B. II only
   C. II and IV
   D. IV only

9. An agent hears a rumor concerning a security and uses it to convince a client to purchase that security. Under the USA, the agent may

   A. recommend the security if it is an appropriate investment
   B. recommend the investment if the rumor is based on material inside information
   C. recommend the security if the source of the rumor came from a reliable source
   D. not recommend the security

10. An agent thinks that a technology stock is undervalued and she actively solicits all her customers. In this situation, the agent

    I. did not violate the USA if she disclosed all material facts
    II. committed an unethical sales practice because her firm has not recommended this technology stock
    III. committed an unethical business practice if she failed to review each account to determine suitability
    IV. did not commit a violation if she accurately informs all her clients of the price of the stock

    A. I, II and IV
    B. I and IV
    C. III only
    D. I, II, III and IV

11. Your customer calls to check on her account value at 9:00 a.m. You were unavailable at the time. It is now 2:00 p.m. and you are able to call her back. Between 9:00 a.m. and 2:00 p.m. her account value dropped from $11,500 to $10,000. What should you say to her?

    A. "At the time that you called, your account had a value of $11,500."
    B. "Your account value cannot be determined until the market closes."
    C. "Your account is valued at $10,000 at this time."
    D. "Your account was down to $9,700 earlier today but is up to $10,000."

12. According to the Uniform Securities Act, an investment adviser may have custody of a customer's funds and securities if

    A. it has received the permission of the Administrator
    B. it has received permission from the SEC
    C. it does not share in the capital gains of the account
    D. the Administrator has been informed of the custody

13. An agent omits facts which a prudent investor requires in order to make informed decisions. Under the Uniform Securities Act, this action is

    A. fraudulent for nonexempt securities only
    B. fraudulent for exempt securities only
    C. fraudulent for both exempt and nonexempt securities
    D. not fraudulent if there was willful intent to omit the information

14. Which of the following actions is not a prohibited practice under the USA?

    A. A market maker fills his firm's order ahead of a customer order at the same price.
    B. A specialist buys and sells stock as principal.
    C. A principal in a broker-dealer allows a rumor to leak out that ABC is going to acquire LMN; after a few days, the broker-dealer sells ABC short for its own account.
    D. A broker sells a customer's stock at the bid price and makes up the difference with a personal check.

15. According to the USA, which of the following is a prohibited activity?

    A. The sales rep enters into an agreement to share in the profits/losses of the customer's account without an investment in the account.
    B. The sales rep and his spouse jointly own their own personal trading account at the firm.
    C. The sales rep, with his firm's and the client's permission, participates in the profits and losses of the account in proportion to his investment in the account.
    D. A sales rep refuses a client's request to share in the performance of the client's account.

16. All of the following are prohibited practices under the USA EXCEPT

    I. borrowing money or securities from the account of a former banker with express written permission
    II. failing to identify a customer's financial objectives
    III. selling rights
    IV. supplying funds to a client's account only when or if it declines below a pre-agreed-upon level

    A. I and II
    B. I, II and III
    C. II and IV
    D. III only

17. Which of the following is(are) prohibited under the USA?

    I. Recommending tax shelters to low income retirees
    II. Stating that a state Administrator has approved an offering based on the quality of information found in the prospectus
    III. Soliciting orders for unregistered, nonexempt securities
    IV. Employing any device to defraud

    A. I only
    B. I and II
    C. I, II and III
    D. I, II, III and IV

18. A federally covered adviser is one who is

    I. registered with the SEC
    II. registered with the state securities Administrator
    III. excluded from the definition of an adviser under the Act of 1940
    IV. required to register with the Interstate Commerce Commission

    A. I and III
    B. I and IV
    C. II and III
    D. II and IV

Series 63 Lesson Exam 4 Answers & Rationale

1. D. An Administrator may deny or revoke an agent's registration if the agent engages in practices that are prohibited by such regulatory agencies as the National Association of Securities Dealers (NASD). All the above practices are prohibited by the NASD but they may not involve fraudulent activity. Fraud must involve willful deceit for profit, e.g., if an agent engages in excessive trading in an account in order to generate commissions (called "churning") with a client's consent, fraud is not involved. The practice is, however, prohibited. If fraud was involved, the practice would be both fraudulent and prohibited. QID: 37185

2. D. Although certain transactions are exempt from filing requirements under the USA, no securities transactions are exempt from its antifraud provisions. QID: 28919

3. D. Failure to bring customers' written complaints to the attention of the agent's broker-dealer is prohibited. QID: 28878

4. B. A representative may not offer services that he cannot perform. Choice A is incorrect because a representative may participate actively in trading a security in which an unusually high trading volume has occurred, provided the trading is not designed to create a false appearance of high volume. C is incorrect because a representative can alter a client's order, even if the effort is not in the interest of the client. D is incorrect because a representative is only required to report written complaints to his employing principal, although it would be wise to report repeated complaints if they are serious. QID: 36368

5. A. An agent may indicate that a security is registered or is exempt from registration. Such representation has no bearing on its quality, safety, or merits. An agent may not represent that an exemption from registration indicates that a security is safer than a nonexempt security. The Administrator does not make a determination that an adviser's qualifications are satisfactory. Registration means only that certain legal requirements have been met in regard to that security or person. QID: 28969

6. A. Creating the illusion of trading activity is market manipulation. Guaranteeing performance of a security and omitting material facts are prohibited practices but do not constitute market manipulation. Trades too large for a customer are also prohibited because they are not suitable. QID: 28886

7. D. All of the practices are prohibited. An agent may not borrow money or securities from a customer unless that customer is a commercial bank in the business of lending money. Selling speculative or "hot" issues to a retired couple of modest means is an unsuitable transaction because it is not consistent with the objectives of the client. An agent must follow legal orders of the customer, even if the agent believes the order is an unwise one. An agent may not backdate confirmations for the benefit on the client. QID: 37152

8. C. The Administrator may prohibit advisers from having custody of client funds or securities. If no such prohibition applies, the Administrator must be notified in writing if an adviser has custody. Whether the adviser is registered or not is irrelevant. Discretionary authority does not affect an adviser's ability to have custody. QID: 31203

9. D. The use of information, such as a rumor, that has no basis in fact is prohibited. QID: 28909

10. C. Agents must always determine suitability before soliciting purchases or sales. Not to do so is an unethical sales practice. QID: 28873

11. C. All other choices are clearly a misrepresentation of account status. QID: 31849

12. D. As long as retaining custody of funds is not prohibited, an investment adviser may have custody of a customer's account after providing notice to the Administrator. QID: 28945

13. C. The omission of a material fact in the sale, purchase, or offer of a security is fraudulent. This applies whether the security offered is exempt or nonexempt. QID: 28888

14. B. The function of the specialist is to act as a broker for orders left with him by other broker-dealers and to act as a dealer in buying and selling for his own account. His activity is not prohibited. Allowing a rumor to leak out and trading on it is a prohibited practice but is not considered market manipulation. Selling stock at the bid price and making up the difference with a personal check is not market manipulation, but it is a prohibited practice. Filling a firm's proprietary order ahead of a customer's order is a prohibited practice called front running. QID: 28879

15. A. Under the USA, it is a prohibited practice for a sales rep to share in the profits or losses of a customer's account unless the customer and the employer have given written consent and the percentage of participation is proportionate to the percentage of the sales rep's personal funds in the account. A sales rep is permitted to jointly own a personal account at the firm. An agent is permitted to refuse to share in a customer's account. QID: 31824

16. D. It is permissible to sell rights, which are securities. Borrowing money or securities from other than a bank and failing to identify a customer's financial objectives are prohibited practices. Failing to identify a customer's financial objectives and guaranteeing a customer's account against losses are also prohibited practices. QID: 28934

17. D. All of the choices are prohibited. Recommending tax shelters to low income retirees is an example of an unsuitable transaction. Stating that an Administrator has approved an offering based on the quality of information in the prospectus, soliciting orders for unregistered nonexempt securities, and employing a device to defraud are all prohibited practices under the USA. QID: 37142

18. A. A federally covered adviser is one who is registered with the SEC or is excluded from the definition of an adviser under the Act of 1940. QID: 39197

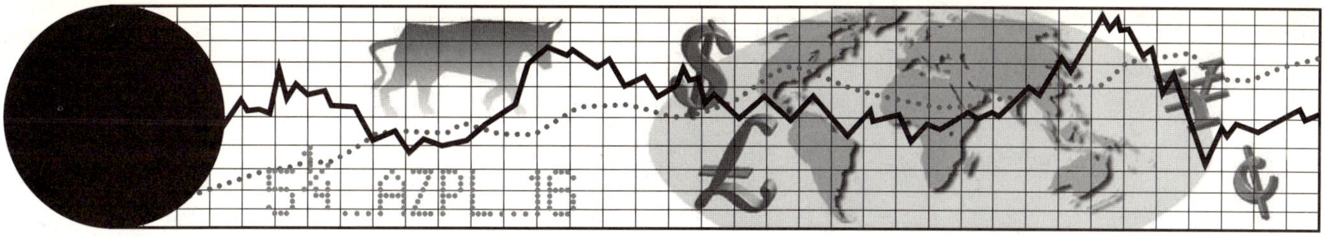

Series 63
Practice Finals 1 - 4

Series 63 Practice Final 1

1. Which of the following activities are violations of the Uniform Securities Act?

   I. Arbitrage
   II. Soliciting investors for unregistered, nonexempt securities
   III. Selling bonds of a foreign government to residents of a state other than the one in which the agent of a broker-dealer is registered and is paid a commission
   IV. Selling T-bonds without being registered as an agent of an issuer and not receiving a commission

   A. I and IV
   B. II and III
   C. II, III and IV
   D. I, II, III and IV

2. Which of the following transactions would constitute a violation of the USA?

   I. Arbitrage
   II. Selling shares of an unregistered, nonexempt security to less than 15 clients
   III. Selling a Canadian government bond to a resident of a state in which the agent is not registered
   IV. Representing an issuer of municipal bonds without being registered as an agent in the issuer's state

   A. I and III
   B. I and IV
   C. II and III
   D. II and IV

3. Which of the following does not have a federally-imposed exemption?

   A. Securities issued or guaranteed by the U.S. government
   B. Securities issued or guaranteed by a state or political subdivision of a state
   C. Promissory notes and bankers' acceptances with maturities of nine months or less and with denominations of at least $50,000
   D. Securities of bank holding companies traded on the New York Stock Exchange

4. Under the USA, if a sales rep is ordered to appear before the Administrator to answer a complaint, and the sales rep refuses to appear, which of the following statements is TRUE?

   A. The Administrator may cancel the registered representative's license within 10 days.
   B. The rep may plead protection under the Fifth Amendment of the U.S. Constitution and refuse to answer questions.
   C. The rep has demonstrated contumacy toward the Administrator.
   D. The Administrator may issue an injunction.

5. Under the USA, a person who has passed the Uniform Securities Agent State Law Examination but whose license has not yet been issued can participate in

   A. prospecting for new clients in person
   B. prospecting for new clients by mail
   C. accepting unsolicited orders
   D. None of the above.

6. The National Securities Markets Improvement Act of 1996 (NSMIA), which amended portions of the USA, allows exemptions from state registration for broker-dealers and their agents for incidental transactions. In which of the following situations is the agent engaged in an incidental transaction?
   A. Alice, an agent with an office in the state of Indiana, executes one trade per year for Mrs. Clark, also a resident of Indiana. All of Alice's other clients are residents of Illinois. Alice claims her transactions with Mrs. Clark are incidental and, as a result, she does not have to register in Indiana.
   B. Tom, a registered agent in California, conducts trades for Terri (a teacher who lives in San Francisco) while on her summer vacation in Utah which lasts from June through August. Tom claims an exemption from registration in Utah.
   C. Patti, a resident of New Jersey, contacts Peter, her registered agent in Short Hills, New Jersey, requesting that he conduct securities transactions for her while she is in California for two weeks. Peter seeks exemption from registration in California because his client, Patti, will only be in California on a temporary basis.
   D. John, an agent only licensed in his home state of Florida, conducts seven trades for Mark, a resident of Georgia, during Mark's two-week vacation in Maine. John claims exemption from registration in Maine because he is licensed in Florida.

7. In the locker room at the country club, an agent overhears that Technotalk (a publicly-traded company) has just lost its biggest account to a competitor. After learning this, the agent discontinues selling Technotalk common stock. In the above situation, the agent has acted
   A. lawfully, because he did not profit from selling Technotalk, Inc. common stock short in his own account
   B. lawfully because he did not take advantage of material, nonpublic information
   C. unlawfully, because he failed to report nonpublic information to the SEC
   D. unlawfully, because he failed to inform his customers of the negative news immediately

8. An issuer employs its officers and directors to sell newly-issued shares of the company and compensates them for the sales. To comply with the USA, the officers and directors would have to be registered as agents of
   A. the issuer
   B. broker-dealer
   C. broker-dealer and the issuer
   D. neither a broker-dealer nor the issuer because the transactions are exempt

9. Which of the following may be required by the Administrator to post surety bonds?

   I. An agent who has custody of or discretion over client funds and securities
   II. A broker-dealer who has custody of or discretion over client funds and securities
   III. A financial adviser who has custody of or discretion over client funds and securities

   A. I only
   B. I and III
   C. III only
   D. I, II and III

10. The Administrator may, by rule,
    A. forbid an adviser from taking custody of client funds
    B. allow an agent to waive provisions of the USA
    C. suspend federal law if the Administrator believes it to be in the public interest
    D. suspend the registration of a federal covered adviser because the contract does not meet the requirements for a state sanctioned investment advisory contract

11. All of the following securities transactions are exempt under the USA EXCEPT a(n)
    A. purchase of stock by an underwriter from the issuer in a firm commitment underwriting
    B. sale of private placement securities to 25 investors in a state that represents the general public
    C. offer of preorganization certificates involving no commission or payment made to five parties
    D. sale of stock to a pension trust

12. According to the Uniform Securities Act, which of the following actions would rectify an inadvertent sale of an unregistered, nonexempt security?

    I. Offering to buy the security back from the customer
    II. Asking the customer to sign a customer agreement that releases the agent from responsibility because the customer is pleased with the security's performance
    III. Registering the stock by notification
    IV. Offering to pay interest as set by the Administrator, less income paid, from the date the security was purchased

    A. I and III
    B. I and IV
    C. II and III
    D. I, II, III and IV

13. In which of the following circumstances has John, a registered representative employed at AAA Securities Corporation, made an offer as that term is defined in the USA?

    I. John calls a long standing client, Mr. Baxter, to indicate that a security on John's firm's "restricted list" is a security that is suitable for Mr. Baxter's portfolio. John indicates that he cannot sell the securities unless Mr. Baxter requests them on an unsolicited basis. Mr. Baxter thinks about making the purchase but ultimately decides not to.
    II. John discovers that Mr. Baxter has inherited shares in a manufacturing firm trading on the New York Stock Exchange. John suggests that Mr. Baxter sell them to him in a private transaction in which no commission would be charged.
    III. John owned XYZ securities for several years. He decided to transfer them to his college's endowment fund, in lieu of giving a cash gift. He then took a tax deduction for the value of the securities transferred.
    IV. Mr. Baxter, as a reward for the years of John's service as his registered representative, transferred $5,000 worth of XYZ Corporation securities to John, claiming the transfer as a business expense on his tax form.

    A. I only
    B. I and II
    C. I, II and III
    D. I, II, III and IV

14. Joe is an agent at a broker-dealer firm and he is very excited about new earnings projections he has received from TechEd. TechEd sells at a market value of $10 and has paid a $1 dividend this past year and earnings projections for the next year amount to an increase of 30%. Joe calls his clients based on this news, soliciting purchases of TechEd stock. In his solicitations, Joe says that if his clients buy now at $10 per share they will realize a yield of 13%. Joe should

    A. show his clients how he came to his calculations, sending them charts that have been approved by his principal
    B. not say anything yet because this is inside information
    C. practice due diligence and call TechEd to verify that these earnings predictions are still current
    D. refrain from making this statement because it is a misrepresentation

15. A corporation's employees sell nonexempt securities to public customers. The corporation receives a commission on the sale of the securities and pays commissions to the employees who sell them. According to the USA, the corporation is a

    A. broker-dealer that must be registered
    B. corporation selling only to sophisticated investors
    C. broker-dealer engaging in exempt transactions
    D. corporation selling to an employee pension fund

16. An Administrator may deny or revoke a security's exemption

    A. if the Administrator, in a court of competent jurisdiction, proves that a security does not qualify for an exemption
    B. if the Administrator determines that an exemption applicable to federal covered securities is inconsistent with state securities law
    C. for a federal covered security if the issuer of that security is in violation of state law
    D. without a hearing providing the issuer is given an opportunity for a hearing after the revocation

17. Under the Uniform Securities Act, the term "security" includes a(n)

    I. single payment insurance contract guaranteed by a highly-rated insurance company
    II. individual retirement account with $200,000 in common stock
    III. valuable collection of coins and currency conservatively valued for estate purposes
    IV. client's $100,000 mortgage on his primary residence

    A. I and II
    B. III and IV
    C. I, II and III
    D. None of the above.

18. All of the following must be specified in the state registration statement of a security EXCEPT

    A. a stop order from another state that affects the offering of the security within that state
    B. the total amount of the security that will be offered in all states
    C. an offering circular or prospectus
    D. all other states where the security is currently registered or will be registered

19. A famous tennis player offers to record a testimonial for an investment adviser for use in a television commercial. Under the USA, the investment adviser may

   A. use the testimonial provided the athlete receives no compensation
   B. use the testimonial and pay the athlete
   C. use the testimonial with the approval of the state Administrator
   D. not use the testimonial

20. Under the USA, agent registrations expire

   A. 365 days after the effective date
   B. each year on December 31st
   C. two years after the effective date
   D. three years after the effective date

21. It is permissible to

   I. solicit transactions in unregistered, exempt securities
   II. open a joint account with a customer with written permission of the customer and the broker-dealer
   III. split commissions with another agent at the broker-dealer firm
   IV. charge larger commissions because of a larger array of services the agent's firm offers

   A. I only
   B. I and II
   C. I, III and IV
   D. I, II, III and IV

22. A rep puts together a recommendation for a customer, but is unexpectedly called out of town and asks another agent at her firm to meet with the customer and present the recommendation. When the other agent makes the presentation, he omits some material facts. According to the Uniform Securities Act, this is

   A. permitted if the recommendation pertains to an exempt security
   B. permitted if the second agent was unaware of the omission
   C. permitted if the second agent receives no compensation for presenting the recommendation
   D. prohibited under any circumstances

23. Which of the following persons is defined as an agent by the Uniform Securities Act?

   A. Silent partner of a broker-dealer
   B. Secretary of a branch office sales manager
   C. Clerk at a broker-dealer who is authorized to take orders
   D. Broker-dealer executive who does not solicit or transact business

24. Who of the following must register as an agent?

   A. An individual representing a broker-dealer who sells commercial paper
   B. An individual who sells commercial paper for ABC National Bank
   C. A government employee who sells Treasury bonds to the public
   D. An individual who is paid a commission to sell certificates of deposit for ABC National Bank

25. Under the USA, which of the following is(are) specifically excluded from the definition of broker-dealer?

I. Investment adviser
II. International bank
III. Issuer
IV. Financial planning company

A. I and III
B. I and IV
C. II and III
D. IV only

26. A sales agent registered in Nebraska works for a broker-dealer registered in all 50 states. A customer who is a resident of Florida calls the rep in Nebraska and offers to purchase securities. Under the Uniform Securities Act, the rep should

A. accept the order because her broker-dealer is registered in all 50 states
B. accept the order because she received it in Nebraska
C. reject the order because she is not registered in Florida
D. reject the order because it was not a wire order

27. Under the USA, all of the following are exempt transactions EXCEPT

A. transactions with a trust company
B. transactions between an issuer and an underwriter
C. private placements
D. the sale of municipal bonds to a retail customer

28. Which of the following would be considered investment representative fraud under the USA?

A. An agent has a large number of clients in a security in which she trades frequently for her own account with no attempt to create an inaccurate impression of trading volume.
B. An investment representative knowingly sold a nonregistered security because he thought it would eventually become registered.
C. An agent who discovers through a private subscription to an online internet legal records service that a company is about to file for bankruptcy and immediately calls her clients recommending they liquidate their holdings.
D. An agent knowingly sells securities in a publicly-traded company in which his family has a beneficial ownership.

29. An individual has passed the appropriate qualifying registration exams in his state, but has not yet been granted a license by the Administrator. The state requires no additional qualification other than passing the Series 63 test. The rep may

A. offer to sell securities to customers but may not sign his trade tickets
B. effect transactions if paid no commission for these trades
C. not effect trades but may make recommendations to customers
D. not function as a rep until registration is granted

30. Which of the following securities is(are) exempt from the registration provisions of the USA?

I. Issue of a savings and loan association
II. General obligation municipal bond
III. Bond issued by a company that has common stock listed on the American Stock Exchange

A. I only
B. II only
C. II and III
D. I, II and III

31. Under the USA, the Administrator may deny or revoke a registration if an agent

I. borrows money from his wealthy clients' accounts
II. solicits orders for nonexempt, unregistered securities
III. buys and sells securities in accounts in order to generate a high level of commissions
IV. alters market quotations in order to induce a client to invest in an attractive growth stock

A. I and III
B. I and IV
C. I, II and III
D. I, II, III and IV

32. Which of the following actions by a sales rep would be considered a violation of the antifraud provisions of the USA?

A. The sales rep recommends a security to a client based on his investigation of the client's financial objectives.
B. The client places an order to buy stock without providing any suitability information; the rep enters the order but marks the ticket discretionary.
C. Upon receiving a signed trading authorization from the customer, the agent effects a discretionary transaction in accordance with the client's investment objectives.
D. After the client places an order, the sales rep discusses and reviews the suitability of the transaction with the client before entering the trade.

33. According to the USA, the sale of a security to an insurance company is

A. an exempt security
B. an exempt transaction
C. always a private placement
D. illegal

34. The Administrator has authority to

I. issue a cease and desist order without a hearing
II. issue a cease and desist order only after a hearing
III. convict violators of the 1933 Securities Act in criminal prosecutions
IV. sentence violators of the USA to three years in prison

A. I and III
B. I and IV
C. II and III
D. II and IV

35. Which of the following is an exempt transaction?

 A. Sale of a municipal bond to a high net worth client resident in the state
 B. Sale of a security issued by the U.S. government to a resident of the state
 C. Sale of a security that has traded in the secondary market for more than 90 days to a resident in the state
 D. Sale of a security issued by a public utility to an investment adviser resident in the state

36. Which of the following may not be used as a basis for a recommendation to customers?

 A. The best estimate of the sales representative's firm regarding the potential movement of a stock
 B. Information obtained while acting in a fiduciary capacity for a corporation that indicates the strong possibility of future mergers
 C. Recommendations of major financial publications generally available through newsstand purchases
 D. Recommendations of private firms charging special fees for such recommendations

37. An agent hears at a social gathering that the chairman of a large manufacturing firm has engaged in erratic behavior. The agent calls his customers who own shares of the corporation and tells them to liquidate their positions. Under the USA, which of the following statements is TRUE?

 A. The agent may have made an error as to the effect of the rumor, so he should wait until he has a better feel for the situation.
 B. This action is based on material inside information, so he must inform all of his customers of this fact.
 C. The agent's action constitutes a prohibited use of rumor to induce a purchase or sale of securities.
 D. This action is legal provided the agent contacts 12 or fewer customers.

38. To protect the public, the Administrator may

I. deny a registration if the registrant does not have sufficient experience to function as a registered representative
II. limit a registrant's functions to that of a broker if, in the initial application for registration as an investment adviser, the registrant is not qualified to act as an adviser
III. take into consideration that the registrant will work under the supervision of a registered investment adviser or broker-dealer in approving a registration
IV. deny a registration, although denial is not in the public's interest if it is prudent in view of a change in the state's political composition

 A. I and II
 B. I, II and III
 C. III and IV
 D. I, II, III and IV

39. A friend of an agent wants to sell a security and asks if the agent can guarantee a certain price. The friend offers to share his profits with the agent in return for a guaranteed price. Is this practice permissible under the USA?

I. No—this is an example of commingling.
II. Yes—if it is disclosed as joint proceeds transaction and has been approved in advance by his principal.
III. No—this is unethical because the rep cannot guarantee trade prices.
IV. No—this is unethical because a rep cannot share profits with a customer.

A. I only
B. II only
C. I, III and IV
D. III and IV

40. Which of the following securities are exempt from registration requirements?

I. Investment contract issued in connection with an employee pension plan
II. Securities issued by St. Paul's Catholic Church in Tempe, Arizona
III. Securities issued by a public utility
IV. Securities issued by the provincial government of Ottawa, Canada

A. I, II and III
B. I and III
C. II and IV
D. I, II, III and IV

41. Which of the following would not be defined as a "sale" under the Uniform Securities Act?

A. A bonus given as a direct result of the purchase of another security
B. ABC attaches warrants to buy common stock of XYZ corporation to a bond issue
C. ABC issues a rights offering
D. ABC issues $1.50 quarterly dividend to existing stockholders of record

42. All of the following activities are prohibited EXCEPT

A. not inquiring into the financial background of a client because the agent is recommending a conservative blue-chip company
B. not determining a client's investment objectives because the agent is recommending an excellent growth stock which has been carefully analyzed by the firm's security analysts
C. recommending the purchase of a security on the basis of an excellent investment rating but not disclosing a change in the number of shares outstanding as a result of a stock split three years ago
D. not indicating the relevant risks of an investment because the agent believes the investment is safe

43. An agent has a good customer with a margin account. The customer informs the agent that he is taking a business trip for a month. He tells the agent to handle the account. While the customer is gone, the stock market goes down and the customer receives a margin call for $1,000. The agent should

A. pay the $1,000 on behalf of his customer and collect at a later date
B. arrange a loan from a local bank to cover the margin call
C. sell some securities in the account and use the proceeds to cover the margin call
D. try to make contact with the customer and, failing that, inform his principal and do nothing until instructed

44. Which of the following is an example of a nonissuer transaction as defined by the USA?

A. Private placement
B. Secondary offering
C. Primary issue of a corporation
D. Preemptive offering

45. All of the following would be considered agents under the USA EXCEPT a person representing a(n)

    A. broker-dealer selling exempt securities
    B. broker-dealer selling nonexempt securities
    C. issuer selling securities in an exempt transaction
    D. issuer selling nonexempt securities to the public

46. Which of the following statements is(are) TRUE?

    I. A person with a place of business in the state who transacts business exclusively for the accounts of banks and savings institutions is not a broker-dealer under the USA.
    II. A person excluded from the definition of investment adviser under the Investment Advisers Act of 1940 who offers investment advice only to investors with less than $25 million in assets is subject to the jurisdiction of the state Administrator.
    III. A person who is excluded from the definition of an investment adviser under the Investment Advisers Act of 1940 who manages funds on a regular basis as a business headquartered in a state is subject to payment of filing fees required by the state Administrator and must submit a consent to service of process.
    IV. Broker-dealers who supply investment advice and make securities recommendations to customers who pay commissions for the execution of their trades are investment advisers subject to state or federal registration.

    A. I only
    B. II and III
    C. I, II, III and IV
    D. None of the above.

47. If an elderly widow with no independent income wishes to invest the proceeds from her recently deceased husband's life insurance, which of the following would be a suitable recommendation?

    A. Call options
    B. Municipal bonds
    C. Oil and gas exploration program that you know is going to strike
    D. Blue-chip income stocks

48. Registration by qualification is effective

    A. when determined by the Administrator
    B. at the same time that the federal registration is effective
    C. 20 days after the filing date
    D. 30 days after the filing date

49. All of the following are exempt transactions under the USA EXCEPT a(n)

    A. executor sells shares of common stock for an estate
    B. agent buys a blue-chip stock in the secondary market
    C. bank buys common shares in a publicly-traded railroad
    D. customer buys a new issue of corporate bonds

50. If a person is exempt from state registration but is a federally registered investment adviser, which of the following actions must the person take to practice within a particular state?

    I. Pay state filing fees
    II. Pass an oral or written examination
    III. Give notice to the state
    IV. Become licensed as a broker-dealer

    A. I and II
    B. I and III
    C. II and III
    D. II and IV

51. Which of the following actions is not a prohibited practice under the USA?

   A. A market maker fills his firm's order ahead of a customer order at the same price.
   B. A specialist buys and sells stock as principal.
   C. A principal in a broker-dealer allows a rumor to leak out that ABC is going to acquire LMN; after a few days, the broker-dealer sells ABC short for its own account.
   D. A broker sells a customer's stock at the bid price and makes up the difference with a personal check.

52. James Jones, quarterback for a National Football League franchise team, deliberately misstated material information in the private sale of securities he owned. Jones claims he is not subject to the antifraud provisions of the USA because he is not a registered agent and, secondly, the securities involved are exempt from registration requirements of the act. Which of the following statements is TRUE?

   A. As a professional athlete, Jones is not in the securities business and, therefore, is not subject to the antifraud provisions of the act.
   B. Jones's failure to accurately state material facts does not constitute fraud because the securities he sold were exempt from registration.
   C. The antifraud provisions of the USA do not apply to Jones because he is not suitably trained nor does he have a securities license.
   D. The antifraud provisions of the USA apply to "any person" who acts fraudulently in connection with the offer, sale, or purchase of a security.

53. A customer buys $20,000 worth of stock with a required 50% initial margin deposit of $10,000 cash. When he places the order, the customer tells the agent he cannot risk more than $4,000 in the stock market. Following a highly unfavorable news release causing a significant price drop, regulators halt trading in the stock. When the stock is permitted to reopen, the stock's price is half the client' purchase price and the client receives a maintenance margin call for $3,000. The customer is outraged that he has (unrealized) loss of $10,000 and must deposit $3,000 more to maintain the position. In the above situation, the agent has acted

   A. lawfully, because the customer agrees to the risk of margin trading upon signing the margin agreement
   B. lawfully, because the agent cannot control regulatory trading halts
   C. unlawfully, because the customer was not urged to enter a stop loss order on the stock
   D. unlawfully, because the agent failed to warn the customer of the true risk of margin trading

54. Which method of securities registration would most likely be used to register an initial public offering?

   A. Coordination
   B. Notice Filing
   C. Qualification
   D. Any of the above.

55. Under the Uniform Securities Act, a registered agent could offer securities for purchase during the underwriting period and before the effective date of registration in which of the following circumstances?

I. Never
II. With the use of a red herring
III. If the securities are not exempt
IV. Only if a bona fide registration statement has been properly filed with the state administrator and the SEC

A. I only
B. II only
C. II, III and IV
D. II and IV

56. Under which of the following circumstances will a private placement fail to qualify for exemption from registration under the USA?

A. The offer is directed to only five individuals during any 12-month period.
B. A bank holding company purchases the offering for trading purposes rather than investment purposes.
C. A modest commission is paid to the agents who sell the offering.
D. Purchasers of the offering have to meet net-worth requirements.

57. Under the USA, a broker-dealer does not include a(n)

A. agent
B. issuer
C. bank holding company that does not own a brokerage subsidiary
D. international bank

58. If an agent unknowingly sells an unregistered, nonexempt security, the agent may rectify this violation of the USA

A. if the client offers to sign a waiver accepting the sale as legal
B. by immediately registering the security in the state and notifying the Administrator
C. if the agent offers (in writing) to repurchase the security plus pay a reasonable rate of interest minus any income derived from the security
D. if the client is compensated for any losses through a waiver of future brokerage or investment advisory fees

59. Under the USA, an investment adviser who has no place of business in a state is exempt from registration in that state if the adviser

A. had no more than five clients in that state within the past 12 months
B. had no more than 10 clients in that state within the past 12 months
C. had no more than 15 clients in that state within the past 12 months
D. is registered as a broker-dealer

60. Which of the following is TRUE?

A. All hearings under the USA must be held in a competent court of jurisdiction.
B. Hearings of an Administrator must be held in public.
C. An Administrator may, at the request of a registrant, hold hearings in private.
D. An Administrator may not refuse the request of a registrant to hold hearings in private.

Series 63 Practice Final 1 Answers & Rationale

1. B. It is a violation under the USA to solicit customers for unregistered, nonexempt securities (such securities should be registered) or to sell securities in states other than where the agent is registered. Arbitrage is not a violation. An individual who sells exempt securities (such as government securities) does not have to register as an agent, provided no commission is collected or he represents the issuer. QID: 28902

2. C. Selling unregistered nonexempt securities is a violation no matter how many or how few clients are solicited and the sale of an exempt security in a state does not excuse the agent from having to register in that state. Representing an issuer of exempt securities does not require registration and arbitrage involves buying and selling the same security in different markets in order to take advantage of small price differences. QID: 39205

3. D. Bank holding companies are not exempt securities—they must be registered with the SEC. However, securities of commercial banks are exempt because they are regulated by the Controller of the Currency. Securities issued or guaranteed by the U.S. government are exempt from registration under federal law. All securities issued or guaranteed by a state or political subdivision of a state have federally imposed exemptions. Promissory notes and bankers' acceptances with maturities of nine months or less and with denominations of at least $50,000 also have federally imposed exemptions. QID: 36375

4. C. The representative has demonstrated contumacy. The Administrator cannot issue injunctions; only a court with jurisdiction can issue an injunction. QID: 31076

5. D. A person who has passed the Series 63 exam cannot transact business until the Administrator grants registration, normally on the 30th day after the application is filed. QID: 28831

6. C. Peter is the only agent listed who has a valid exemption from state registration under the USA. Peter is registered in Patti's home state of New Jersey and can claim the exemption from registration in California because Patti will only be in California on a temporary basis (temporary means thirty days or less). Alice cannot claim an exemption because she conducts business in the state where she has an office. She must register in her home state no matter how infrequently she conducts trades for a client in her state. Tom cannot validly claim an exemption in Utah because his client spends more than 30 consecutive days per year in Utah. John cannot claim an exemption on the basis of incidental trading because he is not registered in Mark's home state of Georgia. The claim would only be valid if John where licensed in Mark's home state of Georgia. QID: 38316

7. B. Having material, nonpublic information makes the agent (sales representative) an insider. An insider may not take advantage of, or repeat (disseminate), nonpublic information. QID: 31837

8. A. Employees who sell shares of their companies to the public for commissions fall under the definition of "agent" under the USA. QID: 28922

9. D. An agent, broker-dealer or financial advisor who has custody of or direction over client funds or securities may be required to post a surety bond. QID: 39216

10. A. The Administrator has considerable discretion to make rules or issue orders. Specifically, the USA allows the Administrator to prohibit custody by rule. However, the USA does not allow the Administrator to waive provisions of the USA, nor can the Administrator suspend federal law. QID: 36703

11. B. Private placements are exempt under the USA only if they are sold to no more than 10 general public investors in a 12-month period. Transactions involving issuers and underwriters, pension trusts, and other financial institutions are exempt. The sale of preorganization certificates is exempt if there is no commission for solicitation, no payment by subscribers, and fewer than 10 subscribers. QID: 31097

12. B. The right of recission is the right of the buyer to recover the purchase price and interest resulting from an illegal sale of securities. The agent may not ask the customer to sign a customer agreement that releases the agent. Registration by notification is not part of the rescission process. QID: 28859

13. B. Under the USA, the term "offer" includes an attempt to dispose of securities for value as well as a solicitation of an offer to buy a security. In choice I, John offers to sell securities for value by indicating to Mr. Baxter that he would accept an order if placed by Mr. Baxter—an actual sale need not take place for an offer to sell to take place. In choice II, John offers to purchase Mr. Baxter's securities—under the USA, an offer to purchase as well as an offer to sell is, under the USA, an "offer." Choices III and IV are gifts of securities, not offers to sell or purchase. QID: 38326

14. D. This is a clear case of misrepresenting dividends and Joe must immediately stop this activity. QID: 31855

15. A. A broker-dealer is an entity in the business of effecting transactions in securities for its own account or for the accounts of others. Broker-dealers pay their sales agents commissions. Under the USA, the broker-dealer must register in the state where business is transacted. QID: 28950

16. D. An Administrator may deny or revoke a security's exemption without a hearing providing the issuer is given an opportunity for a hearing after the revocation. The issuer requesting an exemption must prove the exemption. Proving the exemption is not the responsibility of the Administrator. The Administrator may not revoke exemptions of federal covered securities. QID: 40228

17. D. Single payment insurance contracts, IRA's, collectibles, and mortgages are not among those instruments listed as securities under the act. QID: 37159

18. B. The total amount of the security to be offered in all states need not be included in the registration of a security. QID: 31176

19. D. Testimonials promoting investment advisers' services are prohibited under both state and federal law. Testimonials are prohibited whether or not an athlete receives compensation. QID: 28887

20. B. Every agent registration expires each year on December 31st. QID: 39191

21. D. It is permissible to solicit unregistered exempt securities, open a joint account with written permission of the client and the broker-dealer, and to charge larger commissions when providing additional services. QID: 31868

22. D. An agent making a recommendation to a customer is responsible for presenting all of the material facts. Material facts must be presented to a customer regardless of the type of security sold or whether a commission is to be earned or not. QID: 29001

23. C. Anyone who solicits or receives an order while representing a broker-dealer is an agent. Silent partners, secretaries of branch managers, and executives of broker-dealers are not agents under the terms of the USA because they do not solicit or receive orders. Remember, broker-dealers are not agents; agents represent broker-dealers. QID: 28821

24. A. An individual who represents a broker-dealer who sells commercial paper must register under the USA. The securities (commercial paper) are exempt, nevertheless the representative must

be registered as an agent of the broker-dealer. An individual who sells commercial paper for ABC National Bank would not have to register because both the transaction and security are exempt from state registration requirements. An employee of the federal government need not register with the state because he represents an exempt issuer and is selling exempt securities. An individual who is paid a commission to sell certificates of deposit for a commercial bank does not have to register as an agent. QID: 37162

25. C. The USA specifically excludes issuers and international banks from the definition of broker-dealer. Investment advisers and financial planning firms are not specifically granted exclusions from the definition. QID: 31205

26. C. Both the broker-dealer and the agent must be registered in each state in which they plan to do business. For the agent to accept the order, either she would have to be registered in Florida or the customer would have to be present in her office in Nebraska. QID: 28906

27. D. The sale of municipal bonds to retail customers is not an exempt transaction. The bond is an exempt security. Exempt transactions include transactions between an issuer and an underwriter, transactions with a trust company or savings institution, private placements, and transactions for employees of an issuer where no compensation is paid for solicitation. QID: 39202

28. B. Fraud occurs when a person covered under the USA knowingly violates a provision of the law. The representative knew the security was not registered and therefore fraudulently sold it. It is not unlawful to trade actively in a security; it is unlawful to do so to create a false impression of trading volume in order to generate interest in the security. If an agent has good reason to immediately liquidate clients' positions based upon the information received from the online legal records service, he has not committed fraud. The information is not material inside information because it is both published and generally available. It is not a violation to sell securities in publicly-traded companies in which a representative's relatives own shares. To avoid a potential for a conflict of interest, the representative should disclose the information to clients. QID: 36372

29. D. Although an agent has passed the appropriate examinations, he must wait until the state Administrator grants a license before conducting business. QID: 31078

30. D. Exempt securities are not subject to the antifraud provisions of the USA. QID: 28837

31. D. An Administrator may deny or revoke an agent's registration if the agent engages in practices that are prohibited by such regulatory agencies as the National Association of Securities Dealers (NASD). All the above practices are prohibited by the NASD but they may not involve fraudulent activity. Fraud must involve willful deceit for profit, e.g., if an agent engages in excessive trading in an account in order to generate commissions (called "churning") with a client's consent, fraud is not involved. The practice is, however, prohibited. If fraud was involved, the practice would be both fraudulent and prohibited. QID: 37185

32. B. Failure to obtain suitability information is a violation of the USA, and falsely marking a trade discretionary without a signed trading authorization from the customer is a violation of the antifraud provisions of the USA. The other actions listed are not fraudulent according to the USA. QID: 31827

33. B. Sales of securities to financial institutions or accredited investors are exempt transactions. The sale of securities to an insurance company is not necessarily a private placement. The sales of securities to an insurance company is not illegal. The sale of a security to an insurance company is an exempt transaction. QID: 28933

34. B. The Administrator may issue a cease and desist order without a hearing, but does not have the authority to convict violators of the 1933 Securities Act in criminal prosecutions nor sentence violators of the USA. QID: 39209

35. C. The sale of a security that has traded in the secondary market for more than 90 days is a nonissuer transaction exempt from the advertising and registration provisions of the USA. The other choices are examples of exempt securities, not exempt transactions. Exempt securities are exempt from the registration and advertising provisions of the act; however, the agent selling these securities is subject to the registration provisions of the USA. QID: 37137

36. B. State and federal regulations prohibit actions based on inside information. Recommendations can be based on the best estimate of the sales representative's firm, provided there is an adequate and factual basis for such recommendation. Recommendations can also be based on major recognized financial publications and on information provided by private firms who charge fees for their research. QID: 31096

37. C. Repeating rumors is both misleading and a prohibited business practice under the USA. An agent should not recommend securities transactions to his customers on the basis of rumors. The action is prohibited because it is a misleading use of rumor. The information is not material inside information. The number of customers involved is not relevant. QID: 28844

38. B. The Administrator can deny, suspend, or revoke a registration for many reasons, but they must be in the interest of the public. The Administrator may not deny the registration simply because it is prudent—it must be in the best interest of the public. The Administrator may determine that an applicant, in his initial application for registration for an investment adviser, is not qualified to act as an adviser and thus limit the registration to that of a broker-dealer. The Administrator can also take into consideration whether the registrant will work under the supervision of a registered investment adviser or broker-dealer when approving an application. QID: 38329

39. D. This practice is not permissible under the USA because guaranteeing profits is unethical and agents are not allowed to share profits in a customer account. Commingling is the act of combining customer assets with those of an agent. QID: 31861

40. D. All of the securities listed are exempt from registration under the Uniform Securities Act. QID: 31020

41. D. ABC's issue of a $1.50 quarterly dividend to existing stockholders is not a sale as defined in the Uniform Securities Act. Bonuses, rights, and warrants issued as a result of a purchase of securities are sales under the Uniform Securities Act. QID: 40229

42. C. It is not a prohibited practice to omit all information; however, material information may not be omitted. A stock split three years ago is not considered material. Relying on the reports and ratings of the firm's security analysts is sufficient justification for recommending the security, providing it is a suitable purchase for the client. Remember, an agent must inquire about the client's investment objectives and financial background as well as disclose the relevant risks of an investment (even if the investment is considered relatively safe) to make suitable recommendations. QID: 37155

43. D. If a margin account falls below the minimum maintenance amount required when the customer cannot be reached, the agent should inform his principal who then determines which and how many securities must be sold to maintain the margin requirement as set by Regulation T. An agent may not contribute to a client's account or arrange a loan on behalf of a client. Without written discretionary authority, an agent may not sell securities in a client's account. QID: 31178

44. B. A nonissuer transaction is defined as any transaction in which the process of which do not benefit the issuer. The issuer in a private placement, primary issue of a corporation, or a preemptive offering receive proceeds from the offerings. QID: 28893

45. C. An individual who represents an issuer selling securities in an exempt transaction (e.g., a private placement) would not be considered an agent. QID: 39201

46. D. A person who conducts business exclusively with banks and savings institutions is a broker-dealer under the USA if he has a place of business in state. If the person had no place of business in the state and conducted business exclusively with banks and savings institutions, he would not be considered a broker-dealer subject to the regulatory control of the state Administrator. A person excluded from the definition of investment adviser under the Investment Advisers Act of 1940 who offers investment advice is a "federal covered" adviser not subject to regulation by the state Administrator whether or not he advises investors with less than $25 million. A federal covered adviser is subject to payment of state filing. Broker-dealers who supply investment advice incidental to their business and receive no special compensation for it are not "investment advisers." QID: 36355

47. D. This customer needs income. Of all the answers given, the blue-chip stocks would be most suitable because they would provide income while maintaining relative safety. QID: 28941

48. A. Registration by qualification is effective when determined by the Administrator. QID: 39235

49. D. The purchase of a new issue of corporate bonds involves a transaction in a nonexempt security, and, therefore, would not qualify for an exemption from registration under the act. Sales by a fiduciary (such as an executor of an estate) are exempt from the registration provisions. Sales to financial institutions (such as a bank) are also exempt under the act. Blue-chip securities with long-established trading records on recognized exchanges are exempt from state registration requirements. QID: 37160

50. B. While exempt from state registration, federally registered investment advisers may be required to "give notice" (written) and pay state filing fees to practice within the given states. This is known as notice filing. QID: 31107

51. B. The function of the specialist is to act as a broker for orders left with him by other broker-dealers and to act as a dealer in buying and selling for his own account. His activity is not prohibited. Allowing a rumor to leak out and then trade on it is a prohibited practice but is not considered market manipulation. Selling stock at the bid price and making up the difference with a personal check is not market manipulation, but it is a prohibited practice. Filling a firm's proprietary order ahead of a customer's order is a prohibited practice called front running. QID: 28879

52. D. The antifraud provisions of the USA apply to any person who acts fraudulently in connection with the offer, sale, or purchase of a security. While Jones, as a professional athlete, is not subject to the registration provisions of the act, he is liable for fraud when selling securities, whether registered or not. The fact that Jones is not trained in the securities business does not exempt him from the prohibition against fraud when engaged in the sale of securities. QID: 38320

53. D. The agent (sales representative) acted unlawfully by not fully informing the customer that trading on margin involves leverage that could lead to substantial loss. The agent failed to fully disclose the facts and circumstances of a securities transaction. QID: 31846

54. A. Coordination is concurrent registration with the SEC and the state for initial public offerings. QID: 31072

55. A. During the cooling-off period, indications of interest may be solicited with the use of a red herring. No offers or sales may be made prior to the registration's effective date. QID: 28914

56. C. A private placement will lose its exemption if those who sell the offering are paid commissions. For a private placement to be exempt, the offer cannot be directed to more than 10 persons during a 12-month period. Noninstitutional buyers must sign an investment letter indicating they are purchasing the offering for investment, not trading, purposes only. Institutional purchasers do not have to purchase the offering for investment purposes. In private placements, investors must meet net worth requirements. QID: 37175

57. C. A bank holding company that does not own a brokerage subsidiary is excluded from the definition of a broker-dealer. QID: 31822

58. C. The agent may offer to rescind the trade by offering in writing to repurchase the security, plus pay a reasonable rate of interest minus any income derived from the security. This is called rescission. An agent may not suspend provisions of the USA whether the client agrees or not. QID: 36386

59. A. An adviser who has no more than five clients in a state within the prior 12-month period or deals exclusively with institutions, is not required to register in a state in which the adviser has no place of business. QID: 39208

60. C. An Administrator has the discretion to hold hearings in private. A registrant cannot demand that a hearing be held in private; the Administrator must consent to a private hearing. Hearings are administrative actions and, therefore, are not held in courts. QID: 40230

Series 63 Practice Final 2

1. Which of the following is a fraudulent or prohibited activity under the USA?
   A. Using the dividends paid in the last 12 months to determine the current yield of a common stock
   B. Implying that registration of a security means approval of the security
   C. Selling common stock to a customer with income objectives
   D. Stating that zero-coupon bonds pay no current interest

2. An Administrator may summarily suspend a registration pending final determination of proceedings under the USA. However, the Administrator may not enter an order without

   I. appropriate prior notice to the applicant as well as the employer or prospective employer of the applicant
   II. opportunity for a hearing
   III. findings of fact and conclusions of law
   IV. prior written acknowledgment of the applicant

   A. I only
   B. I and II
   C. I, II, and III
   D. I, II, III and IV

3. A sales agent's registration may be suspended by the Administrator under the USA for all of the following reasons EXCEPT
   A. the agent is enjoined by a court of law from engaging in the securities business
   B. it has been discovered that the agent is not qualified on the basis of training, knowledge, or qualifications
   C. the agent is accused of violations of the antifraud provisions of the USA
   D. the agent is convicted of willful violations of the USA

4. According to the USA, a person would be required to register as a broker-dealer in a state if the person has

   I. no place of business in the state but has directed offers to 25 residents of that state
   II. no place of business in the state and deals exclusively with broker-dealers in that state
   III. no place of business in the state and effects transactions exclusively with issuers of securities in that state
   IV. a place of business in the state

   A. I, II and IV
   B. I and IV
   C. II and III
   D. I, II, III and IV

5. If an agent in one state would like to do business in another state. Which of the following statements is TRUE?
   A. No registration is necessary in the other state provided the agent's activities are limited exclusively to effecting transactions in certain exempted securities.
   B. No registration is necessary if no commission or other remuneration is paid or given directly or indirectly.
   C. If the agent is a partner, an officer, or a director and held that position at the time the broker-dealer was registered, the individual need not register separately.
   D. Registration is required only if an offer is directed, accepted, and paid for in that state.

6. If a firm that has registered securities with the SEC is considering registering its securities in a state, the method that it would least likely use would be
   A. notice filing
   B. coordination
   C. qualification
   D. notification

7. All of the following are exempt securities EXCEPT

I. U.S. government securities
II. unsolicited transactions
III. transactions between issuers and underwriters
IV. securities of credit unions

A. I, II and IV
B. I and IV
C. II and III
D. IV only

8. Under the USA, an agent may file for a review of an Administrator's revocation order within how many days of revocation?

A. 30
B. 60
C. 90
D. 270

9. Under the USA, the Administrator may do all of the following EXCEPT

A. suspend an agent's registration without an opportunity for a hearing
B. issue subpoenas to persons residing outside the Administrators state
C. issue cease and desist orders without a hearing
D. conduct investigations of broker-dealers residing outside the Administrators state

10. Under which of the circumstances may an agent enter into a private securities transaction with a customer of the broker-dealer?

I. All risks of the transaction are disclosed to the customer in writing.
II. The broker-dealer has recorded the transaction.
III. The broker-dealer has supervised the transaction.
IV. The broker-dealer offers to redeem the illiquid security from the customer at no less than purchase price.

A. I and III
B. I, III and IV
C. II and III
D. I, II, III and IV

11. States may require investment advisers who are federally registered to

I. file with the state any documents that are filed with the SEC
II. pay state fees
III. file a consent to service of process

A. I and II
B. I and III
C. II only
D. I, II and III

12. The USA prohibits

I. agents exercising discretion in discretionary accounts
II. charging larger than ordinary commissions on certain transactions
III. soliciting orders for unregistered, nonexempt securities

A. I only
B. II and III
C. III only
D. I, II and III

13. A nonexempt company has authorized a stock split in which it will give each shareholder without charging commissions two shares for every one share owned. This transaction

    A. must have the prior written approval of each state Administrator in which the shares trade
    B. must be registered because it is the issuance of new nonexempt securities
    C. need not be registered because it is an exempt transaction
    D. need not be registered because the shares of the corporation have already been registered

14. An agent has raised capital from his customers with which he and his brother-in-law will build a small shopping center (although the broker-dealer with whom he is registered is not aware of his actions). The customers who contributed the capital received certificates of ownership in the shopping center as well as full disclosure of their risks and participation in income from renting mall space to retail businesses. In the above situation, the agent has acted

    A. lawfully, because risks of the transaction were disclosed to the customers in writing
    B. lawfully, because interests in a shopping mall are not securities
    C. unlawfully, because the agent gave his broker-dealer no opportunity to supervise his activities relative to its customers
    D. unlawfully, because the agent's brother-in-law is not a registered agent (sales representative)

15. Stock of which of following qualifies for the blue-chip exemption provided by the USA?

    A. A corporation with $10 million in net worth
    B. A corporation that is listed on the NYSE
    C. A bank holding company
    D. A municipal issuer

16. An exemption from registration as an investment adviser is granted if the person has no place of business in a state and the person's only clients are

    A. investment companies
    B. other investment advisers
    C. broker-dealers
    D. Any of the above.

17. A consent to service of process allows the Administrator to

    A. verify the accuracy and completeness of registration without obtaining the registrant's prior approval
    B. exercise the power of attorney on behalf of the registrant
    C. ensure that the legal appeal process is expedited as a result of the Administrator's access to information
    D. terminate a registrant's application as the attorney in fact for the registrant

18. If a nonexempt issuer wants to register simultaneously with the state and the SEC, which methods would be used?

    A. Notice filing
    B. Coordination
    C. Qualification
    D. Registration

19. According to the USA, which of the following would be an unlawful activity for an investment adviser?

    A. Entering into an investment advisory contract that does not mention the compensation arrangements
    B. Taking custody of a customer's securities or funds without notifying the Administrator, even though the Administrator has no rule that prohibits such custody
    C. Entering into an investment advisory contract that provides specifically for compensation based on a share of capital appreciation of the customer's funds
    D. All of the above.

20. In following the Howey decision, the USA would consider which of the following a security?

    A. Purchase of a house in a desirable real estate market with the expectation that the house will be resold at a profit within a few years
    B. Purchase of jewelry for speculative purposes as opposed to personal use
    C. Investment in options to acquire a security
    D. Investment in commodities futures

21. All of the following are exempt transactions EXCEPT

    A. sale of securities with manual exemptions
    B. isolated, nonissuer transactions
    C. unsolicited, nonissuer transactions
    D. commercial paper

22. Under the USA, which of the following is(are) not considered a security(ies)?

    I. Secondary sale of a bank mortgage as a pass-through certificate
    II. Limited partnership unit in a cattle-breeding program
    III. Purchase of a condominium as a vacation home
    IV. Franchise agreement where a profit has been promised in the agreement

    A. I and III
    B. I, II and III
    C. I, II and IV
    D. III only

23. Under the USA, the definition of "issuer" includes a

    A. seller in a transaction on the floor of an exchange
    B. officer or director of a company that is offering new shares to the public
    C. person proposing to issue a security
    D. market maker for a new issue

24. Which of the following is(are) prohibited under the USA?

    I. Recommending tax shelters to low income retirees
    II. Stating that a state Administrator has approved an offering based on the quality of information found in the prospectus
    III. Soliciting orders for unregistered, non-exempt securities
    IV. Employing any device to defraud

    A. I only
    B. I and II
    C. I, II and III
    D. I, II, III and IV

25. Under the USA, private placements are exempt from state registration if they solicit no more than how many clients within one year?

    A. 6
    B. 10
    C. 25
    D. 30

26. According to the USA, under what circumstances is an employee of a licensed broker-dealer in a state allowed to sell exempt securities as an unregistered agent?

    A. The securities are exempt.
    B. The transaction is exempt.
    C. The employee is not paid any commission or salary.
    D. Under no circumstances.

27. Under the USA, which of the following is an agent?

A. Joe Smith who represents the city of Albany, New York, in the issuance and sale of its new general revenue bonds to the public.
B. Smith represents, for a fee, the XYZ Corporation in its transactions with underwriters with offices in XYZ's home state.
C. Mr. Smith represents AAA National Bank, member of the Federal Reserve System, in the issuance of AAA preferred stock to residents of his home state. Mr. Smith is paid commissions for his services.
D. Mr. Smith, an employee of XYZ Manufacturing Corporation, receives commission compensation when he represents XYZ in the issuance of securities exclusively to existing employees, partners, and directors of the corporation.

28. Mrs. Abbot, a customer, has a joint account with her sister. She enters a sell order in the account and instructs that the proceeds check be made out to her. Your firm sends the check but makes it payable to both Ms. Abbot and her sister. This is an example of

A. not following instructions, a prohibited practice under the USA
B. an unfortunate error that can be reconciled with the broker-dealer through a process called reclamation
C. a normal joint account procedure
D. an unlawful practice because the transaction was unauthorized

29. It is legal under the USA for a registered investment adviser to tell a client that

A. a registered security may lawfully be sold in that state
B. an exempt security is not required to be registered because it is generally regarded as being safer than a nonexempt security
C. her qualifications have been found satisfactory by the Administrator
D. a registered security has been approved for sale in the state by the Administrator

30. A broker-dealer's agent's license is in effect until

A. the renewal date specific to each state
B. December 31st unless renewed
C. withdrawn by the agent or revoked by the Administrator
D. for the length of the agent's employment by all broker-dealers

31. Which of the following statements is(are) TRUE?

I. It is unlawful for anyone to conduct business as a broker-dealer in a state unless also registered as an agent.
II. A registration statement may be filed by an issuer itself, any other person on whose behalf the offering is to be made, or by a broker-dealer.
III. Registration of an agent is not effective when the agent is not associated with a broker-dealer registered under the act.
IV. Registrations are automatically renewed one year after approval providing no violations occurred during the year.

A. I only
B. I and III
C. II and III
D. II, III and IV

32. What is the official designation of the person or agency that enforces the USA in each state?

A. Transfer agent
B. Registrar
C. Issuer
D. Administrator

33. According to the USA, market manipulation includes all of the following EXCEPT

A. buying on one exchange and selling on another
B. withholding a material fact from a buyer
C. buying and selling intentionally to show market activity
D. giving a false quote

34. A federally covered adviser is one who is

I. registered with the SEC
II. registered with the state securities Administrator
III. excluded from the definition of an adviser under the Act of 1940
IV. required to register with the Interstate Commerce Commission

A. I and III
B. I and IV
C. II and III
D. II and IV

35. Which of the following regarding unsolicited, nonissuer transactions is(are) TRUE?

A. An agent may not accept unsolicited orders unless the transaction directly benefits the issuer.
B. An agent can only accept unsolicited orders in exempt securities.
C. An agent may only accept unsolicited orders with prior approval of a principal.
D. An Administrator may require representatives to obtain customer signatures acknowledging that orders were unsolicited.

36. Aaron Jones is a client of XYZ Financial Services. Over the past several years, Aaron has been suspicious of possible churning of his account, but has taken no action because account performance has been outstanding. After reviewing his most recent statement, Aaron suspects that excessive transactions have occurred. He consults his attorney who informs him that under the USA, any lawsuit for recovery of damages under the USA must be started within

A. one year of occurrence
B. two years of occurrence
C. three years of occurrence or two years of discovery, whichever occurs first
D. two years of occurrence or three years of discovery, whichever occurs last

37. Which of the following activities are prohibited practices under the principles of the Uniform Securities Act?

I. Buying and selling the same stock on the same day on different exchanges
II. Offering shares of an unregistered, nonexempt security to customers
III. Offering a Canadian government bond to a resident of a state in which the agent of a broker-dealer is not registered

A. I only
B. II only
C. II and III
D. I, II and III

38. Thomas Smith, a registered agent of XYZ Broker-Dealer (a member of the NASD), received very competent market insight from a well-known market strategist who indicated that economic indicators were much worse than the public realized. Smith, in an effort to protect his best client, Mr. Story (who maintains a strict buy and hold strategy), told Mr. Story that his major stock position was selling at 5% higher than the current market quotation and that he should sell his stock now. Based on this information, Mr. Story sold his stock. In this situation, the agent

    I. acted in a dishonest and unethical manner
    II. made an untrue statement in connection with the sale of a security
    III. engaged in fraud in connection with the sale of a security
    IV. provided investment advice while acting in a sales capacity, which is a prohibited practice

    A. I only
    B. I and II
    C. I, II and III
    D. I, II, III and IV

39. An agent tells her customer of the long-term growth potential of ABC Company but points out the significant risk of buying the stock. She explains the risk of using simple averages to analyze the company's earnings by indicating to the customer that earnings fell 50% two years ago and that last year's 100% increase in earnings offset the earlier reduction. In this situation, the agent has acted

    A. lawfully, because the risk and earnings volatility was disclosed
    B. lawfully, because it is generally understood that growth stocks experience earnings volatility
    C. unlawfully, because averages represent a form of technical analysis with which the customer may be unfamiliar
    D. unlawfully, because the agent's bullishness on the stock is a prohibited projection of performance

40. According to the USA, a person representing an issuer of which of the following securities would have to be registered as an agent?

    I. Commercial paper
    II. Municipal bonds
    III. Securities of a U.S. bank
    IV. Investment contracts issued in connection with an employee stock purchase, savings, pension, profit-sharing, or similar benefit plan

    A. I and II
    B. I, III and IV
    C. II and IV
    D. None of the above.

41. Which of the following are required to provide a consent to service of process to the Administrator in a state in which registration is sought?

I. An agent whose is employed out of state but seeks registration in a state in which business is conducted
II. A federal covered investment company not required to be registered in a state in which business is conducted but required to supply notice filing materials by the state Administrator
III. A broker-dealer registered in twenty-five states that seeks registration in a twenty-sixth state
IV. An investment adviser with less than $25 million under management not covered by federal legislation

A. I and III
B. II and IV
C. I, II and IV
D. I, II, III and IV

42. Which of the following is a prohibited practice?

A. Buying a security on behalf of a customer then reselling it prior to settlement date
B. Buying a security on one exchange and simultaneously selling it on another prior to settlement of the purchase
C. Purchasing a security in a discretionary account while awaiting written receipt of trading authority
D. Disclosing to a client an adviser's impaired financial ability yet continuing the relationship on the same basis as before

43. Which of the following is a state securities Administrator required to enforce with respect to federal covered investment advisers who practice within their state?

A. Code of Procedure adopted by regulatory agencies
B. Conduct Rules adopted by NASD
C. Antifraud regulations
D. Nonfraud related SEC requirements

44. It would not be considered unlawful under the USA if an agent

A. makes an untrue statement of a material fact
B. omits a material fact because she knew she did not have time to cover everything in a short presentation
C. deliberately fails to follow a customer's instructions
D. actively solicits orders in unregistered exempt securities

45. Which of the following securities is(are) exempt from registration under the USA?

I. Mr. Jones, president of XYZ National Bank, sells one million shares of XYZ bank stock to Mrs. Smith, a fellow resident of California, for the quoted market price of $20 per share plus $5,000 in commissions.
II. Mrs. Peterson, a registered nurse resident in California, sells one million shares of XYZ National Bank stock to Mr. Jones, for $20 per share with no commission.
III. Mr. Smith, a vice-president of ABC Manufacturing Corporation, represents ABC Corp. in the sale of one hundred shares of ABC Corp. to Mrs. Peterson, an employee of ABC, without charging her a commission.
IV. Mr. Smith, a vice-president of ABC Manufacturing Corporation, represents the ABC corporation in the sale of one million shares of ABC Manufacturing Corp to ABC's underwriters.

A. I only
B. I and II
C. III and IV
D. II, III, and IV

46. Under the USA, an example of an investment adviser is a

A. lawyer
B. publisher of a magazine
C. person who is paid a fee for advising customers on securities
D. person who is paid a commission for selling securities

47. An agent hears a rumor concerning a security and uses the rumor to convince a client to purchase the security. Under the USA, the agent may

A. recommend the security if it is an appropriate investment
B. recommend the investment if the rumor is based on material inside information
C. recommend the security if the source of the rumor came from a reliable source
D. not recommend the security

48. Under the USA, all of the following are exempt transactions EXCEPT

A. isolated nonissuer transactions
B. unsolicited customer orders
C. transaction executed by a trustee in bankruptcy
D. a sale of a primary offering registered with the SEC

49. All of the following are required for private placements to be exempt under the USA EXCEPT

A. the offer must not be directed to more than 10 persons in the state during any 12 consecutive months
B. the seller believes that all buyers of the private placement are purchasing for investment rather than trading purposes
C. no commission or remuneration is paid for soliciting any buyer
D. no more than 10 banks, savings institutions, trust companies, insurance companies, investment companies, pension or profit sharing trusts, or other financial institutions may be solicited

50. Under the USA, which of the following are grounds for suspension, denial, or revocation of an issuer's registration statement?

I. Incomplete information
II. Unreasonable compensation to the underwriters
III. Failure to pay filing fees
IV. The security is subject to an administrative stop order in a federal court

A. I, II and III
B. I and III
C. II and IV
D. I, II, III and IV

51. An agent is asked by a customer to open an account and buy stock for the customer's spouse. According to the USA, which of the following statements regarding this action is TRUE?

    A. The agent could be liable if the stock declines in value.
    B. This practice is ordinary and acceptable.
    C. This action is prohibited unless the spouse signs a trading authorization.
    D. This action is prohibited unless the customer signs a trading authorization on behalf of his spouse.

52. Two agents of a broker-dealer agree to work together, as a partnership, in soliciting business and they agree to split commissions. This practice is

    A. permitted
    B. in violation of the USA's prohibition against sharing in the profits of an account
    C. permitted only if a principal of the firm audits the partnerships financial performance
    D. not permitted under the terms of the USA

53. According to the USA, a person would be required to register as a broker-dealer in a state if he has

    I. no place of business in the state but has directed offers to clients with more than 30 days of temporary residency
    II. no place of business in the state and deals exclusively with broker-dealers in that state
    III. no place of business in the state and effects transactions exclusively with issuers of securities in that state
    IV. a place of business in the state

    A. I, II and IV
    B. I and IV
    C. II and III
    D. I, II, III and IV

54. Harry has been Sam's customer for nine years. While Harry is in Europe, two limit orders fill resulting in a $750 margin call to Harry, and Sam is unable to contact Harry. Sam deposits his personal check into Harry's account so the account is not sold out for failure to satisfy margin requirements. When Harry returns from Europe, he gives Sam a check for the $750. In this situation, the agent has acted

    A. lawfully, because he served the customer's interest
    B. lawfully, because the margin call was less than $1,000
    C. unlawfully, because the agent's funds must never be commingled with those of the client
    D. unlawfully, because the agent was not operating under a trading authorization (power of attorney)

55. All of the following statements regarding the selling of private placements under the USA are true EXCEPT that

    A. they can be offered without limitation to institutional investors
    B. they cannot be offered to more than 35 nonaccredited persons in 12 consecutive months
    C. the seller must reasonably believe that all buyers are purchasing for investment purposes only
    D. no commission or other remuneration may be paid for soliciting buyers

56. Which of the following would be an agent under the terms of the USA?

I. A sales representative of a licensed broker-dealer who sells secondary securities to the general public
II. An assistant to the president of a broker-dealer who, for administrative purposes, accepts orders on behalf of the senior partners
III. A subsidiary of a major commercial bank registered as a broker-dealer that sells securities to the public
IV. An issuer of nonexempt securities registered in the state and sold to the general public.

A. I and II
B. III and IV
C. I, II and III
D. I, II, III and IV

57. Which of the following is a prohibited activity for an agent according to the USA?

A. The sales rep enters into an agreement to share in the profits and losses of the customer's account without an investment in the account.
B. The sales rep and his spouse jointly own their own personal trading account at the firm.
C. The sales rep, with his firm's and the client's permission, participates in the profits and losses of the account in proportion to his investment in the account.
D. A sales rep refuses a client's request to share in the performance of the client's account.

58. An agent's former college roommate urges him to invest capital in his privately-owned toy company. The toy company has no plans to issue its securities to the general public; it intends to stay private. The agent and his spouse invest in the business. The agent does not recommend investment in the company to any of his customers and does not discuss this private investment with his firm. In this situation the agent has acted

A. lawfully, because the toy company is privately held with its shares not available to the general public
B. unlawfully, because the issuer had no intention to offer securities to the general public.
C. unlawfully, because the transaction involved unregistered, nonexempt securities
D. unlawfully, because the agent did not receive permission from the firm (broker-dealer) prior to entering the transaction

59. Investment advisers, as fiduciaries, have ethical obligations to act in their client's best interests and in an ethical manner. Which one of the following practices would be unethical, although not fraudulent, for an investment adviser to engage in?

I. Lending money to a client with full and fair disclosure
II. Recommending securities transactions based on research supplied to him by a third party without disclosing this fact to his clients
III. Supplying to his clients research reports prepared by a third-party firm without disclosing the source of the report
IV. Charging significantly higher fees for the identical services offered by other advisers

A. I only
B. II only
C. I, III and IV
D. I, II, III and IV

60. A state securities Administrator may do all of the following EXCEPT

A. levy fines as determined by the Uniform Securities Act
B. issue an injunction after a hearing
C. issue subpoena to registrants who are out of state
D. issue interpretive opinions

Series 63 Practice Final 2 Answers & Rationale

1. B. Registration of a security with the SEC or the state implies neither approval nor disapproval. To state otherwise is fraudulent. Dividends paid in the last 12 months determine the current yield of a common stock Selling common stock to a customer with income objects is not a fraudulent activity if suitable to the client's objectives. Zero-coupon bonds pay no current interest and to state so is not a fraudulent activity. QID: 28855

2. C. With the exception of those proceedings awaiting final determination, the Administrator must provide an appropriate prior notice to the applicant as well as the employer or prospective employer of the applicant and provide the opportunity for a hearing. In addition, the Administrator may only issue a stop order after findings of fact and conclusions of law. An applicant is not required to provide written acknowledgement before an order is issued. QID: 38330

3. C. An accusation is not grounds for suspension under the USA. Convictions, court injunctions, and lack of qualifications are reasons for suspension of registration. QID: 31842

4. B. The term "broker-dealer" does not include a person who has no place of business in the state; who effects transactions exclusively through issuers, other broker-dealers, or institutions; or directs an offer in the state to an existing customer who is not a permanent resident of the state where the offer is received. QID: 28948

5. C. Both the broker-dealer and the agent must be registered in the state where business is to be transacted, even if the securities or the transactions are exempt from registration. At the time the broker-dealer is registered, officers of the firm who act as agents will be automatically registered as agents. QID: 28833

6. C. Registration by qualification is the most difficult form of registration because it requires elaborate disclosure. Notice filing and coordination are much simpler because they involve submission of documents filed with the SEC. QID: 37164

7. B. Both unsolicited transactions and transactions between issuers and underwriters are exempt transactions, not exempt securities. U.S. government securities and securities of credit unions are exempt securities, not exempt transactions. QID: 31175

8. B. An agent may appeal a final order of the state Administrator. A written petition must be filed with the appropriate court within 60 days of the entry of the Administrator's order and the court may then affirm or set aside the revocation order. QID: 28881

9. A. If the Administrator suspends an agents registration, the opportunity for a hearing must be provided. Under the USA, a hearing must be provided within 15 days of a written request by the suspended agent. QID: 39204

10. C. It is permissible for an agent to "trade privately" with customers if such transactions are supervised by the broker-dealer and recorded on its books. With few exceptions, a broker-dealer may not guarantee to repurchase a security at a given or minimum price. QID: 31865

11. D. The state may require federally-covered advisers to pay filing fees and provide consent to service of process as well as documents filed with the SEC. QID: 31018

12. C. The USA prohibits soliciting orders for unregistered nonexempt securities. The act does not prohibit agents from exercising discretion or from charging larger than ordinary commissions when justified. QID: 28841

13. C. Shares issued as a result of a stock split need not be registered because transactions between issuers and existing shareholder are exempt if no commissions are charged. Issuance

of additional shares as a result of a stock split need not have the prior written approval of the state securities Administrator. Since the transaction is exempt, it need not be registered even though the securities of the corporation are nonexempt. The transaction would have to be registered if commissions or other remuneration were paid for the distribution of the shares. QID: 37178

14. C. The agent has acted unlawfully in effecting private securities transactions involving the broker-dealer's customers without proper supervision by the firm. Interests in a shopping center generally fall under the definition of a security. QID: 31820

15. B. Companies whose securities are listed on a national exchange, such as the NYSE or AMEX, qualify for the blue-chip exemption. Companies that are listed must provide periodic reports concerning their firms and the reports must be available to prospective investors. A company with $10 million in net worth is not of itself evidence that the company has a blue-chip exemption. Municipal issuers are not given a blue-chip exemptions because they are exempt securities to begin with. QID: 28913

16. D. Provided its clients are institutional investors and the adviser has no place of business in a state, it is not required to register as an investment adviser. QID: 39224

17. B. The consent to service of process provides the Administrator with power of attorney for registrants. This power of attorney does not grant the Administrator the authority to terminate the registration at will nor does it empower the Administrator to verify information or expedite the registration process. QID: 36700

18. B. Coordination is the simultaneous (concurrent) registration of an initial public offering (IPO) with the state and SEC. QID: 31100

19. D. Each of the answers listed is an example of an unlawful activity by an investment adviser. QID: 28847

20. C. The investment in options is the only choice that meets the definition of a security. It is an investment in a common enterprise with the expectation that the owner will profit as a result of the managerial efforts of others. The purchase of a house or jewelry is a purchase of a real asset or product that may result in a profit for the owner but not as a result of the managerial efforts of a third party. Commodities futures contracts are specifically excluded from the definition of a security. Options on futures, however, are securities under the USA. QID: 38315

21. D. While all of the items listed are exempt, commercial paper is an exempt security, not an exempt transaction. A manual exemption is the same as a blue-chip exemption. QID: 31832

22. D. A vacation home is not a security; it is real estate. QID: 28918

23. C. The term "issuer" includes any person who issues or proposes to issue any security. QID: 28826

24. D. All of the choices are prohibited. Recommending tax shelters to low income retirees is an example of an unsuitable transaction. Stating that an Administrator has approved an offering based on the quality of information in the prospectus, soliciting orders for unregistered nonexempt securities, and employing a device to defraud are all prohibited practices under the USA. QID: 37142

25. B. The USA states that private placements are exempt from registration if they solicit no more than 10 nonaccredited clients within the year. QID: 31111

26. D. It is unlawful for a person to transact business on behalf of a broker-dealer unless that person is registered as an agent in the state. QID: 28869

27. D. Smith acts in the capacity of an agent when he represents a nonexempt issuer for compensation in transactions with existing employees, partners, and directors of the corporation.

Had Smith not received compensation, he would not have been an agent. When Smith represents the city of Albany, he is representing an exempt issuer and, therefore, not defined as an agent. When Smith represents the XYZ Corporation, a nonexempt issuer, in transactions with underwriters, he is not considered an agent because he is dealing with underwriters as opposed to the general public. When Smith represents the AAA National Bank, member of the Federal Reserve System, an exempt issuer, he is not defined as an agent. Note that when Smith is representing issuers with the underwriters he is not an agent. When Smith represents a nonexempt issuer without compensation he is not an agent; however, if he receives compensation he is an agent. QID: 38324

28. C. In joint accounts, either party may act. However, by law, all checks must be made payable to all owners. The firm is following required procedure. QID: 31840

29. A. An agent may indicate that a security is registered or is exempt from registration. Such representation has no bearing on its quality, safety, or merits. An agent may not represent that an exemption from registration indicates that a security is safer than a nonexempt security. The Administrator does not make a determination that an adviser's qualifications are satisfactory. Registration means only that certain legal requirements have been met in regard to that security or person. QID: 28969

30. B. Registrations expire on December 31st of each year unless renewed. QID: 28834

31. C. It is unlawful for anyone to conduct business as a broker-dealer in a state unless registered as a broker-dealer, not as an agent; remember, an agent is not a broker-dealer. A registration statement can be filed by an issuer itself or any other person on whose behalf the offering is to be made, or by a broker-dealer. Registration of an agent is not effective when the agent is not associated with a broker-dealer registered under the act. Registrations expire December 31st unless renewed, whether violations have occurred or not. QID: 37156

32. D. The USA specifies that a state's Administrator (also called the commissioner or secretary) has the authority to enforce the act in that state. A transfer agent is the person or corporation responsible for recording the names and holdings of registered security owners. The registrar is the organization responsible for accounting for all of the issuer's outstanding stock and certifying that its bonds constitute legal debt. The issuer is the corporation or municipality that offers its securities for sale through an underwriting. QID: 31170

33. A. Buying on one exchange and selling on another is called arbitrage, not market manipulation. Arbitrage is an accepted business practice. Withholding a material fact from a buyer is unlawful behavior not necessarily market manipulation. Giving a false quote is a form of market manipulation. QID: 28882

34. A. A federally covered adviser is one who is registered with the SEC or is excluded from the definition of an adviser under the Act of 1940. QID: 39197

35. D. Administrators are authorized by the USA to require agents to obtain client written acknowledgment of unsolicited transactions. An agent may accept unsolicited orders in secondary transactions in either exempt or nonexempt securities. An agent may accept unsolicited orders without prior approval of a principal. QID: 36366

36. C. Under the USA, the lawsuit for recovery of damages must commence within three years of occurrence of the offense or two years of its discovery. QID: 31001

37. C. Broker-dealers and agents must be registered in each state where offers or sales occur. Also, every security must be registered unless it is an exempt security. Buying a security on one exchange and selling it on another is an arbitrage activity and not a violation of the USA. QID: 28838

38. C. Smith acted in a dishonest and unethical manner, made an untrue statement in connection with the sale of a security, and engaged in fraud in connection with the sale of a security. The advice to sell the securities was good investment advice but the sales method was fraudulent. QID: 38310

39. A. The agent (sales representative) has disclosed ABC's earnings volatility by pointing out the 50% drop. In this scenario she tells the customer not to rely on average earnings as simple averages are not real technical analysis. Many customers are unaware of volatile earnings associated with growth stocks. In merely offering a favorable opinion about a stock's potential growth, the agent is not projecting performance. QID: 31829

40. D. An individual is not considered an agent when representing the issuer in each of the cases cited. For purposes of the exam and unless otherwise stated, all commercial paper is considered to mature in 270 days or less. QID: 28921

41. D. Every legal or natural person seeking registration or making a notice filing must supply a consent to service of process with their registration applications. For example, a federal covered investment company, while covered under federal law, need not register with the state Administrator but must submit notice filings materials that include a consent to service of process. QID: 40212

42. C. Written receipt of trading authority is required prior to conducting any trade on a discretionary basis. Verbal approval is not sufficient; it must be in writing. It is not a prohibited practice to sell a security prior to settlement date. Arbitrage (buying securities on one exchange and selling them on another to take advantage of temporary price differences) is also an acceptable practice. Disclosing an adviser's impaired financial ability is required, but the client may continue the relationship on the same basis as before. QID: 36367

43. C. With the adoption of NSMIA, state Administrators are no longer able to exercise full jurisdiction over federally registered advisers. However, Administrators must enforce all antifraud regulations for investment advisers practicing in their states, federally covered or otherwise. QID: 31108

44. D. Securities that do not require registration under the USA are exempt securities. Although the securities are exempt, the agent who makes the solicitation and his broker-dealer must be registered. An agent may not make an untrue statement of a material fact. In addition, he may not omit a material fact simply because there was not sufficient time in a presentation. An agent may not deliberately fail to follow a customer's instructions. QID: 28848

45. B. Bank securities are securities that are exempt from state registration. The securities of the ABC Corporation are not exempt securities; however, the transactions between the issuer, ABC Corporation, and existing employees where no commission is charged is an exempt transaction. A sale between the issuer and underwriter, is also an exempt transaction. QID: 38322

46. C. An investment adviser is any person who is in the business of selling investment advice and is paid a fee for doing so. QID: 31834

47. D. The use of information, such as a rumor, that has no basis in fact is prohibited. QID: 28909

48. D. Exempt transactions include an infrequent nonissuer (secondary market) transaction; transactions between an issuer and an underwriter; transactions by an executor, Administrator, sheriff, marshal, trustee in bankruptcy, guardian, or conservator; any sale or offer to a bank, savings institution, investment company, or other financial institution; and private placements. QID: 39210

49. D. For a private placement to be exempt from state registration, it may not be directed to more than 10 persons in the state during any 12 consecutive months other than the following insti-

tutions: banks, savings institutions, trust companies, insurance companies, investment companies, pension or profit sharing trusts, or other financial institutions. QID: 37140

50. D. Incomplete information on the registration statement, unreasonable underwriting compensation, failure to pay filing fees, and a security subject to an administrative stop order in federal court are all grounds for suspension, denial, or revocation of an issuer's registration statement. QID: 31043

51. C. Effecting transactions without specific written authority from the beneficial owner of the account is prohibited. A customer cannot sign a trading authorization on behalf of a spouse. The spouse must sign the authorization. QID: 28842

52. A. There is nothing in the USA that prohibits agents from forming a partnership in order to conduct business or solicit clients. Under the USA, a principal of the firm need not audit the financial performance of such an arrangement. QID: 37167

53. B. The term "broker-dealer" does not include a person who has no place of business in the state; who effects transactions exclusively through issuers, other broker-dealers, or institutions; or who directs an offer in the state to an existing customer who has less than 30 days of temporary residency within the state where the offer is received. QID: 31815

54. C. An agent depositing a personal check into a customer's account constitutes commingling of funds and is prohibited. This prohibition prevails regardless of whether the account is discretionary or not. QID: 28928

55. B. This question distinguishes the differences in federal and state requirements for private placements. Under state law, a private placement can be offered to no more than 10 nonaccredited investors in 12 consecutive months. QID: 28871

56. A. Under the USA only individuals can be agents. A person who sells securities for a broker-dealer is an agent. An administrative person, such as the assistant to the president of a broker-dealer, is considered an agent if he takes securities orders from the public. Corporate entities are excluded from the definition of an agent. QID: 37144

57. A. An investment rep may not share in the profits with a client without an investment on the part of the agent. An investment rep is permitted to own an account jointly with his spouse for personal trading purposes. A rep may refuse a client's request to share in the performance of the client's account. QID: 31119

58. A. The agent acted lawfully because the investment was in a privately held company that does not offer its shares to the general public. The agent acted lawfully in not recommending the shares to his clients. QID: 31850

59. C. Lending money to a client (even with full and fair disclosure), supplying to his clients research reports prepared by a third-party firm without disclosing the source of the report, and charging significantly higher fees for the identical services offered by other advisers are all considered unethical although they are not fraudulent practices. Recommending securities transactions based on research supplied to him by a third party without disclosing this fact to his clients is not unethical or deceptive. QID: 38350

60. B. A state securities Administrator may not issue injunctions; these must be issued by courts of competent jurisdiction. Administrators may issue cease and desist orders to prevent potential violations of the Uniform Securities Act and may levy fines as determined by the Uniform Securities Act, issue subpoenas to registrants who are out of state, and issue interpretive opinions. QID: 40257

Series 63 Practice Final 3

1. Under the Uniform Securities Act, secondary trades are also known as

   A. private placements
   B. issuer transactions
   C. nonissuer transactions
   D. exempt transactions

2. An investment adviser must disclose which of the following legal or disciplinary actions to clients and prospective clients if they occurred within the last 10 years?

   I. Conviction of a misdemeanor involving an investment related business
   II. SEC or other federal regulatory agency proceedings in which the person was found to have violated an investment-related statute
   III. A proceeding before the NASD in which the adviser was barred or suspended from membership
   IV. Conviction of a misdemeanor in a civil action regarding payment of motor vehicle violations

   A. I and II
   B. II and III
   C. I, II and III
   D. I, II and IV

3. An agent who carefully evaluates a client's risk tolerance, financial situation, and investment objectives engages in an unethical practice when he

   A. buys or sells securities with exceptionally high commissions or transaction costs
   B. fails to discuss a company's working capital position (because the client does not want to be bothered by details) if the securities are fundamentally suitable for his portfolio
   C. automatically recommends securities that are highly regarded by investment reps in the office
   D. underestimates a company's interest rate risk as a result of cautious accounting practices recently adopted by the company

4. An investor who trades for her own account is a

   A. broker-dealer and must register with the state
   B. sales rep for a broker-dealer and must register in each state doing business
   C. public customer who does not need to register
   D. broker-dealer who does not need to be registered at state level

5. According to the USA, a consent to service of process must accompany a(n)

   I. agent's registration application
   II. civil complaint against a broker-dealer
   III. broker-dealer's initial registration application

   A. I only
   B. I and III
   C. II and III
   D. I, II and III

6. Which of the following is NOT a security?

   A. A commodity options contract
   B. Interest in a merchandising marketing scheme
   C. Common stock of ABC National Bank that is a member of the Federal Reserve System
   D. Annuity with a fixed payment plan

7. An investment adviser who is exempt from state registration but federally registered must

   I. pay state filing fees
   II. pass an oral or written examination
   III. give notice to the state
   IV. become licensed as a broker-dealer

   A. I and II
   B. I and III
   C. II and III
   D. II and IV

8. An agent receives inside information concerning an impending merger. Under the USA, the agent may divulge the information to

   A. his best customers three days prior to a public announcement
   B. anyone three days prior to a public announcement
   C. the broker-dealer three days after public notice
   D. anyone after public notice

9. Under the USA, the term "sale" means

   A. an attempt to dispose of a security for value
   B. a contract to dispose of a security for value
   C. a solicitation of an offer to sell
   D. an offer to sell

10. Which of the following transactions is NOT exempt?

    I. A sale of nonexempt securities by a trustee in bankruptcy which involves numerous commissions
    II. A New York Stock Exchange manufacturing company sells its securities to 12 of its employees in a state without charging commissions
    III. A manufacturer listed on the New York Stock Exchange offers its securities only to its employees in a state through an agent who charges commissions
    IV. A bank headquartered in New York State sells securities of the bank to its employees only through an agent who charges commissions

    A. I only
    B. II and III
    C. II and IV
    D. IV only

11. The USA allows investment advisers to share in profits and losses in a customer's account if

    A. they are sharing only in realized capital gains and not unrealized gains
    B. the investment adviser and the customer have a written contract
    C. the advisory fee of the investment adviser is subtracted from his share of the profits earned
    D. Such sharing is never permissible under the act.

12. Which of the following statements regarding licensing and registration under the Uniform Securities Act are TRUE?

I. When an agent's license is suspended, the broker-dealer's is also suspended.
II. When a broker-dealer's license is suspended, the agent's registration is also suspended.
III. The Administrator may suspend or revoke registrations whenever the public's good is the sole consideration.
IV. If a principal's license is suspended, the broker-dealer's license is also suspended.

A. I and II
B. II and III
C. II and IV
D. III and IV

13. Under which of the following circumstances has an agent committed a fraudulent act as opposed to a prohibited business practice?

A. An agent sells securities for the benefit of a client on the basis of carefully guarded inside information
B. An agent sells a highly rated income fund to a client who seeks growth without concern for risk
C. A broker commingles its funds with those of its clients
D. An agent knowingly indicates to a client that a mark-up was less than it actually was

14. An agent solicits orders for a primary nonexempt security (underwriting) in his home state. Within days, he learns that the underwriting is not registered in that state. Relieved that no customer orders were placed, he ceases soliciting orders in this security. In this situation, the agent has acted

A. lawfully, because he ceased soliciting orders immediately upon learning that the security is not properly registered
B. lawfully, because no customer orders were executed
C. unlawfully, because he did not mark the orders "solicited"
D. unlawfully, because soliciting orders in nonexempt unregistered securities is prohibited

15. An individual would not be considered an agent under the USA if he engaged in

I. an isolated nonissuer transaction
II. transactions between an issuer and ordinary investors in which the individual is paid a commission by the issuer
III. a transaction between an issuer and the underwriters
IV. transactions between an issuer and savings institutions or trust companies

A. I, III and IV
B. II and III
C. II and IV
D. I, II, III and IV

16. An Administrator can deny an investment adviser's registration for all of the following reasons EXCEPT

A. lack of experience
B. failure to post a surety bond
C. failure to pass a written exam
D. not meeting minimum financial standards

17. Investment advisory contracts
    A. are cancelable for 48 hours after the customer signs
    B. must list each state in which the adviser is registered
    C. cannot be assigned without the Administrator's approval
    D. must contain a description of fees

18. An agent of a broker-dealer has raised capital from his customers with which he and his brother-in-law will build a small shopping center. The customers who contributed the capital received certificates of ownership as well as full disclosure of the risks involved. The broker-dealer was unaware of the agent's activities. In the above situation, the agent has acted
    A. lawfully, because risks of the transaction were disclosed to the customers in writing
    B. lawfully, because interests in a shopping mall are not securities
    C. unlawfully, because the agent gave his broker-dealer no opportunity to supervise his activities relative to its customers
    D. unlawfully, because the agent's brother-in-law is not a registered agent (sales representative)

19. According to the USA, the investment adviser brochure must include the business background of
    A. the investment adviser
    B. employees of the adviser
    C. an affiliated broker-dealer
    D. institutional clients

20. AAA Investment Advisers has a performance based fee compensation arrangement with the multimillion dollar RRR Family Foundation. Which of the following need not be stated in the written agreement with the RRR Foundation?
    A. The AAA Advisers fee arrangement may create incentives to make investments in more speculative securities than would be the case without a performance fee.
    B. AAA Advisers may receive increased compensation as a result of unrealized appreciation as well as capital gains.
    C. AAA Advisers will compute the advisory fee based on the quarterly returns of the account beginning on the date the contract is executed.
    D. AAA Advisers will not invest in securities whose volatility exceeds that of the Dow Jones Industrial Average.

21. An agent showed the account statement of his best and wealthiest customer to a more experienced agent for advice on additional securities to recommend to the customer. Some of the securities discussed were non-exempt, unregistered private placement securities. In this situation, the agent has acted
    A. lawfully, because seeking advice from a more experienced agent is in the customer's best interest
    B. lawfully, because the customer's high net worth made it suitable to purchase additional securities
    C. unlawfully, because some of the securities considered were unregistered, non-exempt private placements
    D. unlawfully, because the agent did not receive permission to reveal his personal financial information to the other agent

22. A security that is exempt from the registration requirements of the USA is also exempt from the act's

I. civil liabilities provisions
II. antifraud provisions
III. requirements for filing advertising and sales literature

A. I and II
B. I and III
C. III only
D. I, II and III

23. Under the USA, which of the following are considered securities?

I. Commodity option contract
II. Treasury stock
III. Keogh plan

A. I and II
B. I and III
C. II and III
D. I, II and III

24. Which of the following transactions are exempt from registration under the USA?

I. A trustee of a corporation in bankruptcy liquidates securities to satisfy debt holders
II. An offer of a securities investment is directed to 10 persons in the state during a 12-month consecutive period
III. An agent frequently engages in nonissuer transactions in unregistered securities on an unsolicited basis
IV. Agents for an entrepreneur offers preorganization certificates to less then 10 investors in the state for a modest commission

A. I and II
B. I and IV
C. II and IV
D. I, III and IV

25. Which of the following statements regarding registration of securities by coordination is(are) TRUE?

I. The registration statement must be on file for 10 days or shorter period if Administrator allows.
II. The registration statement must contain or be accompanied by consent to service of process.
III. State registration must be effective prior to federal registration.
IV. The registration becomes effective at the state level in conjunction with SEC registration if the Administrator has not entered an order to deny it.

A. I, II and IV
B. II and III
C. III and IV
D. I, II, III and IV

26. Under the USA, which of the following materials can be distributed if an issuing company has applied for registration but not yet cleared for sale?

I. Tombstone advertising
II. Red herring
III. Application with down payment
IV. Registration statement

A. I only
B. I, II and IV
C. II and III
D. II and IV

27. If it is in the public interest, the Administrator may

I. deny an application of an individual who has the required training and knowledge but lacks experience
II. restrict an application for investment adviser to broker-dealer activities if the applicant lacks the experience to function as an investment adviser
III. not enter an order against a broker-dealer on the basis of lack of qualification of any person other than the broker-dealer himself if he is an individual or an agent of the broker-dealer
IV. not enter an order against an investment adviser on the basis of lack of qualification of any person other than the adviser himself if he is an individual or an agent of the adviser

A. I only
B. II only
C. II, III and IV
D. I, II, III and IV

28. An agent needs to borrow some money for a business venture he wants to invest in. Which of the following customers could he borrow from?

I. An established customer with whom the agent has been doing business for at least one year
II. Any accredited investor
III. A lending institution
IV. Borrowing from customers is always prohibited.

A. I, II and IV
B. I and II
C. III only
D. IV only

29. Under the USA, what are the maximum penalties for a securities-related felony?

A. $3,000 and five years imprisonment
B. $3,000 and three years imprisonment
C. $5,000 and five years imprisonment
D. $5,000 and three years imprisonment

30. Under the USA, which of the following types of transactions can be entered into legally with unregistered, nonexempt securities?

A. Public offering
B. Private placement
C. Rights offering
D. Offering to employees of the issuer

31. To transact business in a state as an investment adviser representative, a person must

A. be registered as representative of a brokerage house and have passed the Uniform Securities Agent State Law exam
B. be registered as a representative of an investment adviser and have passed the Uniform Securities Agent State Law exam as well as any oral or written exams required by the state Administrator
C. have passed the registered representative exam and taken no other exams
D. be employed by a commercial bank located in the state

32. Which of the following statements regarding state registration of securities is TRUE?

A. Registration by filing is effective when so ordered by the Administrator.
B. Registration by coordination is effective concurrently with federal registration.
C. Registration by qualification is effective after 30 days.
D. Registration by coordination is effective when so ordered by the Administrator.

33. Directors of an issuer sell stock to employees for which the directors receive commissions. Under the USA, the directors

    I. are agents of the issuer
    II. are agents of a broker-dealer
    III. need not be licensed
    IV. must be licensed

    A. I and III
    B. I and IV
    C. II and III
    D. II and IV

34. Open-end investment companies that register their securities by notice filing must comply with all of the following EXCEPT

    A. have registered securities in the state for at least the preceding 24 months
    B. be in compliance with al material terms of the prior registration
    C. have no material change in the method of selling the securities
    D. have changed the fund's objectives

35. Under the USA, it is unlawful to sell

    A. security registered in the state under the USA but not registered in any other state
    B. federal covered security not registered in the state
    C. nonexempt, nonregistered security issued by a foreign corporation from a country with which the U.S. government maintains diplomatic relations
    D. security of a commercial bank not registered in the state

36. Which of the following transactions are exempt from the registration provisions of the USA?

    A. Isolated nonissuer transactions
    B. Unsolicited nonissuer transactions effected through a broker-dealer
    C. Transactions between issuers and underwriters
    D. All of the above.

37. A customer within one year of retirement informs his agent that he wants to use the equity in his house to make enough money within the year to fully fund his retirement. According to the USA, the agent should

    A. construct a growth-oriented portfolio
    B. urge the customer to reconsider his investment strategy
    C. invest in an ultraconservative portfolio of municipal bonds
    D. invest the money in high tech securities because of their unlimited potential

38. Which of the following constitutes either an offer or a sale?

    A. Mrs. Smith pledges her portfolio to secure a loan for her son Charles who plans to use the proceeds of the loan to buy a major interest in a publicly-traded company.
    B. Marge, a large client, receives saleable stock in lieu of a cash dividend as a result of her large holdings in ABC.
    C. Thomas is offered warrants (rights to purchase a stock at a future date) by his registered agent as the best way to take a position in the XYZ Corporation.
    D. Peggy receives a gift of nonassessable securities.

39. An agent sells her customer $10,000 of 30-year U.S. Treasury bonds. The agent tells the customer this is the best investment due to the "absolute safety" of Treasury securities. In this situation, the agent has acted

    A. lawfully, because Treasury securities carry no default risk
    B. lawfully, because Treasury securities are the safest among all domestically available debt instruments
    C. unlawfully, because allocating the customer's entire $10,000 into bonds ignores the customer's need for diversification
    D. unlawfully, because "absolute safety" implies that the customer will make money

40. Which of the following advisory fee structures is not allowed?

    A. Fees based on a percentage of the change in value of funds from year to year
    B. Fees based on a fixed dollar schedule for funds under management, with payment tied to account performance
    C. Fees based on a fixed dollar schedule tied to the value of funds under management
    D. Fees based on a percentage of the aggregate value of funds under management

41. An employee of an issuer who sells common stock to trust companies and savings institutions for commissions is

    A. a broker-dealer and must be registered as such
    B. an agent of the issuer and must register as such
    C. an agent of the issuer but need not be registered as an agent
    D. not an agent of the issuer

42. An Administrator in conducting investigations may do all of the following EXCEPT

    A. make public or private investigations both inside or outside the state to determine if a registrant has violated the USA
    B. require or permit any person to file a statement in writing under oath or otherwise whether or not professionally related to the party under investigation
    C. publish information concerning any violation of the USA or of any rule whether or not the party investigated objects
    D. revoke immunity from prosecution from a party who is compelled to testify over Fifth Amendment objections

43. What is the difference between an offer and a sale?

    A. An offer is the attempt to sell and a sale is a binding contract to transfer a security for value.
    B. An offer is a binding proposal to sell and a sale is a nonbinding proposal to sell.
    C. An offer can be made only by a customer and a sale can be made only by a broker-dealer.
    D. An offer must be approved by a branch manager and a sale needs no approval.

44. According to the USA, which of the following is an example of market manipulation?

    A. Creating the illusion of active trading
    B. Omitting material facts in a presentation
    C. Guaranteeing performance of a security
    D. Transactions in excess of a customer's financial capability

45. Peter Smith, an officer in Smith's Securities Corporation with all of its offices located in California, acts as a broker-dealer under the USA when he

    A. sells non-exempt securities to the largest clients of the firm that bears his name
    B. sells exempt securities in California to the best clients of the firm
    C. signs contracts with other NASD member firms to purchase securities research
    D. sells securities on behalf of his firm exclusively to other NASD member firms located in Nevada

46. An agent's customer wishes to purchase a small amount of a thinly-traded stock that is only available through a regional exchange of which your firm is not a member. Because of the extra work involved, your firm must charge higher than normal commission rates. After the agent discloses the higher rates to your customer, she instructs the agent to proceed with the order, which is then executed. In the above situation, the agent has acted

   A. lawfully, because the higher than normal commissions were justified and disclosed to the customer in advance of entering the order
   B. lawfully, because firms may charge according to the services provided
   C. unlawfully, because commissions may not exceed normal range
   D. unlawfully, because a broker-dealer may not accept an order for a stock traded on an exchange on which it holds no membership

47. An agent may inform a customer that the customer will always be able to sell a mutual fund at a profit, if

   A. the agent does not use the word "guaranteed"
   B. the agent further explains that dividends reinvested are not taxable income
   C. the fund is a no-load fund
   D. This is not permitted.

48. Under the USA, for a private placement to be considered an exempt transaction, it can be directed to

   I. no more than 10 persons
   II. no more than 15 persons
   III. in nine consecutive months
   IV. in 12 consecutive months

   A. I and III
   B. I and IV
   C. II and III
   D. II and IV

49. Under the terms of the USA, an agent who sells shares of a New York Stock Exchange listed security to an insurance company has engaged in a(n)

   A. unsuitable transaction
   B. sale of a security exempt from the registration and advertising provisions of the USA
   C. unlawful transaction
   D. issuer transaction

50. Persons who act in an investment advisory capacity in states that do not require registration must

   A. register with the SEC
   B. register with the NASD
   C. pass the Series 7 General Securities Representative Examination
   D. pass the Series 65 Uniform Investment Adviser Law Examination

51. An agent thinks that a technology stock is undervalued and she actively solicits all her customers. In this situation, the agent

   I. did not violate the USA if she disclosed all material facts
   II. committed an unethical sales practice because her firm has not recommended this technology stock
   III. committed an unethical business practice if she failed to review each account to determine suitability
   IV. did not commit a violation if she accurately informs all her clients of the price of the stock

   A. I, II and IV
   B. I and IV
   C. III only
   D. I, II, III and IV

52. Which of the following is exempt from state registration under the USA?

    A. Common stock of a manufacturing company whose shares are not registered with the SEC and will only be sold to residents of the state
    B. The sale of a interests in limited partnership to 500 individuals in an offering available to the general public
    C. Common stock of the First National Bank of France, a major foreign commercial bank
    D. Sale of variable annuities offered to the general public by a corporation not required to be registered in the state

53. Which of the following conditions must be met in order for a sales rep/agent to be permitted to share in the profits or losses of the customer's account?

    I. The sales rep/agent has the employer's written consent.
    II. The sales rep/agent has the customer's written consent.
    III. The sales rep/agent has a capital stake invested in the account.
    IV. The percentage of the profits/losses shared is proportionate to the rep's personal investment in the account.

    A. I and II
    B. I, II and III
    C. II, III and IV
    D. I, II, III and IV

54. XYZ common stock is listed for trading on the NYSE. Under the USA, which of the following XYZ securities other than common shares are exempt from state registration?

    A. Mortgage bonds
    B. Warrants
    C. Preferred stock
    D. All of the above.

55. Under the USA, which of the following activities is an example of churning?

    A. Frequent purchases one day and sales of the same stock the next day to align with a customer's investment objectives
    B. Bond swaps
    C. Frequent purchases and sales of front-end load mutual fund shares in a single account
    D. Day trading

56. Which of the following are prohibited practices?

    I. An investment adviser representative transferred an account to a brokerage house because the account went below the firm's minimum size and then informed the client
    II. An investment representative employed by an investment advisory partnership did not inform his clients of the departure of a partner who had only a very small interest in the firm
    III. An investment adviser representative employed by an investment subsidiary of a publicly traded bank holding company failed to inform his clients of the departure of the chairman and major stockholder of the firm
    IV. An agent exaggerated the earnings projections of an excellent company in order to convince the client to make a very wise investment decision

    A. I and II
    B. I, II, and III
    C. I, II, and IV
    D. I, II, III and IV

57. Which of the following would not be a market manipulation?

    A. Three market markers intentionally start buying and selling the same security simultaneously in their own accounts.
    B. A specialist buys and sells stock for his own account.
    C. A principal in a broker-dealer allows a rumor to leak out that ABC is going to acquire LMN. After a few days, the broker-dealer sells short LMN for its own account.
    D. All of the above.

58. Which of the following statements regarding an investment adviser representative is TRUE?

    A. The adviser is not subject to the antifraud provisions of the USA when engaged in securities sales activities.
    B. The adviser is exempt from the USA's antifraud provisions, if the adviser has fewer than three clients residing in the state.
    C. It is unlawful under the USA for an adviser to deceive another person when engaged in nonsecurities-related activities.
    D. It is unlawful under the USA for an investment adviser representative to deceive another person when engaged in securities-related sales activities.

59. Which of the following statement(s) is TRUE?

    I. A registered representative may never be employed by two broker-dealers at the same time
    II. A registered representative must submit separate registrations for each broker-dealer he is registered with
    III. A registered representative may be prevented from multiple registration in those states that prohibit dual or multiple registration
    IV. A registered representative who sells securities in several states must be registered with different broker-dealers in each state

    A. I only
    B. II and III
    C. II, III and IV
    D. IV only

60. Under the USA, all of the following issues would be exempt from registration EXCEPT

    A. stock issued by a Canadian corporation
    B. bonds issued by a municipality
    C. an investment contract issued in connection with an employee stock purchase plan
    D. stock issued by an insurance company authorized to do business in the state

Series 63 Practice Final 3 Answers & Rationale

1. C. Secondary transactions are also known as nonissuer transactions because the proceeds do not benefit the issuer. Private placements, issuer transactions, and exempt transactions are primary transactions in which the proceeds go to the issuer. QID: 28896

2. C. An investment adviser must disclose to clients and prospective clients adverse regulatory events only if they occurred within the last 10 years, such as a conviction of a misdemeanor involving an investment related business, SEC, or other federal regulatory agency proceedings in which the person was found to have violated an investment-related statute, or proceedings before the NASD in which the adviser was barred or suspended from membership. Misdemeanors regarding noninvestment-related actions are not considered material and, therefore, need not be disclosed (such as a motor vehicle violation). QID: 38352

3. C. It is a prohibited practice to automatically recommend securities without having a reasonable basis for the recommendation. Other agents recommending the security is not a reasonable basis for recommendation. Purchasing securities with high transaction costs is not prohibited provided that disclosure is made to the client. An adviser is not required to describe all facts surrounding an investment but must present all those that are material. The representative did not misrepresent a material fact that would have otherwise precluded the client from purchasing the security. QID: 36370

4. C. Investors who trade solely for their own accounts are public customers who do not need to register. QID: 31077

5. B. A broker-dealer, an agent, or a state-registered investment adviser must file a consent to service of process with the Administrator upon filing a registration application. The consent to service of process gives the Administrator the right to process legal complaints against the applicant. QID: 28832

6. D. Variable annuities are securities while fixed annuities are not. Options contracts, interests in merchandising marketing schemes, and common stock are specifically listed as securities under the USA. QID: 37161

7. B. While exempt from state registration, federally registered investment advisers must give notice (written) and pay state filing fees to practice within a given state. Federally registered investment advisers are not required to pass an oral or written examinations or required to become licensed broker-dealers. QID: 31818

8. D. After the inside information has become public, it may be disseminated to anyone. QID: 28911

9. B. A sale means a contract, verbal or otherwise, to dispose of a security for value. QID: 39199

10. B. A New York Stock Exchange manufacturing company that sells its securities to more than 10 persons (whether or not they are employees) is not an exempt transaction, whether commissions are charged or not. In addition, a manufacturer listed on the New York Stock Exchange who offers its securities only to its employees in a state through an agent who charges commissions is not an exempt transaction. A sale of nonexempt securities by a trustee in bankruptcy which involves numerous commissions is an exempt transaction. A bank headquartered in New York State that sells securities to its employees through an agent who charges commissions is engaging in an exempt transaction; bank securities are exempt whether or not a commission is charged. QID: 36373

11. D. Under the USA, investment advisers are prohibited from sharing in the gains and losses in a customer's account. QID: 31088

12. C. The suspension of a BD's registration causes the suspension of all agents, and the suspension of a principal's license causes the suspension of the firm's registration. An agent's license may be suspended if the Administrator finds that the order is in the public interest and the agent is guilty of any of the listed offenses. QID: 28858

13. D. Fraud involves knowingly deceiving a person or the willful misrepresentation of a material fact. By knowingly misrepresenting the markup the agent has fraudulently deceived the client. An agent who sells an income fund to a client with growth as an objective has committed a prohibited business practice by selling securities which were not suitable. This is not a fraudulent act but a prohibited business practice. The use of inside information and the commingling of funds are not activities which involve fraud, but are also prohibited business practices. QID: 37184

14. D. Soliciting orders in unregistered, nonexempt securities is unlawful, regardless of whether or not orders are placed. QID: 31836

15. A. An individual who effects securities transactions for compensation is defined as an agent. A person representing an issuer in exempt transactions, in transactions between issuers and underwriters, and transactions with existing employees in which no commissions are paid is excluded from the definition of an agent. QID: 28949

16. A. Lack of experience, by itself, is not cause for registration denial QID: 39207

17. D. All contracts must contain description of how fees are determined. Contracts are valid upon signing and need not list all states in which an adviser is registered and cannot be assigned without the client's approval. Administrator approval is not required. QID: 36702

18. C. The agent has acted unlawfully in effecting "private" securities transactions involving the broker-dealer's customers without proper supervision by the firm. The agent must not just disclose the risks involved but must also inform his employer because interests in shopping centers generally fall under the definition of securities. The agent's brother-in-law, however, is not under the supervision of the agent's employer and is, therefore, free to engage in business activities without approval. QID: 31167

19. A. The business background of the investment adviser must be included in Part II of the Form ADV and in the disclosure brochure. The business background of employees, affiliated broker-dealers, and institutional clients need not be included in the brochure. QID: 28876

20. D. The AAA Advisers need not state that they will invest in securities whose volatility exceeds that of the Dow Jones Industrial Average. The performance-based contract must state that the AAA Advisers fee arrangement may create incentives to make investments in more speculative securities than would be the case without a performance fee; AAA Advisers may receive increased compensation as a result of unrealized appreciation as well as capital gains; and AAA Advisers will compute the advisory fee based on the quarterly returns of the account beginning on the date the contract was executed. QID: 38319

21. D. The agent acted unlawfully in revealing the client's personal or financial information to another agent without permission from the customer. QID: 31852

22. C. An exempt security is only exempt from the registration requirements and the requirements for filing advertising and sales literature. No transaction is exempt from the antifraud provisions of the act and the liabilities that arise from fraudulent practices. QID: 28968

23. A. A commodity option contract and treasury stock are securities under the USA. Note that a commodity option contract is considered a security, while a commodity futures contract is not a security. A Keogh plan is a vehicle for an investment, but it is not a security in and of itself. QID: 28822

24. A. Transactions by fiduciaries, such as a trustee in a bankruptcy reorganization, are exempt from registration. An offer of a securities investment to 10 or fewer persons (called a private placement) is also exempt from registration. Engaging in nonissuer transactions on a regular basis is not exempt from registration, whether or not the trades are unsolicited. Offers of pre-organization certificates are not exempt when commissions are charged. QID: 37153

25. A. Registration on the state level must be coordinated with federal registration. The registration statement must be on file with the Administrator for 10 days. The registration statement becomes effective in conjunction with SEC and must contain or be accompanied by consent to service of process. QID: 31174

26. B. Prior to clearance, a red herring may be distributed to estimate customer interest. Additionally, the registration statement may be distributed (although normally it is not) and a tombstone advertisement published. An application with down payment cannot be made or accepted. A tombstone advertisement is also allowed and the registration statement may be distributed. QID: 28897

27. C. The Administrator may restrict an application for investment adviser to broker-dealer activities, if the applicant lacks the experience to function as an investment adviser. In addition, the Administrator may not enter an order against a broker-dealer on the basis of lack of qualification of any person other than the broker-dealer himself. QID: 38328

28. C. Borrowing from a customer is strictly prohibited unless the customer is a lending institution. QID: 31867

29. D. Under the USA, the maximum penalty is $5,000 and/or three years imprisonment for a securities-related felony. QID: 31082

30. B. Private placements involve the sale of nonexempt securities to qualified investors and are exempt from registration. The USA stipulates that no more than 10 nonaccredited investors may receive offers in any 12-month period, that the purchase be made for the purpose of investment, and that no commissions be paid for solicitation of noninstitutional buyers. A public offering of an unregistered, nonexempt security may not be entered into. A transaction with an unregistered, nonexempt security may not be entered into unless it is a private placement. QID: 28836

31. B. To transact business in a state as an investment adviser representative, a person must be registered as a representative of an investment adviser and have passed the Uniform Securities Agent State Law exam as well as any other exams required by the state Administrator. One is not a registered investment adviser representative as a result of passing the Series 7 Registered Representative exam nor by virtue of employment with a bank. QID: 37157

32. B. Coordination is frequently used to register a security simultaneously under the Securities Act of 1933 and under the USA in a state. If the security's federal registration is pending and the Administrator has received all of the required material, the two registrations can be declared effective at the same time. QID: 31186

33. B. The directors must register as agents because commissions are paid. QID: 28923

34. D. An open-end investment company must have registered securities in the state for at least the preceding 24 months, be in compliance with all material terms of the prior registration, and have no material change in the method of selling the securities. In addition, the fund's objectives cannot have changed. QID: 38621

35. C. Nonexempt, nonregistered securities cannot not be lawfully sold in a state. The fact that they are issued by a foreign corporation is irrelevant; nonexempt securities must be registered. A federal covered security need not be registered in a state if it is properly registered under the Securities Act of 1933 or exempt from registration under the act. Securities of commercial banks have a federally imposed exemption from state securities registration—they are federal covered securities. QID: 36380

36. D. Isolated nonissuer transactions, unsolicited transactions effected through a broker-dealer, and transactions between issuers and underwriters are exempt transactions under the provisions of the USA. QID: 31087

37. B. Making unsuitable recommendations to customers is prohibited. This investor's time frame is unrealistic because the customer cannot meet his objectives in the time allotted. Investment in high tech securities is unsuitable. Advising the customer to invest in an ultraconservative portfolio of municipal bonds will not meet the customer's objective of capital growth. The agent should advise the customer to reconsider his investment objectives. QID: 28843

38. C. The agent who offered Thomas warrants has made an offer of securities under the USA. Mrs. Smith's pledge of securities to her son does not constitute a sale or offer to sell. Marge's receipt of a stock dividend is not a sale or an offer to sell because she did not get anything of value in return for the shares. A gift of non-assessable stock is not a sale; it is a gift. QID: 38317

39. D. Implying or stating to customers that they will profit from a security is prohibited. Although Treasury securities carry virtually no default risk, the customer faces significant interest rate risk, particularly in light of the bonds' 30-year maturity. QID: 31845

40. A. Fees based on a share of capital gains or appreciation in an account are prohibited. A fee based on a fixed-dollar schedule for funds under management is allowed. A fee based on a fixed-dollar schedule tied to the value of funds under management is allowed. A fee based on a percentage of the aggregate value of funds under management is allowed. QID: 28999

41. D. A person is not an agent under the USA when representing issuers in an exempt transaction (in this case, transactions with trust companies and savings institutions). The fact that a commission is paid is not relevant in this case. It would be, however, if the employee sold stock to other employees in nonexempt transactions. QID: 39219

42. D. The Administrator may not revoke immunity from prosecution if a party is required to testify against his will. Any person compelled to testify over objecting on Fifth Amendment grounds cannot be prosecuted on the basis of the information provided. However, the person compelled is not exempt from prosecution for perjury or contempt committed in the course of his testimony. The Fifth Amendment guarantees the right against self-incrimination. The Administrator can make investigations in public or private both inside or outside the state to determine if a registrant has violated the USA. The Administrator may require or permit any person to file a statement in writing under oath or otherwise, whether or not professionally related to the party under investigation and may publish information concerning any violation of the USA. QID: 36385

43. A. An offer is made in an attempt to sell; a sale is the binding contract to sell a security for value. A customer or a broker-dealer can make an offer or a sale. Neither an offer nor a sale requires a branch manager's approval. QID: 31172

44. A. Creating the illusion of trading activity is market manipulation. Guaranteeing performance of a security and omitting material facts are prohibited practices but do not constitute market manipulation. Trades too large for a customer are also prohibited because they are not suitable. QID: 28886

45. C. Smith, in signing contracts with other NASD member firms, is acting as an officer of the firm and, as a result, is acting in the capacity of a broker-dealer under the USA. When Smith sells securities to customers of the firm, he is acting in the capacity of a registered representative, as opposed to that of a broker-dealer. The relevant issue here is that Smith is an agent when he is representing the firm in a securities sales transactions with the public. Note that Smith's firm is not considered a broker-dealer in Nevada because the firm does not have offices in Nevada and deals exclusively with other member broker-dealers. QID: 38323

46. A. Under the USA, larger than normal commission is permissible if justified and disclosed to the customer in advance. QID: 31860

47. D. An agent cannot legally promise profit in a security transaction nor guarantee a return. Profits are not "guaranteed" if the dividends reinvested are not taxable income or if the fund is load or no-load. QID: 28936

48. B. In order to be an exempt transaction, a private placement can be directed to no more than 10 persons in a 12-consecutive-month period. QID: 39206

49. B. An agent who sells shares of a security to an insurance company is engaged in an exempt transaction; that is, a transaction exempt from the advertising and registration requirements of the USA. The sale of a security not required to be registered under the USA is not necessarily an unlawful transaction because the security might either be exempt from registration under the USA or covered (regulated) by federal securities law. QID: 37138

50. A. Those persons who act in an advisory capacity in states that do not require registration must register with the SEC. QID: 31106

51. C. Agents must always determine suitability before soliciting purchases or sales. Not to do so is an unethical sales practice. QID: 28873

52. C. Securities of international banks are exempt from state registration under the USA. Sales of limited partnerships sold to a large number of investors are subject to registration as are variable annuities. QID: 37177

53. D. All of the conditions must be met in order for a sales rep to legally participate in the profits and losses of the customer's account. QID: 31826

54. D. Under the blue-chip exemption, all of the securities of an account issuer listed on a national exchange are exempt from state registration. QID: 31071

55. C. Churning is defined as excessive activity in a customer's account for the purpose of generating commissions. Because mutual funds carry a front-end load and are considered long-term investment vehicles, frequent trades constitute churning. Frequent purchases one day and sales of the same stock the next day in order to align with a customer's investment objectives is not necessarily churning if it is done for the benefit of the customer. A bond swap is not churning. QID: 28901

56. C. An agent need not inform clients of departures of employees, senior or otherwise, from investment advisory firms that are incorporated. Clients must, however, be informed of the departure of any partner if the firm is an investment advisory partnership. Remember the distinction between assignment and notification—an account can never be assigned to another adviser without the express approval of the client. An agent may not exaggerate the earnings of a firm even if it is in the interest of the client. Such a practice is both prohibited and fraudulent. QID: 37154

57. B. A specialist that buys or sells for its own account is not engaged in market manipulation. The function of a specialist normally is to act as a broker for orders other members left with them and to act as a dealer in buying and selling for their own account. Market makers who buy and sell the same security in their own accounts are

manipulating the market by creating false trading volume. A principal in a broker-dealer that trades on a rumor that he allowed to leak out is manipulating the market for personal gain. QID: 31184

58. D. It is unlawful under the USA for an investment adviser representative to deceive another person when engaged in securities-related sales activities. The antifraud provisions of the USA apply to any person advising another person for compensation as to the value of securities. Broker-dealers and sales representatives, although not technically defined as advisers, are subject to the same restrictions on prohibited practices as advisers when they are engaged in advisory activities. QID: 36371

59. B. A registered representative must submit separate registrations for each broker-dealer he or she is registered with and a registered representative may be prevented from multiple registration in those states that prohibit dual or multiple registrations. Some states allow multiple registrations by registered representatives. The representative must register in each state in which he sells securities, not with separate or different broker-dealers in each state. QID: 38619

60. A. Foreign government securities are exempt. However, securities issued by foreign corporations are not. QID: 39226

Series 63 Practice Final 4

1. Under the Uniform Securities Act, which of the following persons is responsible for proving that a securities issue is exempt from registration?

   A. Underwriter
   B. Issuer
   C. State Administrator
   D. There is no need to prove eligibility for an exemption.

2. An Administrator does not have jurisdiction over an offer to sell if the offer is made in a

   I. TV broadcast originating outside the state
   II. newspaper published outside the state
   III. newspaper published inside the state where more than 2/3 of its circulation is outside the state

   A. I only
   B. II only
   C. II and III
   D. I, II and III

3. Which of the following transactions is not exempt from registration and advertising filing requirements?

   A. Transactions between issuer and underwriter or between underwriters
   B. A bona fide pledge of securities
   C. Nonissuer orders solicited by an agent
   D. Transactions with banks, savings and loan associations, and other financial institutions

4. In which of the following situations does the transaction exemption apply?

   I. City of Chicago bond offering
   II. Canadian government bond offering
   III. Offering IBM to only 21 customers
   IV. The sale of an estate's holding of IBM shares by an executor

   A. I and II
   B. I and III
   C. II, III and IV
   D. IV only

5. An employee of a large, publicly-held company effects transactions with existing employees for the purchase of the company's debentures. Under the USA, the employee

   A. must register as an agent of the issuer
   B. need not register as an agent of the issuer
   C. may receive commissions without registration
   D. must register as an agent if he will receive commissions or remuneration, either directly or indirectly

6. An agency cross transaction occurs when a person acts as an investment adviser and a broker-dealer for both the advisory client and the person on the other side of the transaction. In this situation, the USA requires that

   A. the adviser recommend the transaction to both parties
   B. the adviser indicate the number of cross transactions that occurred in a client's account no less than monthly
   C. prior written approval from a principal of the advisory firm is obtained
   D. the advisory client provide prior written consent and that the adviser make prior disclosure

7. Which of the following entities is required to have a Series 63 license?

   A. A broker-dealer
   B. An agent representing a broker-dealer to the public
   C. An agent at a broker-dealer who is a silent partner
   D. An issuer

8. According to the Uniform Securities Act, which of the following are considered securities?

   I. Condominium project with a rental pool agreement
   II. U.S. Treasury bill
   III. Limited partnership in an oil and gas exploration program
   IV. Contract in soybean futures

   A. I and II
   B. I, II and III
   C. III only
   D. I, II, III and IV

9. Under which of the following circumstances must Broker-Dealer XYZ, a registered broker-dealer whose only office is in Texas, also register in Louisiana?

   I. Broker-Dealer XYZ only dealings in Louisiana are with issuers of securities in Louisiana involved in the transactions.
   II. Broker-Dealer XYZ engages in extensive transactions with the largest insurance company in Louisiana.
   III. Broker-Dealer XYZ routinely sells nonexempt securities to extremely high net-worth residents of Louisiana.
   IV. Broker-Dealer XYZ purchases exempt securities from extremely high net-worth residents of Louisiana for resale to residents of Texas.

   A. I only
   B. I and II
   C. III and IV
   D. II, III and IV

10. Which of the following transactions are not exempt from registration and advertising filing requirements?

   I. Isolated nonissuer transactions
   II. Unsolicited nonissuer orders
   III. Transactions with pension or profit-sharing trusts
   IV. Transactions with intrastate manufacturing companies

   A. I only
   B. II and III
   C. III and IV
   D. IV only

11. Under the NSMIA, an investment adviser with $25 million or more in assets under management may register with the

   A. NASD
   B. NASAA
   C. SEC
   D. NYSE

12. An agent registered in Alabama directs a solicitation to a customer who lives in Connecticut while the customer is temporarily in Indiana. The customer does not accept the offer until he arrives back in Connecticut. According to the Uniform Securities Act, the Administrators of which of the following states have jurisdiction?

   A. Alabama and Connecticut
   B. Alabama and Indiana
   C. Indiana and Connecticut
   D. Alabama, Connecticut and Indiana

13. As a result of the National Securities Markets Improvement Act of 1996 (NSMIA), certain issuer offerings are no longer subject to state registration. The shares that no longer need be registered with the state Administrator are those listed on

I. New York Stock Exchange
II. American Stock Exchange
III. Nasdaq National Market System
IV. Nasdaq's Bulletin Board

A. I only
B. I and II
C. I, II and III
D. I, II, III and IV

14. An agent has over 200 customers. After extensive research on initial public offerings issued by solar energy companies, she recommends that each customer purchase shares in Solargen, Inc. The agent discussed the risk of buying Solargen stock with each customer. In the above situation, the agent has acted

A. lawfully, because the risk was presented to the customers
B. lawfully, because the agent performed due diligence analysis on the recommended company
C. unlawfully, because the recommendation does not consider the financial objectives of each customer
D. unlawfully, because solar energy is an industry that is highly dependent on local weather conditions

15. Under the USA, no specific response is required by the state Administrator before which of the following types of securities notice filing or registration become effective?

I. Coordination
II. Qualification
III. Notice Filing
IV. Application

A. I and II
B. I and III
C. II and III
D. I, II, III and IV

16. The Uniform Securities Act grants state securities Administrators all of the following powers EXCEPT the power to

I. conduct investigations involving dealers located in states other than the Administrator's state
II. issue subpoenas to agents and brokers not resident in the Administrator's state
III. revoke or suspend a registration without an opportunity for a hearing because of the confidential nature of the offense
IV. limit the length of an investigation to a reasonable period of time in order not to place a registrant in continuous jeopardy.

A. I and II
B. II and III
C. III and IV
D. I, II and IV

17. Which of the following transactions are prohibited?

I. Borrowing money or securities from a high net-worth customer
II. Selling speculative or "hot" issues to a retired couple of modest means on a fixed income
III. Failing to follow a customer's orders so as to prevent investment in a security not adequately covered by well-known securities analysts
IV. Backdating confirmations for the benefit of the client's tax reporting

A. I and II
B. II and III
C. I, II and III
D. I, II, III and IV

18. Registration statements are effective

A. for a period of time determined by the Administrator for each issue
B. for one year from the effective date
C. for one year from the date of issue
D. until the next registration statement is filed

19. According to the USA, under which of the following circumstances may an Administrator cancel a person's registration?

A. The person is judged to be mentally incompetent.
B. The Administrator determines it would be in the public interest.
C. The person is the subject of an insider trading lawsuit.
D. The person has been terminated from employment at an investment adviser firm.

20. In their advertising campaigns, investment advisers are prohibited from doing all of the following EXCEPT

A. using testimonials
B. guaranteeing future performance
C. offering free services
D. exaggerating the capabilities of the firm and its personnel

21. Pat Conway, a risk-averse investor, has never before invested money outside of bank instruments. Recognizing Pat's conservative nature, his agent recommends that Pat purchase Treasury notes, pointing out that federal government-backed securities are riskless securities. In the above situation the agent has acted

A. lawfully, because Treasury notes are suitable for a risk-averse customer
B. lawfully, because Treasury notes carry no risk of principal default
C. unlawfully, because Treasury notes are unsuitable for a risk-averse customer
D. unlawfully, because the agent failed to disclose that the customer retains interest rate risk

22. A customer places an order for 1,000 shares of stock in a company in which the adviser holds a large block. In compliance with the antifraud provision of the USA, the adviser

A. must disclose that it will act as a principal in the transaction to reduce its position
B. need not disclose the capacity in which it is acting if the adviser maintains the same position in the stock
C. must refuse the order because there is a conflict of interest
D. may execute the transaction without taking further action

23. Under SEC Release IA-1092, an investment adviser is all of the following EXCEPT a

I. broker who charges for investment advice
II. publisher of a financial newspaper
III. person who sells security analysis
IV. CPA who, as an incidental part of his practice, charges a fee for constructing a portfolio of tax-sheltered investments

A. I and II
B. II and III
C. II and IV
D. III and IV

24. All of the following describe exempt transactions EXCEPT

A. ABC, a broker-dealer, purchases securities from XYZ corporation
B. First National Bank sells its entire publicly-traded bond portfolio to Amalgamated National Bank
C. Amalgamated Nation Bank sells its publicly-traded bond portfolio to ABC Insurance Company
D. Joe Smith, an employee of Amalgamated Bank, buys securities from ABC Brokerage Corporation

25. A customer is upset with her agent for not servicing her account properly and sends him a complaint letter about his actions. The agent should

A. call the customer and apologize, promising to do a better job
B. tell the customer he is willing to make recission
C. do nothing and hope that he doesn't hear any more about it
D. bring the customer complaint to his employer immediately

26. An agent tells a customer that one of the customer's stocks is worth $10 more per share than it is really worth in order to encourage the client to sell. This activity is

A. allowed if the agent views the difference as a service charge
B. allowed if the customer ultimately makes a profit in the account
C. a misrepresentation and a fraudulent act
D. a misrepresentation but not a fraudulent act

27. An offer to sell describes the

A. receipt of a stock dividend
B. attempt to dispose of a security for value
C. exercise of warrants
D. purchase of a new issue

28. Which of the following practices is prohibited under the USA?

A. Participating in active trading of a security in which an unusually high trading volume has occurred
B. Offering services that a rep cannot realistically perform because of his broker-dealer's limitations
C. Altering the customer's order at the request of a customer which subsequently results in a substantial loss
D. Failing to inform the firm's principal of frequent verbal customer complaints

29. Which of the following can be substituted for a fidelity bond?

A. Cash or securities
B. Cash
C. Commodities, cash or securities
D. None of the above.

30. Which of the following statements regarding the antifraud provisions of the USA is TRUE?

    A. The only securities exempt from the provisions are those regulated by federal authority.
    B. The only exempt securities are those issued by national governments or political subdivisions of countries that maintain diplomatic relations with the United States.
    C. The only exempt securities are those that are properly registered under blue-sky laws.
    D. No securities are exempt from the antifraud provisions of the act.

31. An Administrator may not cancel an investment adviser's registration under which of the following circumstances?

    A. The adviser has been declared to be mentally incompetent by a court of jurisdiction
    B. The adviser cannot be located after a reasonable search by the Administrator
    C. The adviser is no longer in business
    D. The adviser has been convicted of a non-securities related felony

32. Mrs. Smith, a lifelong friend of an agent, is also that agent's best customer. Due to a substantial stock market drop, the agent receives a maintenance margin call that cannot be satisfied without liquidating securities in the account. Mrs. Smith offers to transfer cash and securities from her own account into the agent's account. Because this offer could be misunderstood, the agent borrows $10,000 from Mrs. Smith under a legal and binding loan agreement specifying the rate of interest the agent will pay on the loan. In the above situation, the agent has acted

    A. lawfully, because the loan operated as a standard business loan by agreement
    B. lawfully, if the agent can substantiate that Mrs. Smith was a personal friend prior to becoming a client
    C. unlawfully, because borrowing money or securities from a customer is prohibited
    D. unlawfully, because neither party was represented by counsel in drawing up the loan agreement

33. According to the USA, after passing the Series 63, 6, 7, or 22 exam, an agent can begin selling

    I. Immediately
    II. When affiliated with a broker-dealer
    III. When granted a registration from the state Administrator
    IV. When permission is received from the principal in the office

    A. I only
    B. I and IV
    C. II and III
    D. II and IV

34. In order for an agent to engage in securities transactions in a state prior to registration, which of the following conditions must be met?

I. The agent must be eligible to register in the state
II. The agent's broker-dealer must be registered in the state
III. The agent must be registered with a national securities association
IV. The agent must be registered in at least one other state

A. I, II and III
B. I and IV
C. II and III
D. I, II, III and IV

35. A current client of an investment adviser must receive a brochure

A. annually if the adviser has neither custody or discretion
B. quarterly if the adviser has both discretion and custody
C. annually whether or not the adviser has custody or discretion
D. within 48 hours of renewal

36. A sales representative solicits nonexempt, unregistered securities for a client. Under these circumstances, which of the following statements is TRUE?

A. The broker-dealer who employs the sales representative may be sued.
B. The sales representative may be subject to criminal penalties.
C. The broker-dealer may be sued if the client loses money, but if money is made the client may keep it.
D. All of the above.

37. An agent learns of material, inside information regarding a company that is publicly held. Which of the following with respect to the information would not violate the USA?

A. Soliciting orders based on this information
B. Trading for the agent's personal account based on this information
C. Discussing the situation with a superior or compliance officer in the agent's firm
D. Discussing the information at a seminar but not making an investment recommendation

38. Which of the following statements are NOT true?

I. A broker-dealer must be a firm or corporation (legal person) as opposed to a natural person (human being).
II. A registered broker-dealer must have registered principals to sell securities to the public in addition to registered representatives who also sell to the general public.
III. An investment adviser must be a firm or a corporation as opposed to a natural person.
IV. An investment adviser representative cannot, under any circumstances, be employed by a registered broker-dealer.

A. I and II
B. I, II and III
C. II, III and IV
D. I, II, III and IV

39. An agent receives a phone call from the husband of one of his customers. Because his wife is stranded while traveling, he instructs the agent to buy 1,000 shares of XYZ stock in her individual account immediately to take advantage of a price drop. In the above situation, the agent should

    A. accept the order and carry out his client's wishes
    B. accept the order only if the husband faxes or e-mails an immediate release to the broker-dealer
    C. refuse the order because the husband is not authorized to enter orders for his wife's individual account
    D. refuse the order because the customer should buy the security for the long term rather than try to time the market by purchasing the stock because of a temporary price drop

40. According to the USA, a private placement investor may receive a

    A. certificate for exempt securities
    B. certificate for nonexempt securities
    C. trust indenture
    D. certificate only if approved by the administrator

41. Hugh Clark, a minority partner in ABC Investment Partner's, a registered investment adviser, withdraws from the partnership in order to form his own separate partnership, Clark Advisers. ABC Investment Partners

    A. must change its name because the partnership has a new mix of partners as a result of Clark's departure
    B. must promptly notify Clark Advisers of Clark's withdrawal from ABC Investment Partners
    C. must promptly notify its clients of Clark's departure
    D. need not notify its clients of Clark's departure because Clark was only a minority partner

42. Which of the following statements regarding registration of securities under the Uniform Securities Act is TRUE?

    I. A state Administrator has the authority to revoke a security's exemption without prior notice to the issuer
    II. An issuer exempt from the registration requirements of the USA cannot be charged for criminal or civil liability
    III. A security exempt from registration requirements must comply with the advertising and sales filing requirements
    IV. An exempt security can only be sold on an unsolicited basis

    A. I only
    B. I and II
    C. I, II and III
    D. I, II, III and IV

43. Under the USA, which of the following are exempt transactions?

    I. A nonissuer sale of an outstanding security subject to reporting and registration requirements under the Securities Exchange Act of 1934 for the past four months.
    II. In an isolated instance, a customer contacts a registered representative and places an order for 500 shares of a stock the rep has never heard of. The rep finds the stock and fills the order.
    III. XYZ brokerage firm underwrites 1,000,000 shares of ABC and distributes them only to other underwriters.
    IV. A broker-dealer places an entire new issue of securities among 15 different insurance companies.

    A. I and III
    B. II and IV
    C. II, III and IV
    D. I, II, III and IV

44. An income-oriented customer has a discretionary account with his agent. If the agent purchases speculative growth stock on behalf of the customer, under the USA, this is considered a(n)

    A. wash sale
    B. unauthorized transaction
    C. acceptable transaction
    D. matching activity

45. All of the following securities are exempt securities EXCEPT

    A. Canadian government bonds
    B. six month commercial paper
    C. bank holding company stock
    D. tax-free municipal bonds

46. Under the USA, no specific response is required from the state Administrator before which of the following types of securities registration becomes effective?

    I. Coordination
    II. Qualification
    III. Filing
    IV. Appropriation

    A. I and II
    B. I and III
    C. II, III and IV
    D. I, II, III and IV

47. All of the following are prohibited practices under the USA EXCEPT

    I. borrowing money or securities from the account of a former banker with express written permission
    II. failing to identify a customer's financial objectives
    III. selling rights
    IV. supplying funds to a client's account only when or if it declines below a pre-agreed-upon level

    A. I and II
    B. I, II and III
    C. II and IV
    D. III only

48. Under the registration provisions of the Uniform Securities Act, it is unlawful for an agent in the state to sell XYZ unless

    A. XYZ is a federal covered security that trades on the NYSE and other major exchanges
    B. XYZ in a nonregistered, nonexempt security
    C. the agent is a nonregistered, nonexempt person
    D. both the agent and XYZ are nonexempt and nonregistered

49. Which of the following is not acting in the capacity of an agent under the USA?

    A. An individual who represents an issuer in effecting transactions with existing employees and who is paid a modest fee
    B. An individual who sells foreign securities required to be registered with the state
    C. A broker-dealer who transacts business with the general public
    D. An individual working for a broker-dealer who sells commercial paper to wealthy individuals

50. What does the term "guaranteed" mean when used to describe a security?

    A. The broker-dealer will buy the security back at the same price or higher.
    B. The security has been cleared and is backed by the SEC.
    C. The security has a backer that guarantees the payment of principal and interest.
    D. The security is an annuity product that guarantees a retirement income.

51. An agent explains dollar cost averaging to a mutual fund prospect, stating that, "If you invest the same number of dollars each month and reinvest the distributions, the value in your mutual fund will increase." In this situation the agent has

A. accurately explained the result of dollar cost averaging
B. accurately explained the result of dividend and capital gain reinvestment
C. made a misleading statement to the customer
D. made a misleading statement to the customer only if the fund has not increased in value within the previous 10 years

52. Peter Smith, a prominent securities lawyer living in Connecticut, conducts his securities law practice full-time in New York State. He must register as an investment adviser in New York State if

A. he advises his wife, who also has an office in New York State, that her investment in 15 technology stocks is too high
B. the clients of Smith's law firm are New York State residents and seek advice on the construction of trust documents that may be helpful in reducing taxes on the securities in their estates
C. the clients of Smith's law firm are all residents of Connecticut but conduct their business with Smith in New York State
D. Smith's clients, none of whom are residents of New York State, receive investment advice as an integral part of Smith's legal services

53. Your friend is a licensed life insurance agent whose client wants to purchase a variable annuity. You are a licensed securities and insurance agent. Your friend wants you to sell the policy and split commissions with him. Is this allowed?

A. Splitting commissions is an allowable activity at all times.
B. Splitting commissions in variable annuities is allowable only if the agents involved are both licensed in life insurance and securities.
C. Splitting commissions is an unethical trade practice.
D. Splitting commissions would be allowable if the securities rep receives at least 60% of the commission and the insurance agent receives no more than 40%.

54. An individual would not have to register as a sales rep in the state if he

A. receives an unsolicited call from a potential customer who wishes to purchase a particular stock which is listed on the NYSE. The broker-dealer is not registered in the state.
B. made a call to a customer in a state where the BD is registered
C. solicited only 10 calls a year directed in-state
D. made solicitations for unregistered, nonexempt securities

55. Under the USA, an agent may not make which of the following statements to a customer?

A. "This security is registered with the state."
B. "This security has been cleared by the Administrator."
C. "This security is approved for sale by the Administrator."
D. "This security is exempt from registration."

56. An individual with $100,000 to invest will require these funds in six months for the purchase of a house. In which of the following circumstances did the agent act correctly? The agent convinced the client to

A. invest in a Treasury bill on the basis of its safety.
B. purchase $100,000 lump sum annuity on the basis of its security and backing by an insurance company
C. invest in a real estate partnership as a hedge against the rise of real estate values until the client purchases the house
D. invest in an IPO on the basis of its high growth prospects

57. According to the USA, which of the following is a prohibited activity?

A. The sales rep enters into an agreement to share in the profits/losses of the customer's account without an investment in the account.
B. The sales rep and his spouse jointly own their own personal trading account at the firm.
C. The sales rep, with his firm's and the client's permission, participates in the profits and losses of the account in proportion to his investment in the account.
D. A sales rep refuses a client's request to share in the performance of the client's account.

58. Broker-dealers and investment advisers must keep all of the following records EXCEPT

A. memoranda
B. correspondence
C. telephone records
D. account books

59. Under the USA, which of the following transactions are exempt?

I. A transaction between and issuer and an underwriter
II. An unsolicited customer order to buy an exempt security
III. The purchase of a U.S. Treasury Bond
IV. The sale of a municipal security

A. I and II
B. III and IV
C. I and III
D. II and IV

60. If information filed with the Administrator changes in a material way, the registrant must

A. amend the registration statement within 60 days of the material change
B. update the information on the registration upon the next annual renewal date
C. amend or update the information promptly regardless of the renewal date
D. submit an entirely new registration form within 30 days of the material change in information

Series 63 Practice Final 4 Answers & Rationale

1. B. The burden of proof for claiming eligibility for an exemption falls to the person claiming the exemption. QID: 28884

2. D. Under the broadcast and publishing exceptions, the Administrator does not have jurisdiction if the offer is made in a TV or radio broadcast originating outside the state or in a newspaper published outside the state. Furthermore, if a newspaper is published inside a state but over 2/3 of its circulation is outside the state, the Administrator does not have jurisdiction. QID: 39212

3. C. Nonissuer orders solicited by an agent are nonexempt transactions—these are simply secondary market trades. Transactions between issuers and underwriters or between underwriters are exempt from registration and advertising filing requirements. A bona fide pledge of securities is also exempt from registration and advertising filing requirements. Transactions with banks, savings and loan associations, and other financial institutions are exempt from registration and advertising filing requirements. QID: 36376

4. D. An exempt transaction relieves the broker-dealer from any state advertising or registration requirements. Transactions by executors and state Administrators are examples of exempt transactions. QID: 31079

5. D. Under the USA, an individual is an agent when effecting transactions with an issuer's existing employees if commissions are paid. QID: 28829

6. D. The adviser must make prior disclosure that an agency cross transaction may be a conflict of interest and that commissions may be collected from both parties to the transaction. That adviser may not recommend the transaction to both parties. The adviser must provide to each client no less than annually a written disclosure statement identifying the number of agency cross transactions and the amount of compensation. The adviser must get prior written consent from the client prior to executing an agency cross transaction. QID: 38311

7. B. An agent who represents a broker-dealer is required to be registered at the state level. A Series 63 is a required part of the state registration process. QID: 31841

8. B. Except for those items specifically exempted from the definition of "security" (such as life insurance), almost anything that can be traded for value and is managed by a third party is a security. However, certain items (such as futures contracts) are not securities. Single stock features are not included. QID: 28915

9. C. Under the Uniform Securities Act, broker-dealers must register in any state in which they are engaged in securities transactions in nonexempt securities with individual investors. The net worth of the individual is irrelevant. Broker-dealers with no offices in the state who engage in transactions in the state with certain institutional investors, such as insurance companies or investment companies, need not register in that state. QID: 40205

10. D. Transactions with intrastate manufacturing companies are not exempt from registration and advertising filing requirements. Isolated nonissuer transactions are given specific exemption under the USA. Unsolicited nonissuer orders and transactions with pension or profit-sharing trusts are given specific exemptions under the USA. QID: 36384

11. C. Investment advisers who manage $25-$30 may register with either the SEC or the state Administrator, not the NASD. Advisers with over $30 million must register with the SEC. QID: 31105

12. D. The Administrator from any state from which an offer is made, directed, or accepted has jurisdiction over the offer. QID: 28860

13. C. The National Markets Improvement Act of 1996 (NSMIA) eliminated duplicate federal and state registration of securities. Those securities registered under federal law are federal covered securities. These federal covered securities include those issuers listed on the New York Stock Exchange, American Stock Exchange, and on the Nasdaq National Market System. Securities offered on the Nasdaq's Bulletin Board are not federal covered securities and therefore must register in the states in which they are sold. QID: 38331

14. C. In recommending the same stock to 200 customers, the agent (sales representative) failed to consider the investment objectives and financial ability of each customer. The chance that an initial public offering is suitable for all 200 of the agent's customers is virtually impossible. QID: 31851

15. B. Notice filing and registration by coordination do not require a response from the state Administrator. However, registration by qualification becomes effective only in an active order of the Administrator. QID: 28956

16. C. State securities Administrators may conduct investigations involving dealers in other states as well as issue subpoenas to agents and brokers not resident in the Administrator's state. Administrators may not revoke or suspend a registration without an opportunity for a hearing. Administrators have no limits on the amount of time they may devote to an investigation of a registrant. QID: 40214

17. D. All of the practices are prohibited. An agent may not borrow money or securities from a customer unless that customer is a commercial bank in the business of lending money. Selling speculative or "hot" issues to a retired couple of modest means is an unsuitable transaction because it is not consistent with the objectives of the client. An agent must follow legal orders of the customer, even if the agent believes the order is an unwise one. An agent may not backdate confirmations for the benefit on the client. QID: 37152

18. B. A registration statement remains effective for one year from the effective date. QID: 31173

19. A. Registration may be cancelled by the Administrator if the registered person has been judged mentally incompetent. The Administrator cannot cancel a registration solely on the basis that it is in the public interest to do so. A person's registration may not be cancelled simply because he or she is the subject of a lawsuit. A person's registration is not in effect when the person is not associated with an firm. QID: 28875

20. C. It is not unethical to offer free services in advertising the benefits of using a firm, providing those services are indeed supplied. Not to supply services offered as free is unethical. Using testimonials, guaranteeing future performance, and exaggerating the capabilities of the firm and its personnel are unethical. Note that none of these practices are fraudulent. QID: 38351

21. D. Although Treasury securities (such as T-notes) issued by the federal government do not carry default risk, the customer who buys them retains interest rates because the value of the notes will fall if interest rates rise. The agent (sales representative) has acted unlawfully in not disclosing this to the customer. QID: 31866

22. A. The antifraud provisions of the USA require an investment adviser to disclose before the completion of a transaction whether it will act as a principal or an agent. The adviser must disclose the fact that the adviser is a principal in the transaction whether the position is maintained or not. The adviser need not refuse the order but must disclose the conflict of interest to the client prior to execution of the trade. The adviser must disclose the conflict of interest to the client prior to executing the trade. QID: 29002

23. C. A publisher of a financial newspaper and a CPA who, as an incidental part of his practice, constructs portfolios of tax-sheltered investments is not an investment adviser. QID: 28823

24. D. The purchase of securities from a broker-dealer by an employee of a bank is a nonexempt transaction—it is a sale of a security by a broker-dealer to a member of the public and is therefore not exempt. Transactions between brokers and issuers; transactions between banks; and transactions between banks and insurance companies are exempt because they are transactions between financial institutions. In most cases, exempt transactions are those that do not affect the public. QID: 37170

25. D. Failure to bring customers' written complaints to the attention of an agent's broker-dealer is prohibited. QID: 31183

26. C. The agent has committed a fraudulent act by misrepresenting the value of the stock in order to encourage the customer to sell a security. QID: 28899

27. B. An offer to sell includes any attempt to dispose of a security for value. A stock dividend is not an offer or sale except in the unlikely case that the stockholder provides value in return. QID: 39211

28. B. A representative may not offer services that he cannot perform. A representative may participate actively in trading a security in which an unusually high trading volume has occurred, provided the trading is not designed to create a false appearance of high volume. A representative can alter a client's order, even if the effort is not in the interest of the client. A representative is only required to report written complaints to his employing principal, although it would be wise to report repeated complaints if they are serious. QID: 36368

29. A. If an investment adviser has custody of securities, a $35,000 cash bond or securities may be used instead of a fidelity bond. Fidelity bonds are also referred to as surety bonds in the USA. QID: 31083

30. D. Neither exempt securities nor exempt transactions are exempt from the USA's antifraud provisions. QID: 28840

31. D. If an adviser committed a felony or participated in unethical business practices, its registration will be revoked, not cancelled. An adviser's registration may be cancelled if the adviser is found to be mentally incompetent, cannot be located, or has ceased to do business. QID: 37183

32. C. Borrowing money or securities from a customer (regardless of friendship) is a prohibited practice. QID: 31830

33. C. Passing the Series 6 (mutual funds and variable annuities), Series 7 (general securities), or Series 22 (direct participation programs) qualifies an individual to solicit security sales on a federal level. The state Administrator must grant registration and the individual must be associated with a broker-dealer before the individual may engage in securities transactions. QID: 28925

34. D. An agent may conduct business in a state prior to registration if a registration is pending and the agent only conducts business with an existing customer or a customer who is in the state temporarily (less than 30 days). QID: 39223

35. C. Current clients must receive a brochure annually regardless of custody or discretion. New customers of an investment adviser must receive a brochure within 48 hours of signing an investment advisory client. These rules apply to both verbal and written contracts. QID: 36701

36. D. Agents are prohibited from soliciting sales for unregistered nonexempt securities. The broker-dealer who employs a rep who sells nonexempt, unregistered securities may be sued. The sales rep may be subject to criminal penalties. If money is made, the client may keep it. QID: 31086

37. C. Discussing the situation with a superior or compliance officer is the appropriate action. An agent may not solicit or trade on the basis of material inside information. Discussing material inside information in a public forum is prohibited whether or not an investment recommendation is made. QID: 28845

38. D. All of the statements are incorrect. A broker-dealer can be a natural person (human being) as opposed to a legal person (corporation or partnership). Although not a common practice, a broker-dealer can also be a sole proprietorship. A registered broker-dealer must have registered principals, but these principals need not sell securities to the public. If a registered principal is selling securities to the public, he is acting in the capacity of a registered representative. An investment adviser need not be a corporation; it can be a natural person. An investment adviser representative can be employed by a broker-dealer because many broker-dealers have subsidiaries that are registered as investment advisers. QID: 38338

39. C. The agent must refuse the order because the customer did not authorize it. The USA prohibits the acceptance of orders on behalf of customers from persons who have not been granted third-party trading authority. QID: 31859

40. B. Under the USA, a private placement is the sale of unregistered, nonexempt securities to 10 or fewer nonaccredited investors in a 12-month period. The security is not exempt, but the transaction is. The investor will receive a certificate for nonexempt securities. QID: 31068

41. C. ABC Investment Partners must promptly notify its clients of Clark's departure. Under the Uniform Securities Act, any change to the membership of a partnership requires the partnership to promptly notify all investors of the change. ABC has no obligation to notify Clark Advisers of Clark's new employment. QID: 40235

42. A. A state Administrator has the authority to revoke a security's exemption without prior notice to the issuer. An exempt issuer can be charged for criminal or civil liability under the antifraud provisions of the USA. A security exempt from registration need not comply with the advertising and sales filing requirements of the act. An exempt security can be solicited. QID: 37151

43. C. Unsolicited secondary market transactions are exempt, as are transactions between issuers and underwriters and transactions between broker-dealers and institutional investors (such as insurance companies). A nonissuer sale of an outstanding security subject to reporting and registration requirements under the Act of 1934 is exempt only if it has been subject to these requirements for 180 days (six months). QID: 31177

44. B. Income-oriented clients authorize their agents to buy income-producing securities not speculative securities. Purchasing speculative securities would therefore be an unauthorized transaction and would not be consistent with the account's objectives. QID: 28883

45. C. The securities of banks, trust companies, and savings institutions are exempt. The securities of bank holding companies are not. QID: 39203

46. B. Registration by coordination and by filing do not require a specific response from the state Administrator. QID: 36354

47. D. It is permissible to sell rights, which are securities. Borrowing money or securities from other than a bank and failing to identify a customer's financial objectives are prohibited prac-

tices. Failing to identify a customer's financial objectives and guaranteeing a customer's account against losses are also prohibited practices. QID: 28934

48. A. If XYZ is a federal covered security listed on the NYSE it is not required to register with the state. Nonexempt securities and nonexempt persons must be registered to be sold (securities) or to do business (persons). QID: 40211

49. C. An agent is any individual other than a broker-dealer who represents a broker-dealer in effecting securities transactions. An individual who sells foreign securities is an agent under the terms of the USA. An individual who sells commercial paper for a broker-dealer is an agent of that broker-dealer. QID: 37158

50. C. The security has a backer (such as an insurance company or a parent company) that has guaranteed the payment of principal, interest, or dividends. A guarantee does not refer to a broker-dealer buying back a security at the same price or higher, or to the retirement income offered by an annuity. The SEC does not back or guarantee securities. QID: 31171

51. C. Implying that dollar cost averaging or dividend reinvestment will automatically produce profit for a mutual fund customer is misleading regardless of the fund's past performance. The statement is misleading whether or not the fund has increased in value within the previous 10 years. QID: 28863

52. D. Smith must register as an investment adviser in New York State when or if he is offering investment advice as an integral part of his practice. Since his place of business is in New York, he must register in New York as an investment adviser, even though his clients are not themselves resident in the state. If Mr. Smith advises his wife, who also has an office in New York State, that her investment in 15 technology stocks is too high, he need not register in New York State because he is not charging his wife a fee for investment advice. Mr. Smith, as a securities lawyer, need not register in New York State as an investment adviser. He is simply practicing law when he advises clients on the construction of trust documents. QID: 38313

53. B. You must be licensed in both insurance and securities to sell variable annuities as well as to split commissions. Commissions on securities transactions may only be split with registered agents. QID: 31843

54. A. An occasional (unsolicited) interstate transaction is an exempt transaction. QID: 31069

55. C. The state Administrator does not approve securities. QID: 28910

56. A. Investment in a Treasury bill is the only suitable investment among the choices listed. Purchase of annuities and a real estate partnership are high commission long-term investments not suitable to an individual who wants to invest funds on a short-term basis. Although an IPO may be liquid, it is not suitable for short-term funds earmarked for the purchase of a house because commissions are high and there is too much risk to capital. QID: 37174

57. A. Under the USA, it is a prohibited practice under the USA for a sales rep to share in the profits or losses of a customer's account unless the customer and the employer have given written consent and the percentage of participation is proportionate to the percentage of the sales rep's personal funds in the account. A sales rep is permitted to jointly own a personal account at the firm. An agent is permitted to refuse to share in a customer's account. QID: 31824

58. C. Telephone company records are not required to be kept unless the Administrator specifically rules that they must be kept. Memoranda, correspondence, and account books must be kept. QID: 36378

59. A. Choices III and IV represent exempt securities, not exempt transactions. A transaction between an issuer and underwriter and an unsolicited customer order to buy an exempt security are exempt transactions. QID: 39220

60. C. When material information changes, the registrant must amend or update the information promptly regardless of the renewal date. The requirement to amend registration upon a material change to the registration also apples to investment advisers, broker-dealers, and securities. However, the Uniform Securities Act does not define the term "promptly." QID: 40239

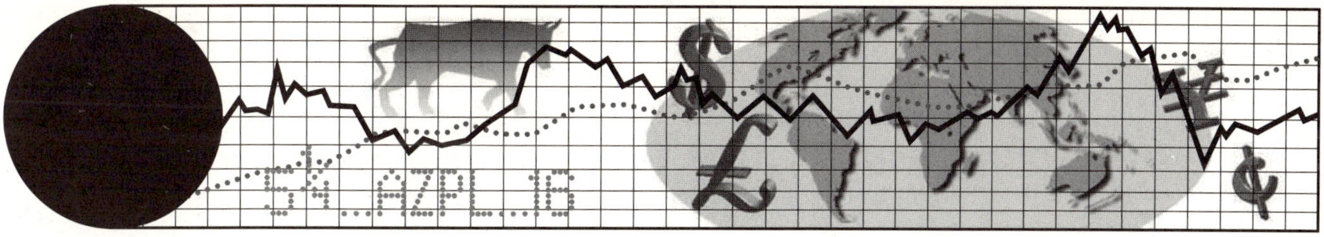

Appendix A

Federal Securities Laws

The following federal laws serve as the regulatory framework for the securities industry.

The Securities Act of 1933

The Securities Act of 1933, also known as the Paper Act, requires companies that intend to sell their securities to the public through interstate commerce or the mail to register the securities with the Securities and Exchange Commission (SEC) by filing a prospectus and a registration statement.

The act requires the full and fair disclosure of relevant information in the prospectus for investors to obtain information necessary to make informed decisions. Its purpose is to prevent fraud in the sale of new issues. The SEC does not review or pass on the investment merit of securities or companies issuing securities.

✓ ***Take Note:*** Certain issuers of securities are not subject to the registration and filing requirements of the Act of 1933. These **exempt issuers** include the U.S. government, municipalities, nonprofit organizations, and banks.

The Securities Exchange Act of 1934

The 1934 Act created the Securities and Exchange Commission which was given responsibility and authority to regulate the securities markets. The

SEC is made up of five commissioners appointed by the President of the United States and approved by the Senate. The SEC's primary responsibility is to enforce the 1934 act, the major provisions of which address the:

- registration and regulation of the exchanges;
- regulation of credit and margin requirements (currently 50%) set by the Federal Reserve Board (FRB) through Regulation T (Reg T);
- registration of broker-dealers that trade securities on national exchanges or over-the-counter (OTC);
- registration of persons effecting securities transactions with the public;
- regulation of insider transactions, short sales, and proxies;
- regulation of trading activities;
- regulation of client accounts;
- customer protection rule;
- regulation of the self-regulatory organizations, such as the National Association of Securities Dealers (NASD) and the Municipal Securities Rulemaking Board (MSRB);
- regulation of the OTC market; and
- net capital requirements for broker-dealers.

The SEC has established rules regarding net capital requirements for broker-dealers, hypothecation (pledging) of customers' securities, commingling (mixing) of broker-dealer securities with those of customers, using manipulative and deceptive devices, and broker-dealer recordkeeping.

The SEC enforces the Securities Exchange Act of 1934 and others by providing rules and prescribing penalties for violations. SROs, such as the NASD, are required to assist the SEC in its enforcement practices by establishing rules and trade practices that their member firms must follow. However, the SEC's jurisdiction does not extend to violations of banking rules. The Commission has preemptive authority over the rules established by the Uniform Securities Act or state securities Administrators.

In addition to the registration of exchanges, the Act of 1934 requires companies that list securities on those exchanges to register with the SEC. Each listed company must file quarterly statements on Form 10Q and annual statements on Form 10K informing the SEC of its financial status.

✓ ***Take Note:*** Although some securities are exempt from the registration provisions of the Securities Act of 1933, no securities are exempt from the antifraud provisions of the Act of 1934. Fraudulent practices never can be used in the sale of any security.

Public Utility Holding Company Act of 1935

The Public Utility Holding Company Act requires the registration of all public holding companies engaged in the electric utility business or in the retail distribution of gas unless exempted by rule or order.

Maloney Act of 1938

The Maloney Act, an amendment to the Securities Exchange Act of 1934, authorized the establishment and registration of national self-regulatory organizations such as the NASD. Broker-dealers must be members of such organizations to transact securities business.

Trust Indenture Act of 1939

The Trust Indenture Act of 1939 requires that each public issue of debt securities exceeding $5 million in a 12-month period be issued under a trust indenture. A trustee must ensure that the indenture includes specific provisions for the protection of the bondholders.

Investment Advisers Act of 1940

The Investment Advisers Act of 1940 provides for the registration and regulation of investment advisers. It prohibits deceptive practices between advisers and their clients and requires that advisers make certain disclosures to prospective clients, including their fees, backgrounds, and methods of transacting business.

Investment Company Act of 1940

The Investment Company Act of 1940 provides for SEC registration and regulation of investment companies, including open-end investment companies (mutual funds), closed-end investment companies, unit investment trusts (UITs), and insurance company separate accounts.

Securities Investor Protection Act of 1970

The Securities Investor Protection Corporation (SIPC) was established in 1970 with the passage of the Securities Investor Protection Act. The purpose of the act is to protect customers of securities firms that go bankrupt.

SIPC oversees the liquidation of bankrupt firms and provides coverage of up to $500,000 in cash and securities to each customer of the firms.

Insider Trading and Securities Fraud Enforcement Act of 1988

The Insider Trading and Securities Fraud Enforcement Act of 1988 expanded the definition of, and the liabilities and penalties for, the unlawful use of nonpublic information prohibited by the Securities Exchange Act of 1934. An insider is any person who has access to nonpublic information about a corporation. Insiders may not use inside information as a basis for personal trading or benefit until that information has been made public.

Written Supervisory Procedures

All broker-dealers must establish, maintain, and enforce written supervisory procedures specifically prohibiting the use of material nonpublic information by all persons interested in, affiliated with, or in any way engaged in the broker-dealers' securities-related activities.

Criminal Penalties

The criminal penalties for violations of securities laws were increased through the 1988 Insider Trading and Securities Fraud Enforcement Act. Persons convicted of violating the act can be fined the greater of $1 million or 300% of profits received or losses avoided, sentenced to prison for up to 10 years, or both.

Telephone Consumer Protection Act of 1991

The Telephone Consumer Protection Act of 1991 (TCPA), administered by the Federal Communications Commission (FCC), was enacted to protect consumers from unwanted telephone solicitations, including recorded autodialer solicitations and facsimile machine and modem (email) solicitations.

The act requires any organization that performs telemarketing (in particular, cold calling) to:

- maintain a *Do-Not-Call* list of customers who do not want to be called and keep a prospective customer's name on the list for 10 years from the time the request is made;
- institute a written policy, available on demand, regarding maintenance procedures for the *Do-Not-Call* list;
- train reps to use the list;
- ensure that reps acknowledge and immediately record the names and telephone numbers of customers who ask not to be called again; and
- call the homes of prospective customers only between the hours of 8:00 a.m. and 9:00 p.m. in the prospective customers' time zones.

✓ ***Take Note:*** This act also applies to broker-dealers.

National Securities Markets Improvement Act of 1996

The National Securities Markets Improvement Act of 1996 (NSMIA) expanded the SEC's role to include improvement and oversight of:

- market efficiency;
- competition in the securities industry;
- capital formation;
- elimination of regulations that no longer serve the public interest; and
- elimination of the dual state and federal regulation.

Under NSMIA, the SEC eliminated the dual regulation of securities by defining those securities covered by federal law as "federal covered securities" which no longer can be subject to state registration.

Because of its role in coordinating the activities of the various securities regulators, this act sometimes is referred to as the Coordination Act.

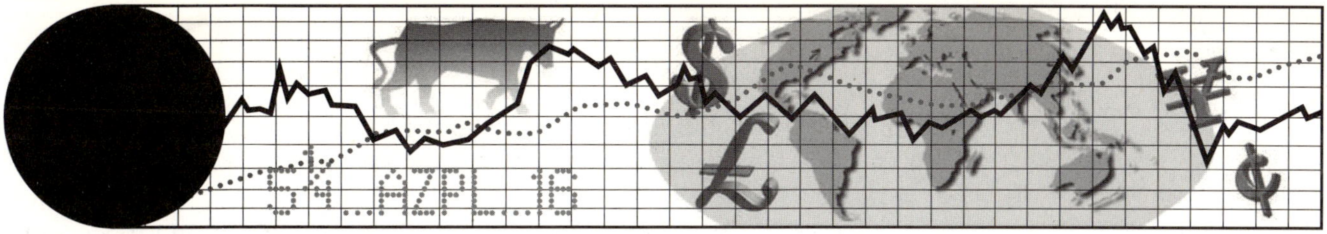

Appendix B

NASAA's Statement of Policy

Dishonest or Unethical Business Practices by Broker-Dealers and Agents in Connection with Investment Company Shares

NASAA Broker-Dealer Sales Practice Committee Adopted 4/27/97

Any broker-dealer or agent who engages in one or more of the following practices shall be deemed to have engaged in "dishonest or unethical practices in the securities business" as used in Section 204 of the Uniform Securities Act and such conduct may constitute grounds for denial, suspension, or revocation of registration or such other action authorized by statute.

A. Sales Load Communications:

1. In connection with the solicitation of investment company shares, failing to adequately disclose to a customer all sales charges, including asset based and contingent deferred sales charges, which may be imposed with respect to the purchase, retention or redemption of such shares.

2. In connection with the solicitation of investment company shares, stating or implying to a customer that the shares are sold without a commission, are "no load," or have "no sales charge" if there is associated with the purchase of the shares: (i) a front-end load; (ii) a contingent deferred sales load; (iii) a SEC Rule 12b-1 fee or a service fee if such fees in total exceed .25% of average net fund assets per year; or (iv) in the case of closed-end investment company shares, underwriting fees, commissions, or other offering expenses.

3. In connection with the solicitation of investment company shares, failing to disclose to any customer any relevant: (i) sales charge discount on the pur-

chase of shares in dollar amounts at or above a breakpoint; or (ii) letter of intent feature, if available, which will reduce the sales charges.

4. In connection with the solicitation of investment company shares, recommending to a customer the purchase of a specific class of investment company shares in connection with a multi-class sales charge or fee arrangement without reasonable grounds to believe that the sales charge or fee arrangement associated with such class of shares is suitable and appropriate based on the customer's investment objectives, financial situation, other securities holdings, and the associated transaction or other fees.

B. Recommendations:

1. In connection with the solicitation of investment company shares, recommending to a customer the purchase of investment company shares which results in the customer simultaneously holding shares in different investment company portfolios having similar investment objectives and policies without reasonable grounds to believe that such recommendation is suitable and appropriate based on the customer's investment objectives, financial situation and other securities holdings and any associated transaction charges or other fees.

2. In connection with the solicitation of investment company shares, recommending to a customer the liquidation or redemption of investment company shares for the purpose of purchasing shares in a different investment company portfolio having similar investment objectives and policies without reasonable grounds to believe that such recommendation is suitable and appropriate based on the customer's investment objectives, financial situation and other securities holdings and any associated transaction charges or other fees.

C. Disclosure:

1. In connection with the solicitation of investment company shares, stating or implying to a customer the fund's current yield or income without disclosing the fund's most recent average annual return, calculated in a manner prescribed in SEC Form N-1A, for one, five and ten year periods and fully explaining the difference between current yield and total return; provided, however, that the fund's registration statement under the Securities Act of 1933 has been in effect for less than one, five, or ten years, the time during which the registration statement was in effect shall be substituted for the periods otherwise prescribed.

2. In connection with the solicitation of investment company shares, stating or implying to a customer that the investment performance of an investment company portfolio is comparable to that of a savings account, certificate of deposit or other bank deposit account without disclosing to the customer that the shares are not insured or otherwise guaranteed by the FDIC or any other government agency and the relevant differences regarding risk, guar-

antees, fluctuation of principal and/or return, and any other factors which are necessary to ensure that such comparisons are fair, complete and not misleading.

3. In connection with the solicitation of investment company shares, stating or implying to a customer the existence of insurance, credit quality, guarantees or similar features regarding securities held, or proposed to be held, in the investment company's portfolio without disclosing to the customer other kinds of relevant investment risks, including but not limited to, interest rate, market, political, liquidity, or currency exchange risks, which may adversely affect investment performance and result in loss and/or fluctuation of principal notwithstanding the creditworthiness of such portfolio securities.

4. In connection with the solicitation of investment company shares, stating or implying to a customer: (i) that the purchase of such shares shortly before an ex-dividend date is advantageous to such customer unless there are specific, clearly described tax or other advantages to the customer; or (ii) that a distribution of long-term capital gains by an investment company is part of the income yield from an investment in such shares.

5. In connection with the solicitation of investment company shares, making: (i) projections of future performance; (ii) statements not warranted under existing circumstances; or (iii) statements based upon non-public information.

D. Prospectus:

In connection with the solicitation of investment company shares, the delivery of a prospectus, in and of itself, shall not be dispositive that the broker-dealer or agent provided the customer full and fair disclosure.

E. Definitions:

For the purpose of this rule, the following terms shall mean:

1. "Recommend": any affirmative act or statement that endorses, solicits, requests, or commends a securities transaction to a customer or any affirmative act or statement that solicits, requests, commands, importunes or intentionally aids such person to engage in such conduct.

2. "Solicitation": any oral, written or other communication used to offer or sell investment company shares excluding any proxy statement, report to shareholders, or other disclosure document relating to a security covered under Section 18(b)(2) of the Securities Act of 1933 that is required to be and is filed with the Commission or any national securities organization registered under Section 15A of the Securities Exchange Act of 1934.

(Note: This Statement of Policy is intended to supplement, not supplant, the NASAA Statement of Policy Regarding the Dishonest or Unethical Business Practices.)

Unethical Business Practices of Investment Advisers

Amended 4/27/1997, Adopted in 1985

A person who is an investment adviser or a federal covered adviser is a fiduciary and has a duty to act primarily for the benefit of its clients. The provisions of this subsection apply to federal covered advisers to the extent that the conduct alleged is fraudulent, deceptive, or as otherwise permitted by the National Securities Markets Improvement Act of 1996 (Pub. L. No. 104-290). While the extent and nature of this duty varies according to the nature of the relationship between an investment adviser and its clients and the circumstances of each case, an investment adviser or a federal covered adviser shall not engage in unethical business practices, including the following:

1. Recommending to a client to whom supervisory, management or consulting services are provided the purchase, sale or exchange of any security without reasonable grounds to believe that the recommendation is suitable for the client on the basis of information furnished by the client after reasonable inquiry concerning the client's investment objectives, financial situation and needs, and any other information known by the investment adviser.

2. Exercising any discretionary power in placing an order for the purchase or sale of securities for a client without obtaining written discretionary authority from the client within ten (10) business days after the date of the first transaction placed pursuant to oral discretionary authority, unless the discretionary power relates solely to the price at which, or the time when, an order involving a definite amount of a specified security shall be executed, or both.

3. Inducing trading in a client's account that is excessive in size or frequency in view of the financial resources, investment objectives and character of the account in light of the fact that an adviser in such situations can directly benefit from the number of securities transactions effected in a client's account. The rule appropriately forbids an excessive number of transaction orders to be induced by an adviser for a "customer's account."

4. Placing an order to purchase or sell a security for the account of a client without authority to do so.

5. Placing an order to purchase or sell a security for the account of a client upon instruction of a third party without first having obtained a written third-party trading authorization from the client.

6. Borrowing money or securities from a client unless the client is a broker-dealer, an affiliate of the investment adviser, or a financial institution engaged in the business of loaning funds.

7. Loaning money to a client unless the investment adviser is a financial institution engaged in the business of loaning funds or the client is an affiliate of the investment adviser.

8. To misrepresent to any advisory client, or prospective advisory client, the qualifications of the investment adviser or any employee of the investment adviser, or to misrepresent the nature of the advisory services being offered or fees to be charged for such service, or to omit to state a material fact necessary to make the statements made regarding qualifications, services or fees, in light of the circumstances under which they are made, not misleading.

9. Providing a report or recommendation to any advisory client prepared by someone other than the adviser without disclosing that fact. (This prohibition does not apply to a situation where the adviser uses published research reports or statistical analyses to render advice or where an adviser orders such a report in the normal course of providing service.)

10. Charging a client an unreasonable advisory fee.

11. Failing to disclose to clients in writing before any advice is rendered any material conflict of interest relating to the adviser or any of its employees which could reasonably be expected to impair the rendering of unbiased and objective advice including:

(a) Compensation arrangements connected with advisory services to clients which are in addition to compensation from such clients for such services; and

(b) Charging a client an advisory fee for rendering advice when a commission for executing securities transactions pursuant to such advice will be received by the adviser or its employees.

12. Guaranteeing a client that a specific result will be achieved (gain or no loss) with advice which will be rendered.

13. Publishing, circulating or distributing any advertisement which does not comply with Rule 206 (4)-1 under the Investment Advisers Act of 1940.

14. Disclose the identity, affairs, or investments of any client unless required by law to do so, or unless consented to by the client.

15. Taking any action, directly or indirectly, with respect to those securities or funds in which any client has any beneficial interest, where the investment adviser has custody or possession of such securities or funds when the advisor's action is subject to and does not comply with the requirements of Reg. 2O6 (4)-2 under the Investment Advisers Act of 1940.

16. Entering into, extending or renewing any investment advisory contract unless such contract is in writing and discloses, in substance, the services to be provided, the term of the contract, the advisory fee, the formula for computing the fee, the amount of prepaid fee to be returned in the event of contract termination or nonperformance, whether the contract grants discretionary power to the adviser and that no assignment of such contract shall be made by the investment adviser without the consent of the other party to the contract.

17. Failing to establish, maintain, and enforce written policies and procedures reasonably designed to prevent the misuse of material nonpublic information contrary to the provisions of Section 204A of the Investment Advisers Act of 1940.

18. Entering into, extending, or renewing any advisory contract contrary to the provisions of Section 205 of the Investment Advisers Act of 1940. This provision shall apply to all advisers registered or required to be registered under this act, notwithstanding whether such adviser would be exempt from federal registration pursuant to Section 203 (b) of the Investment Advisers Act of 1940.

19. To indicate, in an advisory contract, any condition, stipulation, or provisions binding any person to waive compliance with any provision of this act or of the Investment Advisers Act of 1940, or any other practice contrary to the provisions of Section 215 of the Investment Advisers Act of 1940.

20. Engaging in any act, practice, or course of business which is fraudulent, deceptive, or manipulative in contrary to the provisions of Section 206 (4) of the Investment Advisers Act of 1940, notwithstanding the fact that such investment adviser is not registered or required to be registered under Section 203 of the Investment Advisers Act of 1940.

21. Engaging in conduct or any act, indirectly or through or by any other person, which would be unlawful for such person to do directly under the provisions of this act or any rule or regulation thereunder. The conduct set forth above is not inclusive. Engaging in other conduct such as nondisclosure, incomplete disclosure, or deceptive practices shall be deemed an unethical business practice.

The federal statutory and regulatory provisions referenced herein shall apply to investment advisers and federal covered advisers, to the extent permitted by the National Securities Markets Improvement Act of 1996 (Pub. L. No. 104-290).

Dishonest or Unethical Business Practices of Broker-Dealers and Agents

Adopted May 23, 1983

HIGH STANDARDS AND JUST PRINCIPLES. Each broker-dealer and agent shall observe high standards of commercial honor and just and equitable principles of trade in the conduct of their business. Acts and practices, including but not limited to the following, are considered contrary to such standards and may constitute grounds for denial, suspension or revocation of registration or such other action authorized by statute.

1. Broker-Dealers

a. Engaging in a pattern of unreasonable and unjustifiable delays in the delivery of securities purchased by any of its customers and/or in the payment upon request of free credit balances reflecting completed transactions of any of its customers.

b. Inducing trading in a customer's account which is excessive in size or frequency in view of the financial resources and character of the account.

c. Recommending to a customer the purchase, sale or exchange of any security without reasonable grounds to believe that such transaction or recommendation is suitable for the customer based upon reasonable inquiry concerning the customer's investment objectives, financial situation and needs, and any other relevant information known by the broker-dealer.

d. Executing a transaction on behalf of a customer without authorization to do so.

e. Exercising any discretionary power in effecting a transaction for a customer's account without first obtaining written discretionary authority from the customer, unless the discretionary power relates solely to the time and/or price for the executing of orders.

f. Executing any transaction in a margin account without securing from the customer a properly executed written margin agreement promptly after the initial transaction in the account.

g. Failing to segregate customers' free securities or securities held in safekeeping.

h. Hypothecating a customer's securities without having a lien thereon unless the broker-dealer secures from the customer a properly executed written consent promptly after the initial transaction, except as permitted by Rules of the Securities and Exchange Commission.

i. Entering into a transaction with or for a customer at a price not reasonably related to the current market price of the security or receiving an unreasonable commission or profit.

j. Failing to furnish to a customer purchasing securities in an offering, no later than the due date of confirmation of the transaction, either a final prospectus or a preliminary prospectus and an additional document, which together include all information set forth in the final prospectus.

k. Charging unreasonable and inequitable fees for services performed, including miscellaneous services such as collection of monies due for principal, dividends or interest, exchange or transfer of securities, appraisals, safekeeping, or custody of securities and other services related to its securities business.

l. Offering to buy from or sell to any person any security at a stated price unless such broker-dealer is prepared to purchase or sell, as the case may be, at such price and under such conditions as are stated at the time of such offer to buy or sell.

m. Representing that a security is being offered to a customer "at the market" or a price relevant to the market price unless such broker-dealer knows or has reasonable grounds to believe that a market for such security exists other than that made, created or controlled by such broker-dealer, or by any such person for whom he is acting or with whom he is associated in such distribution, or any person controlled by, controlling or under common control with such broker-dealer.

n. Effecting any transaction in, or inducing the purchase or sale of, any security by means of any manipulative, deceptive or fraudulent device, practice, plan, program, design or contrivance, which may include but not be limited to:

(1) Effecting any transaction in a security which involves no change in the beneficial ownership thereof;

(2) Entering an order or orders for the purchase or sale of any security with the knowledge that an order or orders of substantially the same size, at substantially the same time and substantially the same price, for the sale of any such security, has been or will be entered by or for the same or different parties for the purpose of creating a false or misleading appearance of active trading in the security or a false or misleading appearance with respect to the market for the security; provided, however, nothing in this subsection shall prohibit a broker-dealer from entering bona fide agency cross transactions for its customers; or

(3) Effecting, alone or with one or more other persons, a series of transactions in any security creating actual or apparent active trading in such security or raising or depressing the price of such security, for the purpose of inducing the purchase or sale of such security by others.

o. Guaranteeing a customer against loss in any securities account of such customer carried by the broker-dealer or in any securities transaction effected by the broker-dealer or in any securities transaction effected by the broker-dealer with or for such customer.

p. Publishing or circulating, or causing to be published or circulated, any notice, circular, advertisement, newspaper article, investment service, or communication of any kind which purports to report any transaction as a purchase or sale of any security unless such broker-dealer believes that such transaction was a bona fide purchase or sale or such security; or which purports to quote the bid price or asked price for any security, unless such broker-dealer believes that such quotation represents a bona fide bid for, or offer of, such security.

q. Using any advertising or sales presentation in such a fashion as to be deceptive or misleading. An example of such practice would be a distribution of any nonfactual data, material or presentation based on conjecture, unfounded or unrealistic claims or assertions in any brochure, flyer, or display by words, pictures, graphs or otherwise designed to supplement, detract from, supersede or defeat the purpose or effect of any prospectus or disclosure.

r. Failing to disclose that the broker-dealer is controlled by, controlling, affiliated with or under common control with the issuer of any security before entering into any contract with or for a customer for the purchase or sale of such security, the existence of such control to such customer, and if such disclosure is not made in writing, it shall be supplemented by the giving or sending of written disclosure at or before the completion of the transaction.

s. Failing to make a bona fide public offering of all of the securities allotted to a broker-dealer for distribution, whether acquired as an underwriter, a selling group member, or from a member participating in the distribution as an underwriter or selling group member.

t. Failure or refusal to furnish a customer, upon reasonable request, information to which he is entitled, or to respond to a formal written request or complaint.

2. Agents

a. Engaging in the practice of lending or borrowing money or securities from a customer, or acting as a custodian for money, securities or an executed stock power of a customer.

b. Effecting securities transactions not recorded on the regular books or records of the broker-dealer which the agent represents, unless the transactions are authorized in writing by the broker-dealer prior to execution of the transaction.

c. Establishing or maintaining an account containing fictitious information in order to execute transactions which would otherwise be prohibited.

d. Sharing directly or indirectly in profits or losses in the account of any customer without the written authorization of the customer and the broker-dealer which the agent represents.

e. Dividing or otherwise splitting the agent's commissions, profits or other compensation from the purchase or sale of securities with any person not also registered as an agent for the same broker-dealer, or for a broker-dealer under direct or indirect common control.

f. Engaging in conduct specified in Subsection 1.b, c, d, e, f, i, j, n, o, p, or q.

CONDUCT NOT INCLUSIVE. The conduct set forth above is not inclusive. Engaging in other conduct such as forgery, embezzlement, nondisclosure, incomplete disclosure or misstatement of material facts, or manipulative or deceptive practices shall also be grounds for denial, suspension or revocation of registration.

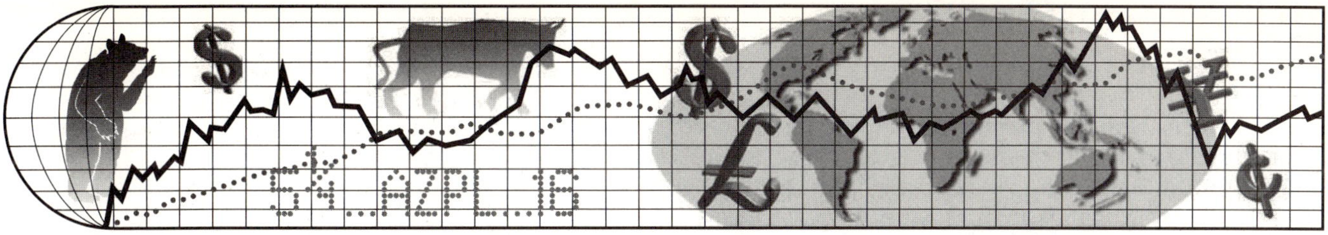

Glossary

A

accredited investor Any institution or individual meeting minimum net worth requirements for the purchase of securities qualifying under the Regulation D registration exemption, as defined in Rule 502 of Regulation D.

An accredited investor generally is accepted to be one who:

- has a net worth of $1 million or more; or
- has had an annual income of $200,000 or more in each of the two most recent years (or $300,000 jointly with a spouse) and who has a reasonable expectation of reaching the same income level in the current year.

administrator (1) A person authorized by a court of law to liquidate the estate of an intestate decedent. (2) The official or agency administering the securities laws of a state.

advertisement Any material designed for use by newspapers, magazines, radio, television, telephone recording, or any other public medium to solicit business. The firm using advertising has little control over the type of individuals being exposed to the advertising. *See also* sales literature.

advertising prospectus An investment company prospectus that includes the fund's performance data, as well as standardized information contained in the summary prospectus.

affiliate Any person directly or indirectly owning, controlling, or holding (with power to vote) 10% or more of the outstanding voting securities of another person. Also, any officer, director, or partner of another entity for which such person acts in such capacity.

When used with respect to a member or sponsor, "affiliate" means any person who controls, is controlled by, or is under control with such member or sponsor and includes:

- any partner, officer, or director (or any person performing similar functions) of such member or sponsor or a person who beneficially owns 50% or more of the equity interest in, or who has the power to vote 50% or more of the voting interest in, such member or sponsor; or
- any person who beneficially owns or has the right to acquire 10% or more of the equity interest in or who has the power to vote 10% or more of the voting interest in, such member or sponsor, or a person who beneficially owns 50% or more of the voting interest in, or who has the power to vote 50% or more of the voting interest in, such member or sponsor.

agent (1) An individual acting for the accounts of others; also, any person licensed by a state as a life insurance agent. *Syn.* broker. (2) A securities salesperson who represents a broker-dealer or an issuer when selling or trying to sell securities to the investing public. This individual is considered an agent whether he actually receives or simply solicits orders. An agent is anyone who receives an order while representing a broker-dealer.

assignment (1) A document accompanying or part of a stock certificate that is signed by the person named on the certificate for the purpose of transferring the certificate's title to another person's name. (2) The act of identifying and notifying an account holder that an option held short in that account has been exercised by the option owner.

associated person of a member (AP) Any employee, manager, director, officer, or partner of a member broker-dealer or another entity (issuer, bank, etc.) or any person controlling, controlled by, or in common control with that member is considered an associated person of that member.

B

blue-sky To qualify a securities offering in a particular state.

blue-sky laws The commonly-used for state regulations governing the securities industry.

broker (1) An individual or a firm that charges a fee or commission for executing buy and sell orders submitted by another individual or firm. (2) The role of a broker firm when it acts as an agent for a customer and charges the customer a commission for its services. *See also* agent.

broker-dealer (1) An individual or a firm that charges a fee or commission for executing buy and sell orders submitted by another individual or firm. (2) The role of a broker firm when it acts as an agent for a customer and charges the customer a commission for its services.

The term "broker-dealer" is defined in the Uniform Securities Act so that it can be determined who must register in the state as a broker-dealer. If the person does not fall under the definition of broker-dealer as defined by the law, the registration process is not necessary. The following persons are not classified as broker-dealers.

- Agents (registered representatives)
- Issuers
- Banks, savings institutions or trust companies
- Persons who have no place of business in the state and who: (a) effect securities transactions in the state exclusively through the issuers of the securities, other broker-dealers, or financial institutions (banks, savings institutions, trust companies, insurance companies, and investment companies) or (b) directs an offer in this state to an existing customer who has less than 30 days' temporary residency in the state where the offer is received.

C

churning A prohibited practice in which a salesperson effects transactions in a customer's account which are excessive in size and/or frequency in relation to the size and character of the account.

commission A broker's fee for handling transactions for a client in an agency capacity.

consent to service of process A legal agreement entered into by all registrants, whereby the administrator is given the power to accept legal papers on behalf of the registrant.

custodian A commercial bank or trust company that holds monies and securities owned by an investment company in safekeeping.

custody Maintaining possession of a customer's money and/or securities. Many states prohibit investment advisors from keeping custody. The others require the adviser to notify the Administrator if it intends to do so.

D

dealer The role of a brokerage firm when it acts as a principal in a particular trade. A firm is acting as a dealer when it buys or sells a security for its own account and at its own risk and then charges the customer a markup or markdown. Any person who is engaged in the business of buying and selling securities for her own account either directly or through a broker, and who is not a bank, is considered a dealer. *Syn.* principal.

debenture An unsecured long-term debt offering by a corporation, promising only the general assets as protection for these creditors.

discretion The authority for someone other than the beneficial owner of an account to make investment decisions for that account regarding the security, the number of shares or units, and whether to buy or sell. Decisions concerning only timing and price do not constitute discretion.

discretionary account An account in which the customer authorizes in writing a registered representative to use his judgement in buying and selling securities, including selection, timing, amount, and price. Judgement as to time and/or price only is not considered discretion.

E

effective date The date on which a security can be offered publicly if no stop order is submitted to the issuer by the Administrator.

exempt security A security exempt from the registration requirements (although not from the antifraud requirements) of the Securities Act of 1933 (e.g., U.S. government and municipal securities).

exempt transaction A transaction exempt from registration, sales literature, and advertising requirements under the Uniform Securities Act. Examples of exempt transactions include:

- isolated nonissuer transactions;
- nonissuer transactions in outstanding securities (normal market trading);
- transactions with financial institutions (banks, savings institutions, trust companies, insurance companies, pension or profit-sharing plans, broker-dealers, etc.);
- unsolicited transactions;
- fiduciary transactions;
- private placement transactions;
- transactions between an issuer and its underwriters; and
- transactions with an issuer's employees, partners or directors if no commission is paid directly or indirectly for the soliciting.

Exemption from the act's registration and advertising requirements does not mean that a transaction is exempt from the act's antifraud provisions.

F

fidelity bond *See* surety bond.

fiduciary A person legally appointed and authorized to represent another person and act on their behalf.

fraud The deliberate concealment, misrepresentation, or omission of material information or the truth to deceive or manipulate another party for unlawful or unfair gain.

G

government security An obligation of the U.S. government, backed by the full faith and credit of the government, and regarded as the highest grade or safest issue (i.e., default risk-free). The U.S. government issues short-term Treasury bills, medium-term Treasury notes and long-term Treasury bonds.

guaranteed Securities that have a guarantee, usually from a source other than the issuer, as to the payment of principal, interest or dividends.

I

inside information Material and nonpublic information obtained or used by a person for the purpose of trading in securities. *See also* material fact.

insider Any person who has nonpublic knowledge (material information) about a corporation. Insiders include directors, officers, and stockholders who own more than 10% of any class of equity security of a corporation.

institutional account An account held for the benefit of others. Examples include banks, trusts, pension and profit-sharing plans, mutual funds, and insurance companies.

institutional investor A person or an organization that trades securities in large enough share quantities or dollar amounts that it qualifies for preferential treatment and lower trade costs (commissions). Institutional investors are covered by fewer protective regulations because it is assumed that they are more knowledgeable and better able to protect themselves.

investment adviser Any person who, for compensation (a flat fee or a percentage of assets managed), offers investment advice. For investment companies, the adviser has the day-to-day responsibility of investing the cash and securities held in a mutual fund's portfolio. The adviser must adhere to the objectives as stated in the fund's prospectus. This definition includes persons who issue written reports or analyses for compensation. The term "investment adviser" does not include:

- institutions such as banks, savings institutions, or trust companies;
- professionals such as lawyers, accountants or teachers whose performance of these services is solely incidental to the practice of their profession;
- broker-dealers that offer investment portfolio advice as part of their business of being broker-dealers and that receive no special compensation for that service;
- publishers of any financial publication of general, regular, and paid circulation; however, a

person who sells subscriptions to investment advisory publications (market letters) is considered an investment adviser under the USA;
- persons whose investment advice relates only to U.S. government securities and certain municipal securities; and
- persons having no place of business within the state and whose activities are limited to (a) professional clients (institutions) or (b) a very few solicitations or sales to clients other than those mentioned above. (e.g., less than six clients in any 12 consecutive months).

The term "investment adviser" can exclude any person that the state Administrator of the USA decides not to include.

investment adviser representative Any partner, officer, director or other individual employed by or associated with an investment adviser who (1) gives investment advice or makes recommendations, (2) manages client accounts or portfolios, (3) determines which investment recommendations or advice should be given, (4) offers or sells investment advisory services, or (5) supervises employees involved in any of these activities.

Investment Advisers Act of 1940 Legislation passed by Congress that requires all investment advisers to register as such with the SEC and to abide by the Investment Advisers Act of 1940 and all other applicable federal acts.

investment company A company engaged primarily in the business of investing and trading in securities, including face-amount certificate companies, unit investment trusts, and management companies.

Investment Company Act of 1940 Congressional legislation enacted to regulate investment companies that requires any investment company in interstate commerce to register with the SEC.

issuer (1) The corporation or municipality that offers its securities for sale; also, the creator of an option (the issuer of an over-the-counter option is the option writer and the issuer of a listed option is the Options Clearing Corporation). (2) According to the USA, any person who issues or proposes to issue any security.

When a corporation or municipality raises additional capital through an offering of securities, that corporation or municipality is the issuer of those securities. An issuer transaction is also called a **primary transaction**. There are two exceptions to the basic definition of **issuer**. In the case of voting-trust certificates or collateral-trust certificates, the term "issuer" refers to the person who assumes the duties of depositor or manager. There is considered to be no issuer for certificates of interest or participation in oil, gas, or mining titles or leases where payments are made out of production.

M

market maker (principal) A dealer willing to accept the risk of holding securities to facilitate trading in a particular security(ies).

material fact Information required to be included in a registration statement that a knowledgeable investor would deem significant in making an investment determination. *See also* inside information.

municipal security A debt security issued by a state, a municipality, or another subdivision (such as a school, a park, or a sanitary or some other local taxing district) to raise money to finance its capital expenditures. Such expenditures might include the construction of highways, public works, or school buildings.

N

net capital Liquid capital (cash and assets readily convertible into cash) maintained by a broker-dealer.

nonissuer A person other than the issuer of a security. In a nonissuer securities transaction, for example, the issuer is not one of the parties in the transaction, and the transaction therefore is not, according to the law, directly or indirectly for the benefit of the issuer. When the USA refers to a nonissuer transaction, it is referring to a transaction in which the proceeds of the sale go to the selling stockholder. Most nonissuer transactions also are called **secondary transactions**.

O

offer (1) An indication by an investor, a trader or a dealer of a willingness to sell a security or commodity. (2) Under the USA, every attempt to solicit a purchase or sale in a security for value.

P

person An individual, a corporation, a partnership, an association, a fund, a joint stock company, an unincorporated organization, a trust in which the interests of the beneficiaries are evidenced by a security, a government, or a political subdivision of a government.

private investment company An unregistered investment company whose investment objective is to raise capital for business ventures. Qualified purchasers are eligible to invest in private investment companies.

private placement An offering that complies with Regulation D (Rule 505 and Rule 506); generally, the offer of an unregistered security to no more than 35 nonaccredited investors or to an unlimited number of accredited investors. The USA's private placement provision allows an exemption from full state registration for a security that is sold in that state to no more than 10 nonaccredited investors.

prospectus The legal document that must be given to every investor who purchases registered securities in an offering. It describes the details of the company and the particular offering. *Syn.* final prospectus.

Q

qualified purchaser A sophisticated investor who invests in a private investment company. This includes a(n):

- individual with $5 million or more invested;
- family-owned business with $5 million or more invested;
- trust established by qualified purchasers; and
- company that invests on a discretionary basis a minimum of $25 million in investments.

R

registered investment company An investment company, such as an open-end management company (mutual fund) or closed-end management company, that is registered with the SEC and exempt from state registration and regulation.

registered representative All associated persons engaged in the investment banking and securities business for NASD registration and exam and licensing purposes. This includes:

- assistant officers (who are not principals);
- individuals who supervise, solicit, or conduct business in securities; and
- individuals who train people to supervise, solicit, or conduct business in securities.

Anyone who is not a principal and not engaged in clerical or brokerage administration is subject to registration and exam licensing as a registered representative—except for foreign associates. *Syn.* account executive, stockbroker.

registration by coordination A security is eligible for blue-sky registration by coordination in a state if the issuer files for registration of that security under the Securities Act of 1933 and files duplicates of the registration documents with the state Administrator. The state registration becomes effective at the same time the federal registration statement becomes effective.

registration by filing A security is eligible for blue-sky registration by filing in a state if the issuer files for registration of that security under the Securities Act of 1933, meets minimum net worth and other requirements, and notifies the state of this eligibility by filing certain documents with the state Administrator. The state registration becomes effective at the same time the federal registration statement becomes effective.

registration by qualification A security is eligible for blue-sky registration by qualification in a state if the issuer files registration documents for that security with the state Administrator; meets minimum net worth, disclosure, and other requirements; and files appropriate registration fees. The state registration becomes effective when the Administrator so orders.

registration statement Before nonexempt securities can be offered to the public, they require registration under the Securities Act of 1933. The registration statement must disclose all pertinent information concerning the issuer and the offering. This statement is submitted to the SEC in accordance with the requirements of the 1933 Act.

S

sales literature Any written material used to help sell a product and distributed by the firm in a controlled manner. *See also* advertisement

Securities Act of 1933 The federal legislation requiring the full and fair disclosure of all material information about the issuance of new securities.

Securities and Exchange Commission (SEC) The commission, created by Congress to protect investors, that enforces the Securities Act of 1933, the Securities Exchange Act of 1934, the Trust Indenture Act of 1939, the Investment Company Act of 1940, the Investment Advisers Act of 1940, and other securities laws.

Securities Exchange Act of 1934 The federal legislation establishing the Securities and Exchange Commission that regulates securities exchanges and over-the-counter markets and that protects investors from unfair and inequitable practices.

security Under the Act of 1934, any note, stock, bond, investment contract, debenture, certificate of interest in profit-sharing or partnership agreement, certificate of deposit, collateral trust certificate, preorganization certificate, option on a security, or other instrument of investment commonly known as a **security**.

Also categorized as securities are interests in oil and gas drilling programs, real estate condominiums and cooperatives, farmland or animals, commodity option contracts, whiskey warehouse receipts, multilevel distributorship arrangements, and merchandising marketing programs.

In general, a security can be defined as any piece of securitized paper that can be traded for value, except an insurance policy or a fixed annuity. As established by the federal courts, the basic test for determining whether a specific investment falls within the definition of security is whether the investor invests his money in a common enterprise and is led to expect profits from the managerial efforts of the promoter or a third party.

self-regulatory organization (SRO) An entity that is accountable to the SEC for the enforcement of federal securities laws, as well as for the supervision of securities practices, within an assigned field of jurisdiction. Eight SROs function under the oversight of the Commission. Selected jurisdictions include the following.

- New York Stock Exchange (NYSE) which governs all matters related to trading in NYSE-listed securities and the conduct of NYSE member firms and associated persons.
- National Association of Securities Dealers (NASD) which governs all matters related to investment banking (securities underwriting), trading in the over-the-counter market and the conduct of NASD member firms and associated persons.
- Municipal Securities Rulemaking Board (MSRB) which governs all matters related to the underwriting and trading of state and municipal securities.
- Chicago Board Options Exchange (CBOE) which governs all matters related to the writing and trading of standardized options and related contracts listed on that exchange.

sell The act of conveying ownership of a security or other property for money or other value; every contract to sell a security or an interest in a security. Sales include the following.

- Any security given or delivered with, or as a bonus for, any purchase of securities is considered to have been offered and sold for value.
- A gift of assessable stock is considered to involve an offer and sale.
- Every sale or offer of a warrant or right to purchase or subscribe to another security is considered to include an offer of the other security.

Sales do not include bona fide pledges or loans or stock dividends if nothing of value is given by the stockholders for the dividend.

surety bond (1) A bond required by NYSE Rule 319 for all employees, officers and partners of member firms to protect clients against acts of misplacement, fraudulent trading and check forgery. (2) The blanket surety bond that indemnifies against losses due to check forgery, lost securities, or fraudulent trading that every member firm required to join the Securities Investor Protection Corporation (that is, any firm doing business with the public) must purchase and maintain. *Syn.* fidelity bond.

T

transfer agent A person or an organization responsible for recording the names of registered stockholders and the number of shares owned, seeing that the certificates are signed by the appropriate corporate officers, affixing the corporate seal, and delivering the securities to the transferee.

U

underwriter The entity responsible for marketing stocks, bonds, mutual fund shares, etc.

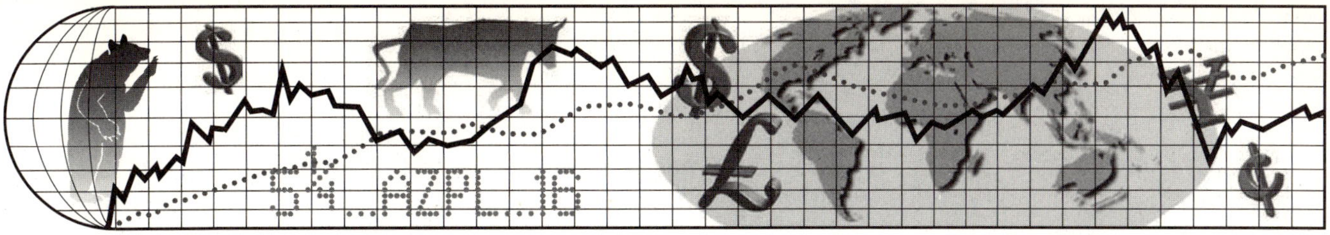

Index

The Administrative Provisions of the USA HotSheet

USA as Model Legislation:	• USA is not *actual* but *model* legislation for each states' own legislation
NSMIA of 1996:	• Eliminates state and federal registration duplication
Securities Litigation Uniform Standards Act (1998)	• Class actions governed by federal standards
Federal Covered Securities:	• Covered by national, not state, regulation • Includes securities listed on U.S. exchanges, issued by investment companies, or sold to qualified purchasers
Administrator:	• State official responsible for the implementation of the USA
Powers of the Administrator:	• Make rules and orders • Conduct investigations and issue subpoenas • Issue cease and desist orders and seek injunctions • Deny, suspend, cancel, or revoke registrations
Fifth Amendment Protection:	• Forced testimony given immunity under the Fifth Amendment
Fraud:	• Willful misrepresentation for unlawful gain
Civil Liabilities:	• Attorney's costs *plus* losses on investment *plus* interest *minus* any income earned
Recission	• Right to rescind a fraudulent trade
Criminal Penalties:	• Fines or imprisonment, or both
Statute of Limitations:	• Time limits for bringing suit in a case • **Civil**—three years from date of sale or of rendering of advice or two years after discovering violation, whichever occurs first • **Criminal**—five years after date of the transaction

Securities HotSheet

Investment Contract (Howey Decision):
- Investment of money
- Common enterprise
- Expectation of profits
- Solely from efforts of others

Nonexempt Security:
- Must register

Issuer:
- Company, government, or government subdivision that offers or proposes to offer securities

Nonissuer:
- Secondary market transaction
- Proceeds do not go to issuer

Primary Offering:
- Initial public offering

Methods of Registration:
- Coordination, Qualification

Notice Filing:
- Federal covered investment company securities – sole documents with states

Exempt Security:
- No registration under USA required
- Still subject to antifraud provisions

Exempt Transaction:
- Transaction need not be registered under USA

Registration of Persons HotSheet

Person:
- Individual, company, or government

Broker-Dealer Registration:
- Must register in state where business is done unless exempt
- Effective after Administrator notification; expires December 31st

Exempt from State Registration as a Broker-Dealer:
- Banks, savings institutions, other financial institutions, agents, issuers
- BDs with no office in state only doing business with institutions
- BDs registered in another state transacting business with a current client passing through a different state

Exemptions from Agent Registration:
- Represents issuer in exempt transaction
- Represents issuer in bankers' acceptances, and commercial paper (270 days or less)
- Represents issuer in sale of employee benefits plans

Agent Registration:
- Broker-dealers can only employ registered agents
- Agents must be registered in state of residence, where securities are offered, and where securities are sold
- Agents who represent broker-dealers must be registered if they sell exempt or nonexempt securities
- Agents who represent issuers must be registered if they sell nonexempt securities
- Effective after Administrator notification; expires December 31
- Notification by agent & old & new employer for employment change
- Automatic registration of partners, officers, and directors when new broker-dealer registers

Investment Adviser Registration:
- Federally registered if adviser manages more than $30 million
- State registered if adviser manages less than $25 million
- Choice between federal and state if adviser manages between $25 and $30 million
- Investment company advisers are always federally registered
- File form ADV and appropriate fees
- Audited balance sheet if custody; unaudited balance sheet if not
- Effective after Administrator notification; expires December 31

Investment Adviser Exemptions:
- No office in state and communications directed to 5 or fewer clients in 12 months
- No office in state and clients are institutions, broker-dealers, or investment advisers only

Investment Adviser Recordkeeping:
- All specific customer and investment adviser records kept for 5 years; must be kept in investment adviser's office for the first 2 years

Business Practices HotSheet

Practices Prohibited of All Securities Professionals:

- Misleading or untrue statements
- Failure to state material facts
- Use of insider information
- Unsuitable transactions
- Market manipulation (pegging, front running, wash sales, matched purchases)

Other Prohibited Sales Practices:

- Unauthorized third-party trading
- Borrowing money from customers who are not banks or lending institutions
- Commingling client funds
- Failing to follow client instructions
- Exercising discretion without authority
- Effecting transactions not on the books
- Failing to report written complaints
- Guaranteeing against loss
- Failing to inform clients of higher than normal charges
- Misrepresenting customer account status
- Creating misleading trading activity
- Promising undeliverable services
- Unauthorized sharing in customer accounts
- Solicitation of unregistered, nonexempt securities
- Misrepresenting Administrator approval

Unlawful or Unethical Investment Advisory Practices:

- Unsuitable investments
- Unauthorized discretion
- Unauthorized third-party transactions
- Excessive trading
- Commingling funds
- Misrepresentation of material facts
- Nondisclosure of information sources
- Excessive fees
- Conflicts of interest
- Unauthorized custody of customer funds
- Operating without advisory contracts
- Performance-based compensation, except under unique circumstances
- Failing to disclose material legal action in past 10 years at least 48 hours before contracting with client
- Failing to disclose principal or agent capacity